The Making of the *Dentiste, c.* 1650–1760

The History of Medicine in Context

Series Editors: Andrew Cunningham and Ole Peter Grell,
Department of History and Philosophy of Science,
University of Cambridge

Titles in this series include:

Medicine from the Black Death to the French Disease
edited by Roger French, Jon Arrizabalaga,
Andrew Cunningham and Luis García-Ballester

*Faith, Medical Alchemy and Natural Philosophy:
Johann Moriaen, Reformed Intelligencer, and the Hartlib Circle*
J. T. Young

*'The Battle for Health': A Political History
of the Socialist Medical Association, 1930–51*
John Stewart

The Making of the *Dentiste*, c. 1650–1760

ROGER KING

Ashgate

Aldershot • Brookfield USA • Singapore • Sydney

Published by
Ashgate Publishing Limited
Gower House
Croft Road
Aldershot
Hants
GU11 3HR
England

Ashgate Publishing Company
Old Post Road
Brookfield
Vermont 05036–9704
USA

The author has asserted his moral right under the Copyright, Designs and Patents Act, 1988, to be identified as the author of this work.

British Library Cataloguing in Publication Data

King, Roger
    The Making of the *Dentiste*, c. 1650–1760.
    (The History of Medicine in Context)
    1. Dentistry—History—17th century.   2. Dentistry—History—
    18th century.   3. Dentistry—France—History.
    I. Title.
    617.6'009032

Library of Congress Cataloging-in-Publication Data

King, Roger, 1955–
    The making of the *dentiste*, c. 1650–1760/Roger King.
    (The History of Medicine in Context)
    Includes bibliographical references and index.
    ISBN 1–84014–653–2 (hb: alk. paper)
    1. Dentistry—France—History—17th century.   2. Dentistry—
    France—History—18th century.   3. Dentists—France—History—17th
    century.   4. Dentists—France—History—18th century.   I. Title.
    II. Series.
    [DNLM: 1. History of Dentistry—France.   2. Surgery—History—
    France.   3. Barber-Surgeons—History—France.   4. History of
    Medicine, 18th century—France. WU11 GF7K5m 1998]
    RK34.F8K56   1998
    617.6'00944'09032—dc21
    DNLM/DLC for Library of Congress   98–27420
                                                                              CIP

ISBN 1 84014 653 2

This book is printed on acid free paper

Typeset in Sabon by Manton Typesetters, 5–7 Eastfield Road, Louth, Lincolnshire, LN11 7AJ
Printed and bound in Great Britain by MPG Books Ltd, Bodmin, Cornwall

Contents

List of Figures

Acknowledgements

When I decided to leave the practice of dentistry in order to pursue my interests in the history of medicine full-time, I was both supported and encouraged by my wife, Morag, to whom I owe a great debt of thanks. I am grateful, too, to my erstwhile dental colleagues, David and Jane Morris, for their friendly support and assistance.

My move into the world of the history of medicine was made enjoyable, exciting and challenging by Andrew Cunningham, whose enthusiasm for the history of medicine has been inspirational and whose careful and attentive supervision of my research I have greatly appreciated. Harmke Kamminga, too, has helped to guide me around the several pitfalls that lie in wait for the fledgling historian, as have other members of the Cambridge Wellcome Unit for the History of Medicine and the Department for the History and Philosophy of Science at Cambridge University.

With regard to the preparation of this book in particular, the list of those who have assisted in uncovering and providing material is long: I have endeavoured to acknowledge as many of them as possible at the appropriate points in the various chapters. Special thanks are, however, due to Roy Porter and Colin Jones for their constructive and critical examination of the research upon which this book is based, and for their helpful indication of likely directions further work should take. Thanks are also due to Adrian Wilson for personal communications regarding his own research, and to François Vidal for providing me with access to his own valuable publications. I am also grateful to Christine Hillam for her work in establishing connections between historians of dentistry in England and France, and for the contacts she has thus enabled me to make. Of these, special thanks are due to Pierre Baron of the Société Française d'Histoire de l'Art Dentaire for giving me details of his studies of archive material for Paris and Lyon, and to Xavier Deltombe for providing me with similar material for Rennes. I am also grateful to Claude Rousseau of the Musée Pierre Fauchard in Paris for supplying material relating to Fauchard, and to Christine Hillam and Anne Hargreaves who have been most helpful in allowing me access to their own research.

For their courteous, efficient and painstaking assistance my thanks are also due to the staff of the library of the British Dental Association, London; the Cambridge University Library, in particular the rare books room; the Whipple Library of the Department of History and Philosophy of Science, University of Cambridge; the Musée Pierre Fauchard,

Paris; the Wellcome Institute Library; the Archives Nationales, Paris; the library of the Royal College of Surgeons of England; the library of the Royal College of Surgeons of Edinburgh; the National Library of Scotland; the History Faculty Library of the University of Cambridge; the Société d'Ingénierie et de Microfilmage, Neuilly-sur-Marne; and the Audio-Visual Department of Cambridge University.

I could not have embarked upon the research which led to the writing of this book without the financial support of my wife, Dr Morag King. I am also indebted to the Wellcome Trust for their generous provision of a grant to finance the final year of the doctoral research from which this book has grown.

I am grateful to the following for providing me with copies of pictures and the permission to use them, in both this work and in allied publications: the Syndics of Cambridge University Library, for 'The Mountebank and his Merry-Andrew', taken from Henry Morley's *Memoirs of Bartholomew Fair* (Figure 1.1), table XXXVI from Scultetus's *The Chyrurgeon's Store-House* (Figure 3.2) and Le Grand Thomas, taken from Chevalier's 'Un charlatan du XVIIIe siècle' (Figure 5.3); the Wellcome Institute Library, London, for the surgeon's instruments for use on the teeth, taken from Paré's *Oeuvres* (Figure 3.1), plates XIV and XXXVI from Fauchard's *Le Chirurgien Dentiste* (Figures 5.2 and 6.1) and plate 8 from Bourdet's *Recherches et observations* (Figure 6.3): the Musées royeaux des Beaux-Arts de Belgique for *Un théâtre de comédiens sur la grand'place de Bruxelles*, by Balthazar van den Bossche (Figure 1.2); the Bundeszahnärztekammer of the Institut der Deutschen Zahnärzte, Köln, for *Le Charlatan, à Paris* by Touzét (Figure 1.3); and to Dr Pierre Baron for permission to reproduce the painting by Nicolas Lefebvre (Figure 6.2 and cover).

Note on Aims and Sources

This book is about the way in which the *dentiste* and the practice of the *dentiste* were made in France, more specifically in Paris, around the beginning of the eighteenth century. It contains no definitive lists of practitioners, performs no complex analyses of patterns of practice, and provides no retrospective judgements on ability, morality or legal status. Neither does it attempt to provide an evidence-based analysis of the rise in the numbers of *dentistes* which took place in the latter half of the eighteenth century. A more archive-based analysis, allied to a consideration of the ways in which the French *dentiste* may have influenced the appearance and rise of the dentist in Britain will, I hope, be the subject of a further volume; but it remains the purpose of this book to find some answers to the question of how the *dentiste*, the modern practitioner for the teeth, was made.

The arguments which I shall present in this story are built on a detailed examination of surgery in France around this time, viewed principally through the published writings of surgeons such as Pierre Dionis and, in particular, the *chirurgien dentiste* Pierre Fauchard. As implied above, these arguments are *not* built on a large body of original archive research, but on a technical and social analysis of what those involved were doing: an analysis which has been made easier by drawing on the work of modern historians of medicine such as Colin Jones and Toby Gelfand, and historians of dentistry such as Pierre Baron and François Vidal. More traditional histories, such as the nineteenth-century French historian Alfred Franklin's extensive record of Parisian life have, used cautiously, also been of value; but it is the writings of those at the centre of this story, the surgeons and *dentistes* of early eighteenth-century France, upon which I have placed the most emphasis.

In my use of these materials, I have taken particular care to reproduce spellings, punctuation marks and accents as they appear in the original texts. I have dispensed with *sic* indications, except where absolutely necessary. For English translations of French texts, I have used contemporary translations when they have been available, which I have checked against the original French for accuracy and omissions. In a few instances, translations are my own, for which, of course, I remain solely responsible.

For Morag and Kate

'Problematizing' the History of Dentistry

By the middle of the seventeenth century in France, sufferers from toothache could follow one of four typical courses of action. First, they could endure the pain, in the hope that it would eventually disappear of its own accord; or they could purchase a bottle containing the promise of a cure, perhaps persuaded of its efficacy by the street trader's harangue. If the pain was too severe, or if they had no wish to wait for such a cure to take effect, they could seek a tooth-drawer to perform an extraction; or, finally, they could enlist the services of a surgeon to deal with the offending tooth.

The surgeon's role here has largely been forgotten, but operations on the teeth had long been an integral part of his practice, contributing to the body of operations to be performed on the head. The most common was extraction – but on occasion the surgeon would also perform such tasks as the cleaning of teeth, the removal of decay or the fixing of those that were loose, using particular techniques and instruments which had been designed with these operations in mind. By the final decade of the seventeenth century the possession of such instruments, and of the knowledge of how to use them, was firmly established as a basic (albeit relatively small) part of the surgeon's practice.

But the early decades of the eighteenth century would see the appearance of a completely new type of practitioner who, for some, would present a fifth option: the *dentiste*. The practice of the *dentiste*, although it focused only on the teeth, was nevertheless extensive. In addition to extractions, there was also a wide-ranging field of operations on offer, the performance of which had only been hinted at by the surgeon of the seventeenth century, which could promise relief of pain, repair of damaged teeth, reshaping and straightening of misplaced teeth – even replacement of teeth that were missing. This new sphere of practice represented a radical departure from what had gone before; and, as we shall see, it was all built solidly on sound surgical foundations, with the *dentiste* occupying a respected position within society in general and the medical world in particular.

There are a great many questions which arise from the arrival of the *dentiste*. Some concern the image of the *dentiste* himself, whilst others arise from the medical and social contexts within which this image appeared. The most important of these questions will be: where did the *dentiste* come from? What type of practitioner was he, and what did he do to encourage, or establish, his standing within surgery and society? More generally, if the *dentiste* did indeed appear from within the world of the surgeon, what was happening in surgery to allow such a spectacular rise? What was happening within France itself to allow it? We should perhaps go further: why France? – and why France *at that time*? In other words, taking all these questions together, the theme of this book will be: *how* was the *dentiste* made?

The history of dentistry: 'natural' history and academic history

The history of dentistry has not, to this writer's knowledge, had these questions put to it in this way before. There is, however, a strong tradition of writing on the history of dentistry, commonly by writers who have had an intimate technical knowledge of the dentistry of their own times. Over the course of the last one hundred years, the nature of much of their work has taken the form of a linear account, mapping out the route of an apparent progression of dentistry from ancient times to the sophisticated techniques of the dentist of the late twentieth century, via the supposedly crude methods of the itinerant mountebank and the charlatan. In this way, these writers have generally followed a 'natural' route, identifying images and instances of apparent dentistry in the past, perhaps placing its origins in ancient Egypt[1] and allowing it to reach a triumphant 'peak of development'[2] at the end of the seventeenth century. The story they have presented has been one of continuous development and advancement, with the handing down of the dentist's pliers (as it were) following the progressive course implied by Lilian Lindsay in a paragraph note to her *Short History of Dentistry* of 1933: 'Change of title: tooth-drawer becomes dentist.'[3] This 'natural' story has endured, continuing to follow a smooth transition. Alan Stanley, for example, has followed Lindsay in suggesting that 'The "tooth drawer" ... evolved into the "operator for the teeth" and then into the "dentist".'[4] Important events along the way have been noted, such as the publication in Paris of Pierre Fauchard's book *Le Chirurgien Dentiste* in 1728,[5] or the drawing up of surgical statutes at the beginning of the eighteenth century in France.[6] In most of these 'natural' histories, every last detail has been carefully dissected for examination[7] – but it is this very act of dissection which has allowed the image of the dentist or, more importantly, the *dentiste,* to remain blurred.

What these various types of history have concentrated on has been *teeth* in the past, and on some of those who may have attended to them.

For such stories have picked up anything connected with the teeth and forced it to fit 'the history of dentistry'; but this has led to a situation in which *teeth* have become confused with *dentistry* and, as this book will, I hope, make clear, the two should by no means necessarily be always connected. Perhaps the most obvious example of this, and certainly the most visible, is that which will be addressed in the following chapter – the misappropriation of pictures and paintings of people who have been taken to have been 'doing dentistry' in the fairs and markets of seventeenth- and eighteenth-century Europe. These pictures have been looked at with eyes that have prejudged them as 'dentistry', sometimes even as ready-made *history* of dentistry. The German writer Walter Hoffmann-Axthelm, for example, has suggested that 'Gerhard van Honthorst and Theodor Rombouts, Adriæn Brouwer and David Teniers, Adriæn van Ostade and Jan Steen, [have made] contributions to the history of dentistry through a rich assortment of true-to-life representations of toothdrawers.'[8] The British writer Menzies Campbell, noting the large number of such pictures, has written:

> This particular type of toothdrawer was a familiar figure for many centuries, not only in Britain, but also on the continent of Europe. Fortunately for the student of dental history, world-famed artists depicted them with their patients in the agonies of apprehension and realisation.[9]

But it is highly unlikely that these pictures were made with any dental intention at all, let alone as a record for future students of dental history. Nevertheless, this way of concentrating on teeth in the past has led to attempts to superimpose 'photographic' interpretations where they were never intended, resulting in the labelling of such pictures as readily accessible records of early dentistry.[10] Whilst some writers may see the painting by Balthazar van den Bossche, reproduced as Figure 1.2 on page 22, as depicting 'L'Arracheur de dents sur la Grand Place de Bruxelles',[11] its present keepers know it as *Un théâtre de comédiens sur la grand'place de Bruxelles*[12] – a title which implies a quite different activity altogether. We shall see in the following chapter that such pictures should be viewed more openly, as illustrations of the fairground entertainer's act: they do not belong to the history of dentistry.

Over the last thirty years or so, academic history of medicine has undergone fundamental change;[13] however, within this wider field, the history of dentistry seems to have become the poor relation. Whilst a growing body of painstaking archive-based research has, in recent years, uncovered a picture of various types of practitioner and their patterns of practice in both England and France,[14] no historian of dentistry has considered in detail the question of *how* the *dentiste* (or the dentist) was made – the direct questions posed at the start of this introduction have not, as yet, been asked. The history of dentistry appears only rarely in academic publications, and then usually only in a supporting role to a wider argument.[15] This relative lack of attention is illustrated clearly in John Henry's review of the wide-ranging *Companion Encyclopædia of the History of Medicine*, published in 1993.[16] Henry notes that although he has 'no doubt that everyone concerned with the history of medicine and its cultural context will soon find it [the *Companion*] an indispensable guide',[17] nevertheless 'There is significantly more on diarrhœa than on dentistry.'[18]

Some recent work in the history of medicine will, however, be of great assistance in the construction of the story of the *dentiste*. Toby Gelfand's social and institutional analysis of medicine and surgery in France, published at the beginning of the 1980s, provides a broad platform from which to view the dramatic changes which took place in the first half of the eighteenth century.[19] More recently *The Medical World of Early Modern France*, by Laurence Brockliss and Colin Jones,[20] has provided a detailed view of the social and cultural context within which *ancien régime* surgery was practised. Colin Jones in particular has touched upon the appearance of particular branches within surgery, briefly noting the effect of the publication of Fauchard's *Chirurgien Dentiste* on the number of publications regarding the teeth appearing in the years following;[21] however, he also bemoans the lack of historical analysis of eighteenth-century French surgical practice.[22] Also of great relevance to this story is the work of Jacques Gélis and Mireille Laget, among others, on the activities of another type of surgeon, the *accoucheur*, in seventeenth- and eighteenth-century France.[23] Similarly, Adrian Wilson's work on the making of the man-midwife in England addresses some of the issues relating to early moves towards specialization within surgery, and the reasons for the success of the surgeons involved in that specialization (although not, unfortunately, for those in France).[24] Wilson has built his story on both technical and social foundations and it is perhaps now time that the history of dentistry, lagging twenty years behind, followed his lead.

The making of the *dentiste*

It should now be clear, then, that this book will locate the making of the *dentiste* firmly within the surgical world of early eighteenth-century France. Whilst the crucial events in this story took place in the 1690s and early 1700s, this world was expanding rapidly during the preceding forty years or so, with the surgeon moving away from the practice of a manual trade towards that of an art based on the possession of theoretical knowledge. By taking 1650 as our starting-point, we shall see that the body of knowledge on which this move was based would grow to be so large, of such an 'étenduë infinie' (as the contemporary French surgeon Pierre Dionis would put it),[25] that some surgeons would choose to focus their attention on one particular part of it *only* and, by so doing, would therefore be able to extend that part of surgery still further. The teeth were one such particular part.

The *dentiste* had needed to climb no ladder, either social or medical, in order to gain respectability. With surgery in the ascendant, and with his origins firmly located within it, the *dentiste* was *already* respectable at his first appearance. As we shall see, he would, quite literally, be working alongside the most important medical men in the kingdom within thirty years of his appearance, thus placing himself in a position from which he could criticize with impunity the old types of practitioner for the teeth. We shall also see that by the middle of the eighteenth century, this fifth option for the treatment of teeth would, for some, not even be optional: for the *gens de considération* of Louis XV's Paris, to consult a *dentiste* for matters of the teeth would now be a virtual *necessity*, driven by the powerful need to present a public face which was graced by *l'ornement de la bouche*, and crowned by the royal signalling of approval given by the king's ennoblement of his own *dentiste* in mid-century. Thus, by 1760, the specialist surgeon for the teeth can be taken to have held an established and respected position within both surgery and society in France.

In many fields of historical research, the paths of technical and social history rarely cross; but we may take advantage of the relatively small field presented by the history of dentistry to examine both the technical and the social stories, and to explore their relationship more fully. In order to do this, I shall offer a technical account of the complex and innovative operations for the teeth which the *dentiste* would perform, and I shall examine the social implications of both his contribution to the presentation of a 'fashionable' appearance and of the ennoblement of the king's *dentiste*. It will therefore be possible to place the performance of these operations in their correct surgical *and* social contexts. We shall see that just as 'fashion' (as social strength) did not drive 'science' (as technical innovation, founded on theoretical knowledge), so 'science' did not drive 'fashion'. Each would act in support of the other – and neither would be able to act alone. In order to achieve this balance, I shall combine the archive work and social analyses of others with well-known contemporary material such as Fauchard's *Le Chirurgien Dentiste*; but I shall use Fauchard's writing in a way in which it has not been used before. As a result, we shall see that the *dentiste*, the 'orphan' of academic history of medicine, can contribute an important chapter to the story of the origins of specialization within surgery.

There are, however, certain key points relating to this story whose importance should be made clear. The location of the *dentiste* within the world of surgery, as a practitioner treating the teeth alone, permits us to use the word 'specialization' in its modern sense without anachronism. As a direct corollary to this, therefore, we may also use the term 'general surgeon' to indicate a surgeon who had *not* specialized. Furthermore, we shall see that the activities of both the *dentiste* and the surgeon will involve a *science*, a term which will be italicized throughout to indicate the use of the historical, French form. A *science* was a body of fundamental elements of theoretical knowledge. Laurence Brockliss, discussing higher education in seventeenth- and eighteenth-century France, defines it as follows:

> In early-modern France (as in the rest of Europe) it was customary to separate knowledge into two distinctive categories: the arts and the sciences. The first offered an understanding of how a phenomenon might be applied; the second of how it might be explained. The distinction between the two was precisely delineated in the various editions of Furetières dictionary, first published in 1690. There defined, an art was 'principalement un amas de préceptes, de règles, d'inventions et d'expériences, qui étant observées, font réussir aux choses qu'on entreprend, en les rendant utiles et agréables.' A science was 'une connoissance certaine et évidente par ses causes.'[26]

The final key term is *dentiste* itself, a word which has been responsible for much confusion in traditional histories of dentistry. Before we can approach the *dentiste*, we will need to know *whom* it is we are approaching.

The *dentistes* – literally making a name for themselves

> DENTISTE, f.m. (*Chirur.*) Chirurgien qui s'applique spécialement à la chirurgie des dents, à traiter leurs maladies, & à pratiquer les opérations qui ont lieu par ces parties. Les qualités d'un bon *dentiste* sont premiérement celles d'un bon chirurgien. Il doit être ensuite instruit particuliérement de tout ce qui concerne l'objet de son occupation: il doit avoir le poignet souple & fort, & s'être par conséquent singuliérement exercé à tirer des dents, à en plomber, à en limer, & en un mot à les traiter méthodiquement & avec sûreté.
>
> *Supplément à l'Encyclopédie, ou Dictionnaire Raisonné des sciences, des arts et des métiers, par une société de gens des lettres,*
> Paris, 1776, vol. II.

The above definition of the *dentiste* is taken from the supplement to the *Encyclopédie*, published in 1776. But in the original edition of this work, which was published in 1751, there is no entry under *dentiste* –

why? Had a new word been invented? Or had a pre-existing title assumed a position in the French language which now demanded inclusion in this comprehensive work? If so, how had this come about? *Who* was this *dentiste*, and to what class of practitioner did he belong?

We have already seen that, in 1728, Pierre Fauchard published a book to which he gave the new title of *Le Chirurgien Dentiste*.[27] As its title suggests, this book concerns the application of the skills and theoretical knowledge of the surgeon to a particular part of the body, and for reasons which will become clearer when we examine the work of the surgeon more closely, it will form the focus of the central part of this book. The story of the *dentiste* pivots on the defining date when this title was first used. A precise date for this is difficult to identify with great accuracy, as we do not know for how long Fauchard had used it before writing his book (which had apparently been awaiting publication since 1723[28]) – nor, for that matter, do we know if any other practitioners were using it earlier. However, from evidence provided in the case histories contained within his writing and the account given by Fauchard of the way in which he built his practice, together with accounts of what others were doing in this period (such as the view of the practice and teaching of surgery provided by the surgeon Pierre Dionis's *Cours d'opérations de Chirurgie*,[29] first published twenty years earlier), we shall be safe in taking the year 1700 as the round year in which the making of the *dentiste* started.

In examining this story, we will need to observe 'actors' categories'. If we do, we should not, therefore, apply the term *dentiste* to anyone treating teeth before 1700. Similarly, other actors' categories will need to be observed, such as mountebank, charlatan, empiric, *expert*, *arracheur*, tooth-drawer, *opérateur*, barber-surgeon and surgeon; but these titles should only be used with the express proviso that we are alert to who is *recording* the title. It should, however, be reasonable to adopt the premise that those who took the new title of *dentiste* knew who, or what, they themselves were.

The making of the *dentiste* is not therefore just a discussion of the use of a title – it is a discussion of the identity and arrival of a whole group of practitioners. Words are made to fit a need: the making of such names marks the making of a new identity, indicating (in this case) fundamental change. Fauchard used this title *deliberately* to mark out as new territory what he and his colleagues were doing, as something quite different from what had gone before. This very word, *dentiste*, indicates someone with a particular interest and a particular skill which is focused on the teeth. But it is not a word that is merely *descriptive* of specialization – it is also a *celebration* of that specialization. It describes a particular *type* of practice, involving social as well as technical elements, rather than simply defining the field of that practice. As Andrew Cunningham has pointed out in his work on the surgeons of Edinburgh in the same period, with respect to titles, skills and roles, 'each issue of medical practice has to be reconstructed in its own right if we are to understand it properly';[30] and in this particular reconstruction, we shall see that the *dentiste* – quite literally – made a name for himself. Thus, rather than seeing a development of the ways in which teeth were already being treated, we shall be seeing the making of a new group altogether, whose members intended to make other groups treating teeth, groups which they did *not* replace, appear at best unrefined and 'manual'[31] and, at worst, unrefined and dishonest.

It is these other groups which will serve as the basis on which this story will be built, providing a contrast against which the refinement of the *dentiste* may be seen more clearly. Therefore, in the first part of this book, I shall examine the activities of those treating teeth in France who were *not dentistes*. Who were they, and what should we call them?

We shall see that three distinct types of practice were in existence. The first was the selling of drugs, performed in the fairs and marketplaces of Europe in order to profit from the sale of drugs and cures for the teeth. The second was the practice of drawing teeth, performed by 'official' or 'unofficial' practiticiers – and the third was the practice of surgery as applied to the teeth. *None* of these people were *dentistes*. Following this, and forming the central part of our story, we shall see that in around 1700 a fourth type of practice appeared which would form the origins of the modern practice of dentistry: that of the *dentiste*.

Notes

1. 'The earliest dentist whose name we know is Hesi-Re, who lived [in Egypt] during the reign of Zoser'. Malvin E. Ring, *Dentistry: An illustrated history*, Abrams, New York, 1985, p. 33.
2. Elisabeth Bennion, *Antique Dental Instruments*, Sotheby's, London, 1986, p. 21.
3. Lilian Lindsay, *A Short History of Dentistry*, John Bale, Sons and Danielsson, London, 1933, p. 57, marginal note.
4. Alan Stanley, 'Dentistry – The Dependence upon Medicine and Surgery for its Professional Status', in the *British Dental Journal*, 176 (12), 25 June 1994, 448–50, 448.
5. Pierre Fauchard, *Le Chirurgien Dentiste, ou Traité des Dents*, Mariette, Paris, 1728. Fauchard's work has been taken by some to have laid the foundations of 'scientific dentistry' (V. Guerini, *A History of Dentistry from the Most Ancient Times until the End of the Eighteenth Century*, Lea and Febiger, Philadelphia, 1909, p. 259), which is, to some extent, an accurate assessment, but as we shall see in Chapter Five, the meanings of the words have changed.

6. The surgical statutes of 1699 defined the practice of the *expert pour les dents*, whom we shall meet later, placing them firmly under the control of the surgeons: the French writer François Vidal has stated that, as a result, 'tout au cours du siècle, l'art dentaire est, et reste, l'affaire exclusive des experts' (François Vidal, *Histoire d'un diplôme*, LCD, Paris, n.d. (*c.* 1993), p. 26). We shall see in Chapter Two, however, that these statutes had very little to do with *dentistry* at all.

7. See, for example, André Besombes and Georges Dagen, *Pierre Fauchard, Pere de l'Art Dentaire Moderne (1678–1761) et ses contemporaines,* Société des Publications Médicales et Dentaires, Paris, 1961. In their examination of Fauchard's life, the authors have left no stone unturned: every detail possible has been unearthed, even those relating to his *confrères* and his relatives.

8. Walter Hoffmann-Axthelm, *History of Dentistry*, Quintessence, Chicago, 1981, p. 171.

9. J. M. Campbell, *Dentistry Then and Now,* 3rd edn, private publication, Glasgow, 1981, p. 337.

10. See, for example, Armelle and Pierre Baron's painstakingly researched *L'Art dentaire à travers la Peinture*, ACR, Paris, 1986.

11. Ibid., p. 175.

12. Catalogue entry, Musées royaux des Beaux-Arts de Belgique, Brussels.

13. See, for example, Steven Shapin, 'Discipline and bounding: the history and sociology of science as seen through the externalism–internalism debate', *History of Science*, 30, 1992, 333–69, in which Shapin discusses one of the central elements of this change.

14. See in particular Christine Hillam, *Brass Plate and Brazen Impudence: Dental practice in the provinces 1755–1855*, Liverpool University Press, Liverpool, 1991, and Anne Hargreaves, 'The provision of practical dental treatment in England from the 14th to the mid-18th centuries', unpublished Ph.D. thesis, University of Newcastle-upon-Tyne, 1996. For examples of similar work in France, see Vidal, *Histoire d'un diplôme*, Pierre Baron, '"Dental experts" in Lyon at the end of the eighteenth century', in C. Hillam (ed.), *Dental Practice in Europe at the end of the eighteenth century: transactions of the Paris meeting, September 1994*, pp. 27–34 and Xavier Deltombe, 'The Rennes Guild of Surgeons at the end of the 18th century', in Hillam, *Dental Practice in Europe*, pp. 38–43.

15. See, for example, the excellent (but all too brief) references to dentistry in Charles Webster's *The health services since the war*, vol. I, HMSO, London, 1988.

16. W. F. Bynum and Roy Porter (eds), *Companion Encyclopædia of the History of Medicine*, Routledge, London and New York, 1993.

17. John Henry, review of Bynum and Porter, *Companion Encyclopædia*, in the *British Journal for the History of Science*, 28, pt 3, no. 98, September 1995, 379–81, 381. I am indebted to Dr Harmke Kamminga for bringing this review to my notice.

18. Ibid., p. 380.

19. See Toby Gelfand, *Professionalizing modern medicine: Paris surgeons and medical science and institutions in the eighteenth century*, Greenwood, Westport, 1980.

20. Laurence Brockliss and Colin Jones, *The Medical World of Early Modern France*, Clarendon Press, Oxford, 1997.

21. Ibid., p. 555.

22. Whilst acknowledging it to be a simplification, Professor Jones also suggests that the fundamental development in French surgery during this period lay in consolidating the gains of the past; however, it is hoped that the present work will make clear that detailed technical analysis can reveal, in some parts of surgery at least, a degree of innovation which has hitherto not been acknowledged.

23. See, for example, Jacques Gélis, 'Sages-femmes et accoucheurs: l'obstétrique populaire aux XVIIe et XVIIIe siècles', *Annales Économies Sociétés Civilisations* 32 (5), 1977, 927–57; Gélis, *Accoucheur de campagne sous le roi soleil: le traité d'accouchement de G. Mauquest de la Motte,* Edouard Privat, Toulouse, 1979; and Mireille Laget, 'Childbirth in Seventeenth- and Eighteenth-Century France: Obstetrical Practices and Collective Attitudes', in Robert Forster and Orest Ranum (eds), *Medicine and Society in France: Selections from the Annales,* vol. 6, The Johns Hopkins University Press, Baltimore, 1980, 137–76.

24. Adrian Wilson, *The Making of Man-Midwifery: Childbirth in England 1660–1770,* UCL, London, 1995.

25. Pierre Dionis, *Cours d'opérations de Chirurgie, démontrées au Jardin Royal,* Bruxelles, t'Serstevens et Claudinot, Bruxelles, 1708, p. 416.

26. Antoine Furetière, *Dictionnaire Universel, contenant généralement tous les mots françois, tant vieux que modernes et les termes de toutes les sciences et des arts,* The Hague, 1690; cited in Laurence Brockliss, *French Higher Education in the Seventeenth and Eighteenth Centuries: A Cultural History,* Clarendon Press, Oxford, 1987, p. 1. Brockliss points out that Furetière was the eighteenth-century French equivalent of the *OED.*

27. Pierre Fauchard, *Le Chirurgien Dentiste.* 'It would seem that Fauchard either coined, or was the first to use the title "Chirurgien Dentiste."' Lilian Lindsay, in the translator's introduction to Fauchard, *The Surgeon Dentist* (Lindsay's translation), Butterworth & Co., London, 1946, p. v.

28. 'J'étois prêt en 1723. à faire emprimer mon livre; mais les occupations continuelles que me donne ma profession, m'empêcherent jusqu'en 1728 de le mettre au jour.' Pierre Fauchard, *Le Chirurgien Dentiste* (2nd edn, 1746), vol. II, p. 354.

29. Pierre Dionis, *Cours d'opérations.*

30. Andrew Cunningham, 'The medical professions and the pattern of medical care: the case of Edinburgh, c. 1670–c. 1700', in Wolfgang Eckart and Johanna Geyer-Kordesch (eds), *Heilberüfe und Kranke im 17. und 18. Jahrhundert die Quellen und Forschungssituation,* Münster, 1982, pp. 9–29, p. 26.

31. The implications of 'working with one's hands' in this status-driven society will be considered more fully in a later chapter.

CHAPTER ONE

Pretending to Draw Teeth:
The Mountebank Drug-seller of the
Fairs and Markets

As Matthew Ramsey has said in his study of professional and popular
medicine in France, 'The medical charlatan of early modern Europe was
an immediately recognizable type.'[1] He quotes the eighteenth-century
Dictionnaire de Trévoux's definition of the charlatan: 'Empiric, false
physician, who gets up on a stage in the public square, to sell theriac or
other drugs and who gathers the people by magical tricks and clowning,
to sell his drugs more easily.'[2] Identifying the charlatan more specifically
as the 'itinerant mountebank',[3] Ramsey describes his typical appearances at the fairs and marketplaces of France, moving often from area
to area and frequently accompanied by a large entourage of assistants
and gaily dressed performers.[4]

Closely related to Ramsey's 'classic mountebank'[5] (and, at times, indistinguishable from him) was a type of charlatan whose performance focused
attention on the teeth. As suggested in the Introduction, the activities of
this group have frequently been portrayed in pictures, performing on
their platforms or carts in lavish costume and appearing to work on the
teeth of sufferers from the watching crowd. Their activities have therefore
come to be aligned with the practice of the tooth-drawer – that is, one
who made his (or, less frequently, her) living principally from the removal
of teeth. This interpretation is due to a misappropriation of such images
as depicting 'dental events' – as representing the activities of a group who
were 'doing dentistry' on a gullible public whilst exercising no skill or
theoretical knowledge whatsoever. But far more may be gained from
these pictures if they are viewed more openly as fairground events, designed to entertain and attract the crowd. Watching the charlatans'
performance and listening to their cries will reveal them as mountebanks,[6] for whom the *parody* of the tooth-drawer (rather than their
imitation) was a central part of the act – whilst their principal business
and main source of income was the sale of drugs and secret remedies for
the toothache. For these reasons, I shall use the title of 'mountebank
drug-seller' to describe the members of this group.

The key to a better understanding of the activities of these practitioners lies in the environment in which they worked – the fairs or

marketplaces of Europe. However, a balanced examination of these busy events is not straightforward. Attempts at such a study soon reveal that different national traditions have produced different kinds of evidence: pictures in one case, written records in another. Although these various kinds of sources do not all appear to have been produced (or perhaps to have survived) in any one country, all the evidence they provide relates to fairs held throughout Europe, and is therefore highly relevant to this story.

Most history of fairs and markets, which had grown in number and size throughout Europe over a long period,[7] is economic, focusing on the structure of the merchant's trade.[8] With many decencies now becoming regarded as necessities for some, the expansion in both size and frequency of fairs and markets allowed merchants and farmers easier access to selling, and consumers easier access to consuming. In this way, the fairs were performing a role in accelerating the evolution of need. The Inspecteur des foires at Caen noted that 'L'universalité du luxe, l'extension sans bornes des besoins de la vie', offered at the fair during the 1750s, was encouraging 'l'usage de mille superfluités.'[9] Similarly, the great majority of English fairs had traded principally in horses, cattle, linen, cheese, coopers' ware, china, shoes, hats, pedlary, apparel and 'all sorts of goods from London',[10] but many were becoming associated with the business of enjoyment and entertainment, in some instances exclusively.[11] As we shall see, this element of entertainment would be central to the business of the drug-seller.

The *orviétan* seller of the fair: drugs to cure the toothache

For the travelling seller, transporting his wares from fair to fair in his bag or on his back, the sale of drugs, and his own secret *orviétan*[12] in particular, held out the promise of a good livelihood. The purchase of such cure-alls, commonly from itinerants, was becoming of increasing importance to the trade of the markets and fairs. Every French charlatan had his *orviétan* to sell, often claiming a wide range of cures. Its origins are obscure: James's *Medicinal Dictionary* of 1743 describes 'orvietanum' as 'a celebrated antidote, thus called, according to Lemery, from Orvieto, a City of Italy, where it was first used; but, according to others, from Hieronymus Ferrantes Orvietanus, a celebrated mountebank, who invented it.'[13] According to popular tradition, Orvietanus first made himself famous by taking such things upon the stage, after doses of pretended poisons.[14]

There were several variations on the theme of orvietan, most of which contained theriac, viper's grass, angelica, bitumen, dittany, gentian, acorus and dry vipers, complete with hearts and livers, which, along with many spices, were mixed with a large quantity of honey.[15] James described orvietan as 'highly esteem'd, as good against the Plague, the Small-pox, and the Bites of poisonous animals. It, also, corroborates the Brain, the Heart, and the Stomach. Dose is from one scruple to a dram and a half.'[16] As 'the goodness of the Orvietan is principally estimated by its smell',[17] some recipes drew heavily on the use of aromatics and spices, such as oranges, mace, cinnamon, bay, cardamon and sal ammoniac: the *Electuarium Orvietanum* of Frederic Hoffman included opium and volatile salt of vipers, and required fermentation for some months.[18]

Many such mixtures had the power to cure diseases affecting the teeth. In France Jean Embry, the possessor of many secret cures, could treat corns and verrucae (using a mixture made with vipers' tongues), swelling of the throat, pale complexion, pustules and 'les traces de la variole'; he could also thicken the hair and 'répare les dents'.[19] Some recipes, specifically intended for the teeth only, had endured over the years, including mixtures which could even cause hollow and painful teeth to fall out. Simply by placing them in the hollow of the offending tooth and sealing in with wax, the pain of extraction with an instrument could be avoided:

> Tu prendras deux onces de roses rouges et les sera bouillir avec fort vinaigre l'espace d'un jour et d'une nuit. Après, les secheras, puis en seras fondre que mettras sur la dent, et elle tombera.[20]

> Faites bouillir, puis réduisez en cendre des vers de terre; remplissez de cette poudre la dent creuse, et fermez-la avec de la cire. Elle tombera.[21]

Such mixtures, published in books of remedies, had been 'respectable': they were not solely the province of the mountebank. In the fourteenth century, John of Gaddesden had described the ancient use of the fat of the green tree frog to make teeth fall out, even noting that oxen eating grass would lose the teeth that came into contact with them.[22] This advice would endure, being repeated by the Viennese surgeon Plenk in 1790.[23]

The sale of drugs such as these could be big business at the larger fairs, as Jean-Claude Perrot has shown in his studies of the taxation records of the fairs at Caen and Guibray.[24] Although the greater proportion of all goods sold was not recorded at the time of sale, the officers and agents of the fairs would investigate and estimate the amounts taken by the various traders after the fair had closed, for taxation purposes. In submitting to demands for some indication of their returns from the Inspecteur des foires at Caen in 1754, sellers of drugs declared that they had distributed more than 25 000 *livres*-worth. Although this may well have been a likely underestimate to reduce the demand for tax payments, it was still a high proportion of the total business of the fair.[25]

However, the activities and selling methods of those travellers offering drugs and cure-alls at the fair or the market, and in particular the mountebank drug-sellers, remain outside the scope of detailed economic studies such as those of Margairaz and Perrot. Simply identifying their presence can be problematic: Jean-Pierre Goubert, in discussing popular medicine in France towards the end of the eighteenth century, has shown that the charlatans' position regarding official acceptance was frequently ambiguous, and that their movements from fair to fair usually rendered them invisible to town or parish accounting records.[26] In order to gain a clearer understanding of the activities of those itinerants who appear to have been healers, we must examine the structure and form which the fairs took, looking more carefully at some of those activities which might nowadays be labelled as entertainment rather than as trade.

Entertainment at the fair

Itinerants, both traders and stage performers, were attracted to the larger fairs such as those at Paris, Leipzig, London and Cambridge. Fun was becoming all-important, with the promise of entertainment moving centre-stage in the process of parting the crowd from their money. Stage shows and entertainments of all kinds had been growing in number at the larger fairs for a long time, with many (particularly the smaller attractions) presented by travellers.[27] The diarist Samuel Pepys went twice round Bartholomew Fair on 28 August 1668 which he had been 'glad to see again after two years of missing it by the plague, ... and there did see a ridiculous little stage play called Marry Audrey, a foolish thing, but seen by everybody, and so to Jacob Hall's dancing on the ropes, a thing worth seeing and mightily followed'.[28] Pepys was a connoisseur of 'the dancing on the ropes', attending to watch it regularly each year.[29] Rope-dancing was a favourite with the crowds, a typical show being that of the booth of Barnes and Appleby in 1699. First, the audience would see a little child, using a pole 'not much bigger than a large tobacco stopper',[30] followed by two stout lasses, who 'doffed their petticoats after a gentle breathing'.[31] Then a negro woman and an Irishwoman would perform, followed by 'a man of authority, who with great airs required sundry adjustments of the rope; out of Fair time, this was an "Infallible Physician"'.[32] The tradition was still strong in 1775, when a Turkish artist danced on a rope thirty-eight feet high above the ground.[33] As a result of the growth in amusements, attempts had been made to confine London's Bartholomew Fair to only three days instead of fourteen in 1691 and 1708. The people of Smithfield had complained that the booths were too large, and were not used by dealers and traders (as the organizers thought proper for a fair) but for stage plays, music and the like[34] – however, the attractions were popular.

Typical advice to the would-be showman, including how to attract a large crowd, was recorded in the notebooks of the writer Henry Fielding, who produced many plays at his booth at Bartholomew Fair (the principal London fair) from 1728 to 1737:

> when the fair begins, he should sometimes walk about the stage grandly and show his dress; sometimes he should dance with his fellows; sometimes he should sing; sometimes he should blow the trumpet; sometimes he should laugh and joke with the crowd, and give them a kind of touch-and-go speech, which keeps them merry and makes them come in. Then sir, he should sometimes cover his state robe with a great coat, and go into the crowd, and shout opposite his own booth, like a stranger who is struck with its magnificence: by the way, sir, that is a good trick, I never knew it fail to make an audience; and then he has only to steal away and mount his stage and strum and dance and sing and trumpet, and roar over again.[35]

Fielding's showman would stop at nothing to stir up and attract his audience – and booths such as these presented an ideal opportunity for the satirical treatment of many respected areas of the establishment.[36]

In addition to staged plays, the visitor to the fair could call at many booths offering a wide range of attractions and entertainments, including such performers as acrobats and high-wire artistes, coarse and noisy puppet shows, sword-throwers, contortionists, posture-masters, fire-eaters, bell-ringers, moving waxworks, wrestlers and boxing-booths, performing animals and any number of street performers and tumblers: there were many ways of parting people from their money. The merrier the crowd, the easier this would be, and merrymaking was easy – to assist in the enjoyment at English fairs, for example, any person had the right to sell malt liquor in a booth during a fair.[37] During the day, it was common practice for bargains to be sealed by vendor or purchaser (whichever was mutually agreed to have secured the advantage) by paying for drinks.[38]

The mountebank as entertainer: parodying the physician

How do mountebanks fit into this picture of the fair and its entertainers? Their presence is noted in a 1773 account of Sturbridge Fair, Cambridge, one of the longest-established and most famous fairs in England:

> Goldsmiths, Toymen, Jewellers, Braziers, Turners, Milliners, Haberdashers, Hatters, Mercers, Drapers, Pewterers, China Warehouses, and most trades that can be found in London; but likewise Coffee Houses, Taverns, Eating Houses, Music shops, Buildings for the Exhibition of Drolls, Puppet Shews, Legerdemain, Mountebanks, Wild Beasts, Monsters, Giants, Dwarfs, Rope Dancers & c.[39]

In this list, the mountebanks are placed in a group of what to modern eyes appear to be entertainments: drolls (comic plays or farce), puppet shows, legerdemain, *mountebanks*, wild beasts, monsters etc. They are *not* included in the first list of traders selling their services or products. Why? It seems that the mountebanks' *methods* of selling their cures and treaments may have been considered more noteworthy than the cures themselves.

The principal means by which the mountebank would attract a crowd to buy his mixtures and medicines would be by the performance of a spectacular, and usually extremely verbose, parody of the learned physician. William Eamon, in discussing the rise of the Italian *ciarlatani* of the seventeenth century, has described their parodying of authority:

> One can imagine him in his tight knee-breeches, ruffled doublet, and cloak, holding forth with his learned platitudes and his ridiculous malapropisms. 'He who is sick cannot be said to be well,' he would expound in a mock-serious tone, parodying the physicians, and he would prove it on the analogy that he who walks cannot be said to stand still. In another commedia dell'arte scenario Graziano advises a patient with a toothache, 'Hold a ripe apple in your mouth and put your head in the oven; before the apple is cooked your toothache will be gone.'[40]

Eamon sets great importance on the theatrical performance of the Italian *ciarlatano*, who would parody a quack doctor in a comedy, then peddle his own quack nostrums to the audience in the piazza marketplace, creating 'a stark contrast between the physician's elegant but meaningless prattle and the charlatan's instant, surefire remedies [which] struck a responsive chord in the audience gathered around the mountebank'.[41] Although Eamon is drawing a contrast between official Galenic theory and a convicingly sold instant remedy, we shall see that there is a parallel here with the performance of the charlatan pretend tooth-drawer whose drugs and promises would hold out hope for many of cheating the more conventional, and painful, remover of teeth.

In his *Dictionary of the English Language* of 1755, Dr Johnson described the mountebank as 'A doctor that mounts a bench in the market, and boasts his infallible remedies and cures':[42] a definition which makes no distinction between trader or performer, applying equally well to either, or both. However, examination of some of the statutes and regulations which were applied to fairs shows, again, that mountebanks could be considered primarily as entertainers. In England, sixteenth-century regulations, applied to fairs with the intention of reducing entertainment to encourage trade, had forbidden minstrels, rope-dancers and mountebanks to *perform* in all the fairs of the kingdom.[43] In the *Postman* for 8 September 1702, the Master and Controller of the revels at London's Bartholomew Fair named several of the 'Stage-players, Mountebanks, Rope-dancers, Prize-players, Puppet-showers, and such as make shew of motion and strange sights', who had defied their licence.[44] In France, this positioning with entertainers had been applied to so-called 'tooth-drawers' also, as a Parisian police article of 1635 had grouped both them and drug-sellers with acrobats, puppeteers and singers in addressing 'les vendeurs de thériaque, arracheurs de dents, joueurs de tourniquet, marionnettes et chanteurs de chansons'.[45]

The performance of the mountebank, dressed in his colourful costume, and accompanied by the clowning of his Merry-Andrew or fool, was indeed extravagantly theatrical (see Figure 1.1). The Merry-Andrew, appealing to the crowd's 'predominant delight in jesters',[46] was no stranger to them. The audience knew that the fool, concealed within his clowning, had a licence to speak the truth, with no risk of censure in the fair's atmosphere of fun and revelling.

Playing the Merry-Andrew required unusual talent, as an advertisement from the *Newcastle Courant* of 1761 indicates:

> Wanted immediately a brisk active man to serve a travelling doctor as an Andrew. He must be a person of drollery and ready wit, if he has followed that calling before he will be the more acceptable, or if he plays an instrument. Like wise wanted a second-hand trumpet, cheap.[47]

The fairground favourite of rope-dancing could also feature in the act: after the London mountebank Tom Jones ('Gentlemen, Because I present myself among you, I would not have you to think I am an Upstart, Glisterpipe, Bum-Peeping Apothecary')[48] had given his appeal for the crowd to buy his packets of medicine at a 'Twopenny piece' each, his Jack-pudding (or Merry-Andrew) would dance upon the tightrope for their amusement.

1.1 'The Mountebank and his Merry-Andrew'. The Merry-Andrew appears from behind a curtain, as the mountebank displays his bottles of medicine to the crowd. (Frontispiece to *The Harangues or Speeches of several Famous Mountebanks in Town and Country*, anon., 1725: reproduced in Morley, *Memoirs of Bartholomew Fair*, 1859.)

Such descriptions show the mountebank and his Merry-Andrew to have made an important contribution to the humorous and entertaining atmosphere of the fair. *Fun upon Fun, or the Humours of a Fair*,[49] although probably dating from around 1810, nevertheless provides an example of the typical 'patter' of a mountebank and Merry-Andrew, serving to impart the long-established atmosphere of busy enjoyment and amusement which had prevailed for centuries. The writer described the crowd, setting the scene of fun and gaiety, the dangers of getting caught up in the bustling mob, complaining about the smell of the packed crowd and savouring 'the first thing I saw which gave me pleasure, ... old *Gaffer Gingerbread's* stall'.[50] There were rides, such as roundabouts and the 'Up-and-down', the dangers of which were warned against – it was a wooden 'horse in a box, a horse that flies in the air, like that which the ancient poets rode upon'.[51] Mr Punch 'with his haunch at his back'[52] was there, and the Wheel of Fortune, playing children for oranges, with as many as twenty players at a time being introduced to the horrors of gambling.[53] But it was the mountebank, in his garish attire,[54] that attracted the greatest attention, and his Merry-Andrew that drew the laughter:

> Hey day! Who comes here? Oh, this is the Mountebank. He talks of curing ev'ry sore, but makes you twice as many more. But hear him! hear his speech, and observe the merry Andrew.
>
> *The DOCTOR'S SPEECH.*
> Gentlemen and Ladies, I am the doctor of all doctors, the great doctor of doctors, who can doctor you all. I ease your pains gratis, cure you for nothing, and sell you my packets, that you may never be sick again. (Enter *Andrew* blowing on a scrubbing-broom.) Sirrah, where have you been this morning?
> *Andrew.* Been, Sir! why, I have been on my travels, Sir, with my knife, Sir; I have travelled round this great apple. Besides this, I have travelled through the fair, Sir, and bought all these ginger-bread books at a man's stall, who sells learning by weight and measure, arithmetic by the gross, geometry by the square, and physic and philosophy by the pound. So I bought the philosophy, and left the physic for you master.
> *Doctor.* Why, sirrah, do you never take physic?
> *Andrew.* Yes, master, sometimes.
> *Doctor.* What sort do you take?
> *Andrew.* Any sort, no matter what; 'tis all one to me.
> *Doctor.* And how do you take it?
> *Andrew.* Why I take it; I take it: and put it upon the shelf: and if I don't get well, I take it down again, and work it off with good strong ale. But you shall hear me read in my golden books, master.
> He that can dance with a bag at his back,
> Need swallow no physic, for none he doth lack.
> He who is healthy, and cheerful and cool,
> Yet squanders his money on physic's a *fool*,

Fool, master, fool, fool.
Doctor. Sirrah, you blockhead, I'll break your head.
Andrew. What, for reading my book, Sir?
Doctor. No; for your impudence, puppy. But come, good people.
Throw up your handkerchiefs, you lose time by attending to that
blundering booby, and by and by you'll be in a hurry, and we shall
not be able to serve you. Consider, gentlemen and ladies, in one of
these packets is deposited a curious gold ring, which the purchaser,
whoever it may happen to be, will have for a shilling, together with
all the packet of medicines; and every other adventurer will have a
packet for one shilling, which he may sell for ten times that sum.
Andrew. Master, master, I'll tell you how to get this ring, and a
great deal of money into the bargain.
Doctor. How, sirrah?
Andrew. Why, buy up all of them yourself, and you will be sure of
the ring, and have the packets to sell for ten shillings a piece.
Doctor. That's true: but you are covetous, sirrah: you are covetous
and want to get money.
Andrew. And master, I believe you don't want to get physic.
Doctor. Yes I do.
Andrew. Then 'tis to get rid of it. But,
He that can dance with a bag at his back,
Need swallow no physic, for none he doth lack.
Huzza, halloo boys, halloo boys, halloo![55]

What was the purpose of this performance? The mountebank and the
Merry-Andrew were engaged in a theatrical conversation, telling jokes
at the mountebank's expense, while offering the crowd a game of chance
with the promise of certain gain for those who bought medicine. The
Merry-Andrew played the part of the fool: a court jester, being at once
serious yet silly, building the backdrop of the crowd's laughter. As an
obvious figure of fun, dressed in his check costume and hat and waving
his broom at the crowd,[56] he could tell them that the mountebank's
medicine was a nonsense; it was worthless. His part was clearly intended to be ludicrous, with the joke stated at the outset as he blew on
his scrubbing-broom in parody of the trumpeter preceding an announce-
ment. But both joke and laughter were central to the successful sale of
the mountebank's medicine, which, as he stated at the beginning of his
speech, was the *only* way he made his money – his cures, had he
performed any, were *gratis*.

The mountebank drug-seller as entertainer: parodying the tooth-drawer

If the performance of the mountebank may, therefore, be understood as
an entertainment of the fair, how does this sit with the activities of his

near neighbour the mountebank drug-seller, pretending to remove teeth? Some of the harangues directed at the crowd indicated that these neighbours could often, perhaps unsurprisingly, be one and the same person. In the speech of 'The High German Doctor, and the English Fool',[57] the fool described his master as having been 'three years oculist to the German spread eagle, and seven years operator for the teeth to the King of Spain's white elephants'.[58] He was 'not only learned by his long studies, but reverend, as you may see by his beard; and wise, as you may judge by his silence'.[59] Another harangue described the high German doctor Waltho Van Claturbank as a 'chymist and dentifricator',[60] who, with the benefit of an education which included attendance at twelve universities, could offer cures for 'odontalgick inflammations'[61] in addition to cephalalgias, paralitick paraxysms, illiac passions, hen-pox, hog-pox, and whores-pox. He also sold his stiptick for 'the restoration of maidenhood' alongside the 'Carthamophra of the Triple Kingdom', two drops of which would restore health to any who may 'chance to have his brains beat out, or his head chop'd off'.[62]

Many pictures of the mountebank drug-seller contain suggestions of entertainment or trickery of some sort: some show stages, with rapt or horrified audiences; some show a clown, a fool or a monkey[63] (a symbol of trickery),[64] whilst others show the supposed removal of highly unlikely objects from the 'sufferer's' mouth.[65] Many of those so represented perform their parodies in grand settings (see Figure 1.2), the opulence of the show on the stage suggesting that their business is extremely successful.

Such pictures, far from representing literal images, contain a much richer description of their subjects than a modern photograph could. Far from requiring every element mentioned above, the presence of just one suggests an entertainment of some kind: the monkey, in particular, indicating the mountebank's dupery. But what form would this trickery take? Was the performer pulling teeth, barbarically, and exercising no skill as some writers have suggested,[66] or was he pulling legs – with an almost unrivalled consummate skill?

The fullest descriptions of the mountebank drug-seller of the fair have appeared mostly in France. The historian Alfred Franklin's exhaustive history of Parisian life, written at the end of the nineteenth century, provides a popular view of this type of entertainer performing in the fair-like atmosphere of the Pont-Neuf and amusing the crowds with claims and promises of cures for the toothache.[67] The Pont-Neuf resembled a permanent market, with shops, tents and stalls placed along each side of the bridge, and was an ideal position from which to attract business from the many who passed, whoever they might be: 'Qu'en tout tems qu'on passe sur ce pont, on y trouve toûjours un

1.2   Detail from *Un théâtre de comédiens sur la grand'place de Bruxelles*. (Balthazar van den Bossche, *c*. 1710.)

cheval blanc, un Abbé, et un putain.'[68] Franklin, writing in the 1890s, chose to align the 'tooth-drawers' with mountebanks rather than with surgeons:

> Il semble, en effet, y avoir eu de tout temps des arracheurs de dents qui, comme ceux qui exercent encore aujourd'hui dans les foires, se rapprochaient plus de la classe des saltimbanques que de celle des chirurgiens.[69]

Dressed in spectacular clothing and addressing the crowd from a stage with a resplendent backdrop or a lavishly decorated cart, the supposed tooth-drawer's appearance and behaviour was as theatrical as that of any mountebank, and each would have his own particular method of attracting the crowd to his booth. As with the English mountebank of the fair, a clown would be employed to provide the repartee, and to attract the crowd: 'Chamarrés d'or, l'épée au côté, assistés d'un pitre qui leur donnait la réplique, leurs bouffonneries attiraient autour d'eux une foule empressée'.[70] But crowds could be drawn in many ways. The Parisian Cormier was a mountebank drug-seller who attracted his audience's attention by his astonishing ability to turn water into wine. By adding a powder to a glass of water, the water would turn red: Cormier, taking the part of the jester, told the truth. He assured his audience that he used no magic, sorcery or enchantment – just a little deceit.[71]

But as suggested above, for the mountebank in his parody of the physician, the central part of the mountebank drug-seller's act was to parody the tooth-drawer. For this to succeed, some semblance of removing a tooth would be essential; and many different implements and instruments were employed in the act. Franklin quotes the *Histoire de Francion*, who had witnessed the claims of a pretend-Italian charlatan visiting the Pont-Neuf in the sixteenth century. Loudly proposing questions that his horse might ask of him if it could speak, he claimed to use its bridle to remove teeth:

> – Gentilhomme italien, à quoi est-ce que tu nous peux servir? – A vous arracher les dents, messieurs, sans vous faire aucune douleur, et à vous en remettre d'autres, avec lesquelles vous pourrez manger comme avec les naturelles. – Et avec quoi les ôtez-vous? Avec la pointe d'une épée? – Non, messieurs, cela est trop vieil; c'est avec ce que je tiens dans ma main. – Et que tiens-tu dans ta main, seigneur italien? – La bride de mon cheval.[72]

After 'beaucoup d'autres sottises', a 'sufferer' was displayed, spitting fake blood, from whom the charlatan had supposedly removed at least six teeth earlier: 'tenant un peu de peinture rouge dans sa bouche, il sembloit qu'il crachoit du sang'.[73]

The eighteenth-century Parisian charlatan depicted in Figure 1.3 is using one of the favourite implements of the mountebank drug-seller,

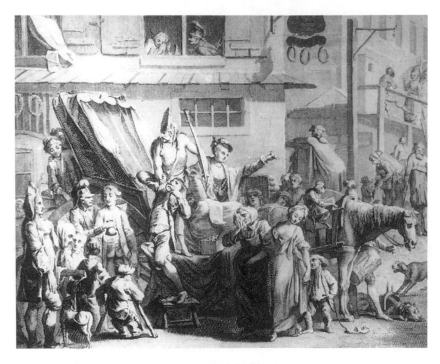

LE CHARLATAN,
à Paris.

L'argent fait à chacun jouer ici son rôle.
Pendant que sur son char cet hardi Charlatan
Enlève avec son sabre, une dent à ce drôle,
Sa belle, à ses côtés, vend son orviétan.
  Un nouveau débarqué qu'un grenadier engage
Par l'appas des ...s perdant sa liberté,

Du métier des héros va faire apprentissage.
  Avec sa Colombine Arlequin en gaieté,
Faisant sur leurs trétaux mille bouffonneries
Excitent des passants la curiosité
Pour se faire payer leurs plates Comédies.

1.3   *Le Charlatan, à Paris*. (Engraving by Touzét, eighteenth century.)

the point of his sword (as dismissed by the charlatan of the *Histoire de Francion* as too old-fashioned), to attract the attention of the crowd. But if he were really attempting to remove a tooth, would he choose such an unlikely implement? The tooth-drawer, who *did* extract teeth, would use specially designed instruments to make the task of tooth removal easier, such as the pelican or the forceps;[74] even the village farrier, called upon occasionally to remove teeth for his neighbours,[75] would perhaps use an instrument from his forge which had been modified to assist him in removing teeth. But the use of a cumbersome sword, long and unwieldy, and held at the point (with all the weight at the other end, making the 'instrument' unbalanced and difficult to hold) appears ludicrous. If a sharp point were deemed necessary for such a task, surely a small, easily handled knife or dagger, as the tooth-drawer may perhaps have used, would have been more suitable?[76] But consider the wielder of the sword as a showman, wishing to attract as much attention to himself as possible, and emphasizing his business as a curer of toothache at the same time. The unsuitability of the instrument begins to make more sense: it is a parody of the tooth-drawer's small knife, which becomes a large pointer, indicating the mouth. As with the English Merry-Andrew blowing on his scrubbing-brush, this particular 'tooth-drawer' plays his joke on the audience by suggesting the use of a ludicrous implement. A flashing and brightly tassled sword would be seen more easily by the crowd, drawing their attention in the most spectacular manner to the open mouth, and doing nothing to make the physical extraction of a tooth seem an attractive prospect for real or potential sufferers – who would now be more easily persuaded to consider a drug as an alternative to calling on the services of a tooth-drawer of *any* description.

Reading the caption to the *Charlatan, à Paris* reveals a picture explicitly intending to show the power of money: 'Money makes everyone here play their part. While on his wagon this audacious charlatan lifts with his sword a tooth from this buffoon, his *belle*, at his side, sells his *orviétan*.' The picture is about money, and money is gained by the sale of *orviétan*. To the left of the cart, a recruit to the army loses his freedom for money, whilst to the right a performer entertains passers-by in order to pay his way. Our eyes, drawn to the man holding the sword in parody of the tooth-drawer, have not moved on as they should: we cannot hear the cry of the woman holding up the bottle for all to see and buy, standing at the very centre of the picture.

Strong support is lent to this reading of the picture of the Parisian charlatan in the contemporary writings of the Parisian surgeon Pierre Fauchard. We shall see that the publication of Fauchard's book, *Le Chirurgien Dentiste,* will provide us with a valuable window on to the making of the *dentiste* in France in the early eighteenth century; and at the same time this window reveals a glimpse of a different kind of practitioner, referred to by Fauchard as a 'pretend-operator'.[77] This type of practitioner, whom Fauchard places typically at the fair on the Pont-Neuf, appears to be a close relative of the performer in the picture above. His performance has little to do with the physical removal of teeth as a cure for genuine sufferers from toothache – but much to do with the successful sale of drugs.

> le prétendu Opérateur, qui tient dans sa main une dent toute prête envéloppée dans une membrane très-fine avec du sang de poulet, ou d'un autre animal, introduit sa main dans la bouche du feint malade, & y laisse la dent qu'il tenoit cachée: Après quoi il n'a qu'à toucher,

ou faire semblant de toucher la dent avec une poudre, ou une paille, ou avec la pointe de son épée: Il n'a même, s'il veut, qu'à sonner une clochette à l'oreille du prétendu patient, qui écrase pendant ce tems là ce qu'on lui a mis dans la bouche: On le voit aussitôt cracher du sang & une dent ensanglantée, qui n'est pourtant que la dent que l'imposteur, ou le supposé malade avoit introduite dans sa bouche. Si dans la foule quelqu'un trompé par ce stratagême, se présente pour se faire tirer une dent, la poudre, la paille, &c. n'étant plus de mise, l'Opérateur ambulant trouvera bien vîte une défaite: Il ne manquera pas de supposer, que la fluxion est trop forte; qu'il faut patienter encore quelques jours, ou bien que cette dent est une dent œillére, qu'il ne faut point tirer; parce que ces sortes de dents, &c. sont, comme ces Empiriques le prétendent, relatives à l'œil, qui seroit, disent-ils, bientôt perdu, si on les ôtoit. ... car pour peu qu'ils en rencontrent qui leur paroissent difficiles à ôter, ils rengainent bien vîte leur épée ... dont ils sont parade dans les Provinces, & à Paris sur le Pont-neuf, théâtre ordinaire de ces imposteurs, qui ayant alarmé les malades par cette fausse opinion des dents œilléres, les assurent après cela que moyennant une certaine somme, ils ne laisseront pas de les guérir, & qu'ils ont pour leur mal, un reméde immanquable, dont ils possédent eux-seuls le secret ... [78]

Fauchard's account shows that this event was not about extracting teeth, but was a typical performance of what had become the charlatans' *théâtre ordinaire* – the Pont-Neuf. The *prétendu opérateur* had his pretend patient, the *feint malade*. With a theatrical flourish, a tooth covered in blood was removed from the supposed sufferer's mouth at the touch of a straw, a powder, the point of a sword or even by the simple act of ringing a bell – but it had *first been placed there* by the sleight-of-hand of the charlatan. This was an entertainment, a comical conjuror's performance, worthy of the mountebank and his Merry-Andrew. But what was the reason for such a ridiculous display of what was clearly *not* tooth drawing? If any member of the crowd should be taken in by the joke, and mount the stage to ask for a tooth to be removed, the mountebank, far from attempting an extraction, would refuse to intervene physically in the patient's suffering. Any excuse would be found – there would perhaps be too much fluxion present, or the painful tooth would instead be identified as an eye tooth, removal of which would surely pull the eye out with it. But there was still hope for the poor unfortunate. Whilst the reluctant 'tooth-drawer' could not possibly physically remove such a tooth without causing more harm than benefit, the sufferer could instead be persuaded to purchase an infallible secret cure for his or her toothache. The charlatan's intention, as Fauchard saw it, should now be clear: he was using a spectacular theatrical parody of the tooth-drawer's performance, aimed purely at increasing sales of his own particular secret remedy for painful teeth – his *orviétan*.

The mountebank drug-seller as part of a 'quack' tradition of treating teeth

Where should we place the image of the mountebank drug-seller, the supposed tooth-drawer of the fair, in the picture of the treatment of teeth in early eighteenth-century France? In his discussion of popular medicine, Jean-Pierre Goubert has described the charlatan as a criminal, either actual or potential, following the pattern: (i) charlatans were not competent, due to a lack of training; (ii) due to this ignorance, charlatans may have caused accidents, or committed crimes; (iii) as a result, they were rogues and swindlers who sought to trick others.[79] But it is difficult to apply such reasoning to the fairground activities of the mountebank drug-seller. Application of the traditional view of the charlatan setting out to perform many unskilled physical extractions of teeth, work that was properly that of the tooth-drawer, could allow for a moulding of the act to fit such an analysis; but viewing the mountebank drug-seller as a showman, using spectacle and parody to advertise the sale of drugs to cure diseased teeth, levels a charge of a different type of deception. Much has been made of the common claim to remove teeth 'sans douleur',[80] the implication being that in the absence of modern analgesia this was impossible, and therefore dishonest.[81] Similarly, the remark 'to lie like a tooth-drawer' has been taken to be proof of dishonesty[82] – but the lie here lay not in the absence of pain; it lay in the absence of extraction. The *suggestion*, an important part of the show, has a modern parallel in the act of the magician, whose audience have 'learned the game' as children, and who enjoy the entertainment with an aura of complicity and ready suspension of belief.

Pictures of the mountebank drug-seller at the fair should now, perhaps, be unlocked from their jealously guarded places in works of dental history, and allowed to be positioned with those of other entertainers and showmen. In our assumption that this type of mountebank is an unskilled and dishonest pretender to the trade of the tooth-drawer, we have ignored the skill, and purpose, of the show. The mountebank drug-seller possessed a different type of skill altogether – and, therefore, was part of a greater quack tradition in the treatment of teeth.

The quack tradition of the itinerant fairground mountebank would continue alongside the practice of the 'real' tooth-drawer and that of the *dentiste* into the nineteenth century, with a plentiful supply of miraculous cures and powders available to the paying public. Roy Porter, in noting that 'Historians have assumed that the itinerant quack was a species dying out like the dodo', has shown that 'It would be wrong, however to kill them off prematurely.'[83] With regard to the mountebank performing on the stage, he has illustrated this using the

young Francis Place's enjoyment of the performance of Dr Bossy, in full
mountebank regalia, in Covent Garden around the turn of the nineteenth century.[84] A new lease of life was given to the mountebanks by
the advent of the railway, by which means they were now able to wend
their way in a leisurely manner from town to town, thereby increasing
their range very effectively.[85] Porter has also pointed out that 'Perhaps
the most flamboyant quack ever to traverse England, "Sequah", surrounded by tribes of "Indian braves", flourished as late as the end of
the nineteenth century.'[86]

But it was not only the mountebank selling physic who would perform on into the next century – the mountebank drug-seller and pretend
tooth-drawer of the fairs and markets would also enjoy continuing
longevity. Matthew Ramsey's work regarding illegal healers in nineteenth-
century France also refutes the suggestion that the old-fashioned
itinerant charlatan disappeared at the end of the eighteenth century,
when the growth of advertising in provincial journals allowed a mail-
order trade in patent remedies to flourish for the first time.[87] And it was
not only the *colporteur* or pedlar who continued to operate – Ramsey,
studying the Bas-Rhin department of France, notes the presence of
groups of 'classic mountebanks',[88] announcing their arrival with printed
flyers, dressed in elaborate costumes and using a carnival barker's techniques to draw large crowds at fairs and other public places. Amongst
his 'classic mountebanks', Ramsey usefully uncovers the activities of
'Tauber' from the Bas-Rhin, appearing in the Napoleonic department of
Mont-Tonnerre as late as 1810. Calling himself (in Ramsey's words)
dentist and oculist, he 'travelled on horseback from village to village,
claiming, among other things, to possess a marvellous specific to cure
chronic illnesses in twenty-four hours, and to make goiters disappear'.
As we shall see, from the middle of the eighteenth century onwards the
natural target for his parody would become the *dentiste*, rather than the
tooth-drawer, however, in true mountebank tradition, 'A buffoon followed him to distribute his flagons.'[89]

Notes

1. Matthew Ramsey, *Professional and popular medicine in France, 1770–
   1830: the social world of medical practice*, Cambridge University Press,
   Cambridge, 1988, p. 132.
2. *Dictionnaire universel françois et latin*, 4th edn, 1743, cited in ibid.
3. Ibid., p. 133.
4. Ibid., 'The charlatans at work', p. 147 ff.
5. Ibid., p. 147.

6. 'Mountebank' will here be taken in its literal meaning, as one who mounts a bench. *OED*, Clarendon Press, Oxford, 2nd edn, 1989.
7. For example, in the 1770s the fair at Beaucaire (which was reputed to be the largest in France) boasted 'cent mille visiteurs par jour'. Dominique Margairaz, *Foires et marchés dans la France préindustrielle*, École des Hautes Études en Science Sociales, Paris, 1988, p. 102.
8. For perceptive research concerning the economics of French fairs and markets, see Margairaz, *Foires et marchés*; Jean-Claude Perrot, *Genèse d'une ville moderne: Caen au XVIIIe siècle*, Mouton & Co. and École des Hautes Études en Sciences Sociales, Paris, 1975, vol. 1; and P. Léon, 'Vie et mort d'un grand marché international: la foire de Beaucaire (XVIIIe–XIXe siècles)', *Revue de Géographie de Lyon*, 28, 1953, 309–28.
9. Perrot, *Genèse d'une ville moderne*, p. 474.
10. As at King's Lynn, each February 2nd. W. Owen, *Owen's Book of Fairs, being an authentic account of all the Fairs in England and Wales*, London, 1773, 6th edn. This book was first published in 1756 as *An authentic account, published by the King's authority, of all the fairs in England and Wales*.
11. According to *Owen's Book of Fairs*, in some areas, for example Essex, toy fairs were more common than any other kind.
12. The French word *orviétan*, describing a secret remedy or antidote, was also used in England – Samuel Johnson gave its meaning as 'a medical composition or electuary, good against poison'. Johnson's *Dictionary of the English Language*, London, 1755. In this work, I shall take it from both languages.
13. R. James, *A Medicinal Dictionary, ... together with a History of Drugs*, Osborne, London, 1743: the 'Lemery' referred to was the author of a pharmacopoeia.
14. Hooper, *Lexicon Medicum*, Longman, Hurst, Rees, Orme & Co., London, 1820, 4th edn.
15. Pierre Pomet, *A Compleat History of Druggs, written in French by Monsieur Pomet, chief druggist to the late French King Lewis XIV*, Bonwicke and Wilkin, London, 1725, and James, *A Medicinal Dictionary*.
16. James, *A Medicinal Dictionary*.
17. Ibid.
18. Ibid.
19. François Vidal (ed.), *Histoire d'un diplôme*, LCD, Paris, n.d. (*c.* 1993), p. 4. Vidal describes Embry as 'a chemist'.
20. *Les secrets du seigneur Alexis*, 1691 edn, p. 351; cited in Alfred Franklin, *La vie privée d'autrefois: Arts et métiers, modes, mœurs, usages des parisiens du XIIe au XVIIIe siècle d'après des documents originaux ou inédits*, vol. 14, *Variétés chirurgicales*, E. Plon, Nourrit et cie, Paris, 1893, p. 139.
21. Mme Fouquet, *Recueil de remèdes faciles et domestiques*, 1678 edn; cited in Franklin, *Variétés chirurgicales*, p. 139.
22. Walter Hoffmann-Axthelm, *History of Dentistry*, Quintessence, Chicago, 1981, p. 125.
23. J. J. Plenk, *Lehre von den Krankheiten der Zähne und des Zahnfleisches*, 1790, cited in Hoffmann-Axthelm, *History of Dentistry*, p. 238.
24. Perrot, *Genèse d'une ville moderne*, p. 468.
25. Ibid., p. 480.

26. See Jean-Pierre Goubert, 'L'art de guérir. Médecine savante et médecine populaire dans la France de 1790', *Annales Économies, Sociétés, Civilisations,* 5, 1977, 908–26.

27. Common usage of 'fair' in present-day England is generally taken to mean a travelling group of entertainments, each typically operated by the members of one family – now also called a 'funfair'. This is balanced by the 'trade fair', usually held indoors and offering exhibitions of services or products from one branch of industry.

28. Pepys's *Diary,* cited in Ian Starsmore, *English Fairs,* Thames and Hudson, London, 1975, p. 13. 'A rope-dancer' was described helpfully by Samuel Johnson as 'An artist who dances on a rope.' More usefully, Johnson also cited *Wilkin's Mathematical Magic*: 'It is a usual practice in these times for our funambulours, or dancers on the rope, to attempt somewhat like to flying', and *Addison's Guardian*: 'Statius, posted on the highest of the two summits, the people regarded with the same terror, as they look upon a daring ropedancer, whom they expect to fall every moment.' Johnson, *Dictionary.*

29. For example, 5 September 1661, 4 September 1663, 2 September 1664 and again on the 7th – 'the best dancing on the ropes that I think I ever saw in my life.' Robert Latham (ed.), *The Shorter Pepys,* Unwin Hyman, London, 1990.

30. An implement for pressing down the tobacco in a smoker's pipe. Henry Morley, *Memoirs of Bartholomew Fair,* Chapman and Hall, London, 1859, p. 345.

31. Ibid., p. 345.

32. Ibid., p. 345.

33. Ibid., p. 453.

34. According to the 'Reasons Formerly published for the PUNCTUAL LIMITING of *Bartholomew Fair* to those *Three Days* to which it is determined by the ROYAL GRANT of it to the City of LONDON', reprinted in 1711, the 'lewd and ravenous crew' from the fair did 'annoy the Commerce of honest Citizens in the Day, and disturb their Repose in the Night'. The fair was declared 'a season of the utmost Disorder and Debauchery, by reason of the Booths for Drinking, Music, Dancing, Stage-plays, Drolls, Lotteries, Gaming, Raffling, and what not'. Morley, *Memoirs of Bartholomew Fair,* pp. 380–81.

35. Cited by Starsmore, *English Fairs,* pp. 13–14.

36. Such as Fielding's production of Molière's *Le Médecin Malgré Lui* at Bartholomew Fair in 1732. Starsmore, *English Fairs,* p. 16. In 1693, after a naval disaster in the bay of Lagos, an entire cast of players from Bartholomew Fair were imprisoned for commenting 'to large applauding audiences, not only on the affairs of the Admiralty, but also on other departments of the State'. Morley, *Memoirs of Bartholomew Fair,* p. 335.

37. Frederick W. Hackwood, *Inns, Ales and Drinking Customs of Old England,* Bracken, London, 1987 edn, p. 113.

38. Ibid., p. 151.

39. Charles Caraccioli, *An Historical account of Sturbridge, Bury, and the most famous fairs in Europe and America; interspersed with anecdotes curious and entertaining,* Fletcher and Hodson, Cambridge, 1773, p. 21.

40. Doctor Gratiano Pagliarizzo, *Secreti nuovi et rari,* Bologna, Milan, n.d., cited in William Eamon, *Science and the secrets of nature: books of*

secrets in medieval and early modern culture, Princeton University Press, Chichester, 1994, pp. 240–41.

41. Eamon, *Science and the secrets of nature,* p. 241.
42. Johnson, *Dictionary.*
43. Caraccioli, *An Historical account,* p. 32.
44. See Morley, *Memoirs of Bartholomew Fair,* p. 359.
45. Franklin, *Variétés chirurgicales,* p. 144.
46. Morley, *Memoirs of Bartholomew Fair,* p. 423.
47. Christine Hillam, *Brass Plate and Brazen Impudence: Dental practice in the provinces, 1755–1855,* Liverpool University Press, Liverpool, 1991, p. 131.
48. Anon., *The Harangues or Speeches of several Famous Mountebanks in Town and Country,* T. Warner, London, n.d. (*c.* 1725), p. 19.
49. Anon., *Fun upon Fun, or the Humours of a Fair, giving a description of the curious Amusements in Early Life: Also an account of a Mountebank Doctor and his Merry Andrew,* J. Lumsden, Glasgow, n.d. (*c.* 1810).
50. Ibid., p. 12.
51. Ibid., p. 32. Pictures of the 'Up-and-down' show a machine similar to the Ferris wheel of the modern fair, with boxes for the passengers to ride in. See ibid., p. 33, or Morley, *Memoirs of Bartholomew Fair,* p. 397, for an Up-and-down of 1728.
52. *Fun upon Fun,* p. 13.
53. Ibid., p. 18.
54. For examples of mountebanks' costumes at the fair, see Morley, *Memoirs of Bartholomew Fair,* pp. 284 and 297 (see Figure 1.1).
55. *Fun upon Fun,* pp. 23–31.
56. See illustration, 'Assembling the people', on p. 27 of ibid.
57. Anon., *The Harangues or Speeches of several celebrated Quack-Doctors in Town and Country,* J. Thomson, London, 1762, p. 11.
58. Ibid., p. 11.
59. Ibid., p. 11.
60. *The Harangues or Speeches of several Famous Mountebanks,* p. 13.
61. Ibid., p. 14.
62. Ibid., p. 14.
63. Examples may be found in Armelle and Pierre Baron, *L'Art dentaire à travers la Peinture,* Paris, 1986, including *Le Marché en Italie,* by Peter Bout and Adrien Boudewyns (p. 122), *Scène de foire,* by Faustino Bocchi (p. 126), *Arracheur de dents sur une foire,* by Christian Wilhelm Dietrich (p. 172), *Le Charlatan,* by Anton Maulpertsch (p. 178), *Arlequin dentiste,* by François Watteau (p. 179) and *Le Charlatan,* by Giandomenico Tiepolo (p. 187). There are also similar pictures to be found in Malvin E. Ring, *Dentistry: An illustrated history,* Abrams, New York, 1985, such as an engraving of a German charlatan (p. 156) and *Le Charlatan, à Paris* (p. 175). Each picture shows at least one of these elements. It should be noted that in each case except the last, the titles have been applied retrospectively.
64. Baron, *L'Art dentaire,* p. 13.
65. For example, in Palizzi's painting titled *Il Caccia-Mole in Carnevale* ('the jaw-breaker at the fair', Palizzi's own title) the charlatan is brandishing before a crowd an entire animal's jaw, which he has supposedly just removed from a human mouth. Reproduced in Ring, *Dentistry,* p. 214.

66. For example, Malvin Ring has described extraction by sword as 'barbaric' yet 'very popular'. Ibid., p. 174. In similar vein, Menzies Campbell has stated that 'tooth-drawing by instalments' would ensue, thereby implying that a lack of 'dental' skill on the part of the mountebank would result in broken-off rather than cleanly extracted teeth. J. M. Campbell, *Dentistry Then and Now*, 3rd edn, private publication, Glasgow, 1981, p. 120.

67. Franklin, *Variétés chirurgicales*, p. 142 ff.

68. Alfred Franklin, *La vie privée d'autrefois: Arts et métiers, modes, mœurs, usages des parisiens du XIIe au XVIIIe siècle d'après des documents originaux ou inédits*, vol. 21, *La vie de Paris sous la Régence*, E. Plon, Nourrit et c^ie, Paris, 1897, p. 202.

69. Franklin, *Variétés chirurgicales*, p. 143.

70. Ibid., p. 143.

71. Ibid., p. 154.

72. Ibid., p. 147.

73. Ibid., p. 148.

74. The pelican was named after the bird, from its resemblance to the shape of the beak, and is first recorded as having been in use in France in the fourteenth century. The forceps 'is probably the oldest of all dental instruments after the fingers', and was well known throughout Europe in the seventeenth and eighteenth centuries. See Elisabeth Bennion, *Antique Dental Instruments*, Sotheby's, London, 1986, chapter 2: Extracting instruments.

75. See, for example, Parson Woodforde's diary: Woodforde called on a farrier to remove a painful tooth for him on 4 June 1776. James Woodforde, *A Country Parson: James Woodforde's diary 1758–1802*, OUP, Oxford, and Century, London, 1985, p. 51.

76. The Dutch surgeon Cornelius Solingen, having described the technique for removing teeth with forceps and pelican in detail, notes in passing that it can be done 'like the quacks and toothdrawers, with the point of a dagger'. Solingen, *Handgriffe der wund-artzney*, Frankfurt, 1693, cited in Hoffmann-Axthelm, *History of dentistry*, p. 185.

77. Pierre Fauchard, *Le Chirurgien Dentiste, ou Traité des Dents*, Mariette, Paris, 1746 (2nd ed.), vol. II, p. 183.

78. Ibid., pp. 183–5.

79. Goubert, 'L'art de guérir', p. 915.

80. See, for example, Cormier, offering extraction 'sans aucune douleur', cited in Franklin, *Variétés chirurgicales*, p. 154, and 'Un homme à cheval' in Paris, who could 'arracher les dents, messieurs, sans vous faire aucune douleur', cited in ibid., p. 147.

81. 'The majority were brazen charlatans with little or no ability except a line of patter about their skill and the painlessness of their ministrations, this giving rise to the popular expression "he lies like a tooth-drawer".' M. Smith, *A Short History of Dentistry*, Allan Wingate, London, 1958, p. 23.

82. 'about this time [1730] a common aphorism referring to the character of the itinerant dentist was often used in continental Europe; "Il ment comme un arracheur des dents"'. Hermann Prinz, 'Pierre Fauchard and His Works', *Dental Cosmos*, LXV, 1923, p. 827. 'Menteur comme un arracheur de dents': see Franklin, *Variétés chirurgicales*, p. 144.

83. Roy Porter, *Health for sale: Quackery in England 1660–1850,* Manchester University Press, Manchester, 1989, p. 61.
84. Ibid., p. 61.
85. Ibid., p. 62.
86. W. Schupbach, 'Sequah: an English American medicine-man in 1890', *Medical History,* **XXIX**, 1985, 272–317, cited in Porter, *Health for sale*, p. 62.
87. Matthew Ramsey, 'Medical power and popular medicine: illegal healers in nineteenth-century France', in P. Branca (ed.), *The Medicine Show: Patients, Physicians and the Perplexities of the Health Revolution in Modern Society,* Science History Publications, New York, 1977, p. 186.
88. Ibid.
89. Ibid., p. 187.

CHAPTER TWO

Drawing Teeth: Practitioners below the Ladder of 'Official' Surgery

Having examined the activities of the mountebank drug-seller of the fair, using his act to promote his principal business of the sale of drugs, we should now consider those practitioners who *did* physically treat teeth in France in the late seventeenth and eighteenth centuries. In this chapter, it will become apparent that such treatment, consisting principally of the removal of diseased teeth rather than their repair, was inextricably linked to the structure of the French surgical profession, from the officially recognized and respected Paris surgeon to the 'unofficial' popular practitioner of the provinces. By the beginning of the eighteenth century, French surgery was becoming highly structured and its practice increasingly regulated as surgeons moved centre-stage in the practice of medicine. In the chapters which follow, this movement and its central role in the making of the *dentiste* will be examined in more detail; but this chapter will focus on the broad and, to us at any rate, often indistinct picture of those practitioners who could not officially take the title of surgeon but who chose to offer the treatment of teeth as an important part of their practice. In the relatively narrow field which is provided by the activity of treating teeth, we shall see that the boundary between official and unofficial practice is, to our eyes, at best highly mobile and at worst completely non-existent – but again, here we must exercise great care. As noted in the discussion of nomenclature in the introduction to this book, the implications of a title will hinge on the viewpoint of the observer; hence we shall come across examples of surgeons described as charlatans, and charlatans who were apparently officially recognized as surgeons. We shall see that the principal activity of the members of this group was the drawing of teeth, and for this reason I shall describe them as 'tooth-drawers'; but how can we obtain a clearer view of them and their activities? Where should they sit in the structure of surgical practice in the *ancien régime*?

In analysing the practice of this type of practitioner, we first need to look closely at the lower levels of official surgery in France in this period. Studies in the history of medicine in eighteenth-century France have naturally tended to focus on the changes occurring at the end of the century, with much of the existing literature denying the existence of a viable and recognizable (to us, that is, structured in the modern style) profession before the French revolution.[1] Over the last thirty years, however, our view of this period has been made much clearer by the increasing interest of professional historians of surgery. Writers such as Toby Gelfand, Matthew Ramsey and Colin Jones have revealed the impact and importance of French surgery on and for the medical profession of the *ancien régime*. Gelfand's somewhat 'surgeon-friendly' work in particular has demonstrated the existence of a broad-based officially regulated hierarchical structure, which became increasingly powerful in the late seventeenth and eighteenth centuries and which would later come together with the practice of the physicians, thereby creating a basis for a new profession.[2] Colin Jones's writing has encouraged a perhaps more balanced approach to the activities of the *ancien régime* surgeon, and of the social and institutional contexts within which those activities should be placed.[3] In an attempt to place the narrower field of practice of the tooth-drawer in a more accurate context than hitherto, I will take 'traditional' sources such as the extensive writings of the nineteenth-century French historian Alfred Franklin, and the valuable archive work of current French writers on dental history such as François Vidal and Pierre Baron, and apply them to Gelfand's model. First, however, we need to examine this model more closely and attempt to identify that part of it which will act as our framework – and, if necessary, extend it further.

Toby Gelfand has argued that beneath the hierarchical rank of the surgeons (that is, master surgeons) there was a group of practitioners constituting what can be considered as a profession, in the sense of an organized occupational group with a broad demand for its services, but that this group was organized in a very different way from the modern medical profession.[4] This group consisted of what Gelfand calls 'ordinary practitioners', those with no university training, whose members were known to eighteenth-century France as the *chirurgien ordinaire* or barber-surgeon. His argument, that there was no sudden birth of a legitimate medical profession at the end of the century but that one legitimate profession was replaced by another (albeit radically different), will be of great assistance here in its uncovering of these 'ordinary practitioners' and the way in which their practice was structured. But to uncover those who were typically treating teeth as a *principal* means to an income, who do *not* appear as surgeons and who did not take their title, we shall need to probe even more deeply. We shall need to examine the large supporting surface immediately *below* the broad-based pyramidal network of official French surgical hierarchy. In order to do this, we shall need to ask how this pyramid was constructed, and on what foundations it was built.

The hierarchical structure of French surgery in the *ancien régime*

The mechanism for the officially regulated structure of French surgical practice, centred in Paris, would enjoy great change and success throughout the eighteenth century. In a later chapter, both the reasons for this success, and some of its implications, will be examined more fully; however, before we can uncover the work of those practitioners who occupied the lower rungs of this framework or, indeed, the ground beneath it, we shall need first to understand the structure itself. In the mid-seventeenth century, the small number of academic surgeons of the college of Saint-Côme had united with the much larger group of barber-surgeons, a trade guild under the jurisdiction of the medical Faculty.[5] Although surgical training in Paris consisted entirely of apprenticeship, with no teaching at Saint-Côme, the academic surgeons were gaining power. Endowments in the 1690s led to the establishment of new teaching and the building of a magnificent amphitheatre at the college.[6] Under the direction of the surgeons, statutes were drawn up in 1699 to regulate the practice of the Parisian surgical community, giving real control to the academic surgeons via royal officials. Whilst the public courses at Saint-Côme received mention in these, attendance was not required – neither did they confer any credit towards surgical mastership.[7] The statutes provided for two routes of apprenticeship for would-be surgeons: a formal contract of two consecutive years, signed before a notary, or an agreement to serve one master surgeon for a minimum of six years, or several masters for seven years. This second route was intended for the *garçons chirurgiens* (surgical apprentices) who could not afford the formal contract, as they would live like domestic servants and pay no fee. After apprenticeship, the young surgeon would become a journeyman or *compagnon*, which would often be the final stage in his career. It was, however, common in Paris for the *compagnons* to leave their masters and set up in illegal practice – a police regulation of 1731 estimated the numbers of these to exceed two thousand.[8]

At the head of this surgical community sat the king's *premier* surgeon. The holder of this title had absolute rule over the practice of surgery, being in an ideal position to secure royal legislation and oversee its implementation. For example, a set of surgical statutes, drawn up in 1699, would be imposed upon the Paris guild despite the opposition of the majority of surgeons.[9] Similarly, the members of the same guild would not be consulted in the establishment of surgical institutions later in the eighteenth century. This lack of consultation is illustrated clearly in the establishment of the Académie Royale de Chirurgie, confirmed in *lettres patentes* of 1731,[10] which had the effect of creating an élite body which would effectively exclude most of the master surgeons in Paris. In addition to his power, the *premier* surgeon accrued enormous revenue, with a vast network of lieutenants and recording secretaries under his command – as Toby Gelfand has said, he was 'a virtual king of surgery'.[11]

The authority of the *premier* surgeon, and the network under his jurisdiction, reflected the organization of the state in the *ancien régime*, giving rise to Gelfand's apt description of a 'monarchical profession'.[12] As we shall see later, this began to develop with increasing speed at the beginning of the eighteenth century, with the cultivation by an élite group of Paris surgeons (led by the *premier* surgeon) of their special relationship with the Crown. By encouraging legislation, they modified the isolated surgical bodies or *communautés* of the country to form a professional network possessing some degree of unification, resulting in the 1723 statutes establishing lieutenants of the *premier* surgeon in each *communauté*. The lieutenants had the power to visit and inspect the credentials and instruments of all practitioners of any branch of surgery within their jurisdiction. But the surgical élite were becoming increasingly unhappy about their inclusion with 'vile' occupations: the surgical *communautés* were classed with *arts et métiers*, the mechanical professions, whilst the medical élite, the physicians, enjoyed high social position. In Paris, the surgeons were addressing this lack of prestige by such means as the creation of five chairs at the École de chirurgie in 1724[13] and the establishment of the Académie in 1731, both royal foundations to stand at the head of the profession. These had some beneficial effects on educational standards, but their principal aims were to raise social acceptability and professional standing of the Paris surgeons, challenging the traditional authority of the physicians and distancing themselves further from the lowly village barber-surgeons.

Further change in surgical regulation came with the legislation of 1730, which defined a three-tier gradation of master surgeons, according to the type of examination passed and the fees paid.[14] At the highest level were the surgeons practising in a city that possessed a surgical *communauté*, followed by those working in other cities and towns only. At the lowest level were the *chirurgiens de petite expérience*, who, as their title suggests, submitted to one rudimentary examination to allow them to 'set up shop and hang out a sign'.[15] Gelfand's analysis of these ordinary practitioners in terms of his 'professional' model (that is, as members of an organized occupational group) demonstrates the features of this lowest level of official surgery. A barber-surgeon, or *chirurgien ordinaire*, would thus have had legal status as a member of an occupational group, the *communauté*, formed along the lines of a guild with statutory codes of practice. It was the *communauté*, presided over by the lieutenant of the *premier* surgeon, which could confer

degrees of 'master' of surgery, control the licensing of ordinary practitioners and oversee the awarding of less prestigious certificates such as
those held by midwives, within its own particular geographical jurisdiction. In order to obtain a licence, the village barber-surgeon was examined
orally for three hours on surgical principles, including bloodletting,
abscesses, wounds and medicaments:[16] this examination conferred legal
status, setting the recipient apart from the many types of 'illegal' ordinary healers.[17] Thus, with this licensing structure in place, the official
practice of surgery, in all its forms, became a giant network with the
premier surgeon at its head, reaching down to a very fine network of
master barber-surgeons in the villages – Gelfand's 'ordinary practitioners' of France.

These ordinary practitioners enjoyed great numerical strength, which
in some regions could even approach one per thousand population. Of
the nearly four hundred surgical *communautés* in the kingdom during
the second half of the eighteenth century, almost half were located in
towns of more than four thousand inhabitants. Thus the surgical network extended to a much finer level than the other two major medical
bodies of the *ancien régime,* the physicians and the apothecaries, and
enjoyed a much wider geographic distribution in the process.[18] This
widely spread profession was of low to modest social origins and status,
similar to skilled artisans, with training by apprenticeship and subsequently by private arrangements as opposed to public (such as schools
or hospitals). Social and moral criteria, such as diligence, obedience and
reliability, were of primary importance in the evaluation of apprentices.
Even when surgical colleges began to replace apprenticeships in Paris
and the large centres, certificates would still attach great importance to
the aspiring surgeon's attendance record. These surgical schools would
have no admission requirements, and could not grant licences to practice, a power which would remain in the hands of the surgical
communautés.

Practice was usually wide-ranging, often exhibiting great versatility in
the types of work undertaken – much of which would not fit in with
modern ideas of medical care. In addition to such treatment as blood-
letting and treating wounds, activities such as barbering, bathing,
cosmetics and tooth treatment would be practised in varying propor-
tions. Some practitioners would perform relatively few different tasks,
travelling in order to find trade, whilst others would offer a wider range
in order to serve a smaller community. Practitioners would enjoy a
relatively equal social relationship with their patients, who could exercise a degree of discretionary power over the form their treatment might
take. This applied at every level of surgery: Gelfand has drawn attention to the patronage system operating at higher levels of medicine,

arguing that this relationship had much in common with the peasant seeking out a barber-surgeon to perform a blood-letting.[19] We shall see later that such a comparison may also be extended to the practice of the *dentiste*, treating members of the court and the aristocracy, and the village tooth-drawer and his patients. In both cases, a social match would be made between patient and practitioner, be they ordinary or extraordinary.

But within this hierarchical structure of surgery there was yet another 'grade' of official practitioner, placed even lower down than the barber-surgeon, and it is within this group that we shall find those whose principal activity was the drawing of teeth: but, as we shall see, the boundary marked by official recognition becomes less distinct.

The *expert pour les dents*: below the 'ordinary practitioner'

Since the beginning of the fourteenth century, the term *expert* had been used in France to describe a person who, by experience, had acquired a particular skill. By the early seventeenth century, it had come to be used frequently in conjunction with a description of a designated part of the body to indicate one who had a particular skill in attending to that part.[20] The term *expert pour les dents*, indicating someone in whom that skill was directed towards the teeth, had been in use throughout the seventeenth century, but carried with it no official recognition within the structure of the surgical hierarchy. François Vidal has described the term *expert*, in its seventeenth-century usage, as a variation on the word *opérateur*, stating that it was an *opérateur, artiste ou expert* who, by empiricism, had acquired a manual dexterity which permitted him to treat sufferers.[21] In the statutes drawn up in 1699 to regulate the practice of surgery in Paris, however, the title of *expert* would now assume a degree of legitimacy, albeit severely limited. By presenting for examination, the successful candidate could now gain official accept-ance in the practice of his or her chosen area of work, taking the title of *expert* for the treatment of that part of the body *only*. Having previ-ously carried no official approval or standing, this title would now endure, to a variable extent, throughout the remainder of the *ancien régime*.

The title *expert* could generally be applied to a wide range of practi-tioners such as midwives, cataract couchers, herniotomists, lithotomists, bone-setters and corn-curers as well as those offering to treat the teeth. Of these, the midwives were the largest group, possessing no guild of their own but now being overseen and licensed by the local surgical *communauté*. Despite their numbers, they would remain essentially uncertified until the Napoleonic era.[22] Many *experts* were itinerant, if they could not hope to find enough clients for their particular field of practice in a single town, and for the same reason many would choose to combine more than one activity. At Quesnoy, for example, it was a mason who 'played the part of dentist',[23] and Matthew Ramsey uses the example of Pierre Guilleminot of Troyes, who offered to treat both hernias and teeth as late as 1797.[24] Other craftsmen, in legitimate exercise of their art, appear to our eyes to have encroached upon the trade of the *expert*: principal amongst these were the *tabletiers*, carvers of ivory and inlaid ware, who had the right to make and sell artificial teeth,[25] and the *barbier-perruquiers*, who in addition to cutting hair and making wigs were entitled to sell powders and pastes to both whiten the teeth and to cure toothache. Barbering, bathing and the selling of cosmetics were entrusted by statute to the members of this trade, which was quite distinct from that of the barber-surgeon. Yet the threshold between the two was frequently crossed, creating the need for regulations to assist the public in distinguishing one from the other. The *barbier-perruquier* was to have

> des marques visibles de leur Art pour la propréte & ornement du corps humain ... [they were permitted] d'avoir des boutiques peintes en bleu, fermées de chassis à grands carreaux de verre, sans aucune ressemblance aux montres des Maîtres Chirurgiens; & de mettre à leurs enseignes des bassins blancs, pour marque de leur Profession, & pour faire différence de ceux des Maîtres Chirurgiens qui en ont de jaunes.[26]

The *maître barbier-perruquiers* were forbidden by law to have more than one blue boutique each in Paris.[27] Although not permitted to treat teeth by removing them, they were, however, authorized to 'vendre en leurs boutiques des poudres, opiats pour les dents, ... & généralement tout ce qui est propre pour l'ornement, propreté & netteté de corps humain',[28] thereby having access to an extremely important part of the tooth trade. It is likely that the variety and combinations of activities performed by some practitioners were indirectly responsible for the occasional need to advertise, in order to refute the damaging claims of others that the advertiser no longer offered particular types of treatment. As we shall see, many of these operators, particularly those who travelled in search of trade, were indistinguishable from empirics; but the surgical statutes for the Paris *communauté* of 1699, which would be extended to cover practice in the provinces in 1730[29] and would become further enlarged in 1768, expressly provided for the officially licensed *expert* working outside the regular corps of surgeons, but examined and approved locally by them.

The official standing of the *expert pour les dents*: the statutes of 1699 and 1768

What place did the *expert pour les dents* hold in the official hierarchical structure of eighteenth-century surgery? The regulations designed to control the practice of all parts of surgery, including those wishing to practice as *experts* (not only *pour les dents*), had been first drawn up in the statutes of 1699, which would govern surgical practice until their modification and reinforcement in 1768. Those wishing to be 'acknowledged as qualified'[30] by the *communauté* were forbidden to practise, or advertise as practising, any part of surgery for which they had not been examined by the premier surgeon or, more likely, his lieutenants. The *renoueurs*, or bone-setters, were required to demonstrate their skills and to pay a duty, whilst the *experts pour les dents, oculistes, lithotomistes* and others were required to follow the procedure laid down in two further articles. No group had the right to form a separate body, nor to assume the right to be *agrégés à la communauté* of master surgeons, nor to take any title other than *expert* for that part of surgery for which they had been officially received:

> ARTICLE CII   Il sera fait défenses à tous Bailleurs, Renoueurs d'os, aux Experts pour les dents, aux Oculistes, Lithotomistes, & tous autres exerçans telle partie de la Chirurgie que ce soit, ... d'avoir aucun étalage, ni d'exercer dans la Ville et Faubourgs de Paris, aucune de ces parties de la Chirurgie, s'ils n'en ont été jugés capables par le P. Chirurgien du Roi ou son Lieutenant, & par les quatre Prévots en charge: scavoir les Bailleurs & Renoueurs d'os en faisant la légère expérience, & payant les droits portés par l'article 123 ci-après; les Experts pour les dents, Oculistes, Lythotomistes [sic] & autres, suivant la forme prescrite par les articles 111 & 112 ci-après; sans que les uns ni les autres puissent former un corps distinct & séparé; ni prétendre au droit d'être aggrégés à la Communauté des Maîtres Chirurgiens; ni prendre d'autre qualité que celle d'*Expert* pour la partie de Chirurgie, sur laquelle ils auront été reçus: & payeront néanmoins les droits de Confrairie & de visite à l'ordinaire.[31]

There was no doubt that this was to be a distinct group from the master barber-surgeons. Article 102 of the statutes also declared

> qu'il n'est nullement question d'assimiler les futurs experts dans le corps des maîtres en chirurgerie.[32]

The paragraph cited above clearly states that, in order to be received (that is, to gain official recognition) as *experts pour les dents*, the prospective *agrégés* must first meet the requirements of two further articles. The first of these lists the ranks of the members of the surgical *communauté* whose presence was required at the candidate's examination, and the second describes the form which that examination should take:

> ARTICLE CXI   L'examen sera fait par le P. Chirurgien du Roi ou son Lieutenant & les 4 Prévôts en charge, en présence du Doyen de la Faculté de Médecine, du Doyen de la Communauté des Chirurgiens, du Receveur en charge, des deux Prévôts et du Receveur qui en sortent, & de tous les Maîtres du Conseil, de deux Maîtres de chacune des 4 classes, qui seront choisis successivement & chacun à leur tour; & de deux Experts aussi successivement.
>
> ARTICLE CXII   Cet examen sera composé d'un seul acte, dans lequel seront lesd. Experts interrogés, tant sur la théorie, que sur la pratique; & payeront les droits portés par l'article 126 ci-après.[33]

As these articles indicate, the examination for the title of *expert pour les dents* would be a single event in which the candidate would be questioned equally on the theory and practice of his, or her, particular part of surgery.

These statutes would be further reinforced by the *lettres patentes* presented at Versailles in 1768. This new legislation implied even greater control of the lower orders of surgery by the *premier* surgeon, via the Crown. Those wishing to gain certification as an *expert* would now have to be received by the college of surgery rather than simply be examined by the *communauté*, and the examination they had to submit to had grown in complexity. They would now be required to present themselves on two different days in the same week, the first to be questioned on theory and the second on practice.

> ARTICLE CXXVI   Ceux qui voudront s'occuper de la fabrique et construction des bandages pour les hernies ou ne s'appliquer qu'à la cure des dents seront tenus, avant d'en faire l'exercice, de se faire recevoir au collége de chirurgie en la qualité d'experts.
>
> ARTICLE CXXVII   Ne pourront aucuns aspirans être admis en ladite qualité d'experts, s'ils n'ont servi deux années entières et consécutives chez l'un des experts établis dans la ville et faubourg de Paris, ou enfin sous plusieurs maîtres ou experts des autres villes pendant trois années: ce qu'ils seront tenus de justifier par des certificats en bonne forme.
>
> ARTICLE CXXVIII   Seront reçus lesdits experts en subissant deux examens en deux jours différens dans la même semaine ... Ils seront interrogés le premier jour sur la théorie, et le second sur la pratique, par le lieutenant de notre premier chirurgien, les quatre prévots et le receveur en charge, en présence du doyen de la Faculté de médecine, du doyen du collège de chirurgie ...
>
> ARTICLE CXXIX   Defenses sont faites auxdits experts, à peine de trois cents livres d'amende, d'exercer aucune partie de la chirurgie que celle pour laquelle ils auront été reçus, et de prendre sur leurs enseignes ou placards, affiches ou billets, la qualité de chirurgiens, sous peine de cent livres d'amende. Ils auront seulement la faculté de prendre celle d'experts herniaires ou dentistes.[34]

This article, number 129, makes clear how much importance was now attached to keeping the *expert* in his, or her, place. Strict limitations were laid down for their field of practice, which could only consist of that part of surgery for which they had been received. Those who transgressed into other fields would have to meet a fine of 300 *livres*. It was also made clear that neither class of *expert* could under any circumstances take, claim or advertise the title of *chirurgien*, on pain of a 100-*livre* fine. They were permitted *only* to take the title of *expert* for their particular part of surgery – carrying with it less status than the lowliest 'ordinary practitioner', the *chirurgien ordinaire* of the towns and villages.

It would seem, therefore, that we shall need to exercise great caution in how we view the use of the title *expert* as applied to this type of practitioner. The word 'expert', as applied to modern medical practice in both France and England, is taken to mean one who has a thorough general knowledge of his particular field of practice, superimposed on which is a high degree of specialized knowledge on one part of that practice in particular. But the 'surgical' *experts* of eighteenth-century France specifically did *not* have general knowledge of surgery – their practice was restricted *to that area in which they worked*. Matthew Ramsey, in his detailed work on the activities of popular healers in the *ancien régime*, has placed the *expert* on the outskirts of official surgery, belonging to a distinct occupation but with no extensive shared fund of theory: he has described them as 'essentially artisans who applied highly developed mechanical skills to certain delicate operations'.[35] Thus, typically, the *expert*'s knowledge did not exceed his or her practice, which would often have a strong family oral tradition. In this manner, they could claim the right to practise in certain areas of surgery but specifically *not* others – a pattern which, as we have seen, would be reflected in the statutes governing their activities. In this way, their practice should therefore be seen as *exclusive* (in the sense of excluding) rather than *specialist* (in the sense of learned and highly skilled), and interpretation of their title treated with an appropriate degree of care.[36]

What, then, did the possession of the title *expert* mean? What particular levels of knowledge or ability would be required of those who chose to take it? Apart from mention of the organization of the examinations, of whose practical content no details are given, it should be noted that none of the regulations regarding the *experts pour les dents* addressed standards of training or education for the prospective *expert*. There were no public courses which dealt with the teeth in particular,[37] and it seems likely that the operations upon which the *expert pour les dents* would be examined consisted of, for the most part, little more than the removal of diseased teeth, the cleaning and removal of scale

and, on occasion, a limited degree of tooth repair.[38] The court surgeon
Pierre Dionis had a low opinion of these 'lesser' examinations in surgery, describing them as 'easy and conniving Admissions and superficial
examinations which have introduced into that Society [meaning, for
Dionis, the society of Parisian surgeons at Saint-Côme] several who
thought themselves not able to incorporate themselves by the Master-
proof'.[39] This dismissal of the examinations as 'superficial' would gain
implied support from the Parisian *chirurgien dentiste* Pierre Fauchard,
who lamented the lack of particular knowledge of the mouth and teeth
on the part of those examining the *experts pour les dents* in the 1720s
and, by extension therefore, a similar lack of knowledge on the part of
those examined:

> mais quoique Messieurs les Examinateurs soient très-sçavans dans
> toutes les autres parties de la Chirurgie, je crois, ... que ne
> s'appliquant pas ordinairement à la pratique de celle-ci, il ne seroit
> pas mal que dans ces occasions on admît un Dentiste habile &
> expérimenté, qui sçauroit sonder les Aspirans sur les difficultez
> qu'un long usage lui auroit fait rencontrer dans son art, ... Par ce
> moyen, on ne verroit pas que la plûpart des Experts pour les dents,
> ne sont munis que d'un sçavoir au-dessous du médiocre.[40]

As we shall see, by the time of Fauchard's writing there would indeed be
several candidates for the title 'Dentiste habile & expérimenté' who
could have assisted in conducting these examinations.

It would seem, then, that this 'tightening up' of control over the
practice of the *expert* was designed principally to protect and enhance
the status of the Paris surgeons, underlining their increasing control
over the lower orders of surgery, who had traditionally been subordinate to the physicians of the medical faculty. If an applicant wished to
become an *expert*, he[41] was required to be received by the college (and
pay a fee), serve as an apprentice[42] (either paying a fee or acting the role
of domestic servant) and to protect in law the practice, income and
reputation of the surgeons by non-encroachment. But were these statutes effective, and how would they relate to the practitioner offering to
treat teeth? Would he now be able to reap some degree of advantage
conferred by official acceptance, or would he continue to inhabit the
marginal shadows at the lowest reaches of the surgical hierarchy? Unfortunately, little evidence which could, perhaps, have thrown some
light on the answers to these questions seems to have survived for the
early part of the eighteenth century. But by looking, after this period, at
the evidence provided by the Comité de salubrité enquête of 1790–91,
one aim of which was to identify those practising varieties of medicine
throughout France, we can see that by the later decades of the century
the majority of surgical *communautés* had refused to receive *experts* of

any kind – Gelfand has noted that out of nearly four hundred, only *sixteen* would do so.[43] Who *was* treating teeth in these areas of France, and where did they stand on the hierarchical ladder of surgery in the *ancien régime*?

Medical jurisprudence of eighteenth-century France understood the label *charlatans, empiriques, ou gens à secret* (literally, persons with secrets) to fit all those who practised any part of the healing art without the certification of a *communauté* of physicians or surgeons.[44] It is within this group, whose members Jean-Pierre Goubert has described as 'other practitioners',[45] that the overwhelming majority of tooth-drawers (or *arracheurs*) operated. Gelfand's uncovering of only sixteen *communautés* which would receive *experts* as late as 1790 implies that all the rest regarded them as charlatans – and, as we shall see, the two groups cannot necessarily be considered as having separate identities.

The Enquêtes du Contrôle Général et du Comité de Salubrité: charlatans, *experts* or surgeons?

Dr Guillotin, president of the Enquête du Comité de salubrité of 1790–91, asked fourteen questions of *communautés*, lieutenants and surgeons concerning the practice of surgery throughout France. Of these, only two paid attention to the activities of 'other practitioners' or charlatans.

> *12e question* : « Reçoit-on à part d'autres praticiens, sous les noms particuliers de dentistes, oculistes, herniaires, rebouteurs, pédicures, etc? »
> *14e question* : « Les charlatans, les empiriques et gens à secret sont-ils répandus dans votre arrondissement? Quel est le degré de tolérance qu'on leur accorde? »[46]

Although these questions were asked towards the end of the century, the information they provided, and that provided by an earlier *enquête* of the Contrôle Général of 1786, is of great help in attempting to determine who had been practising what, and with whose authority, in the *ancien régime*. The evidence provided by the *enquêtes*, which covered all of France, may be placed into three distinct groups with regard to charlatans:

1. 27 per cent of surgical regions, which reported high numbers of charlatans in that region;
2. 32.2 per cent of surgical regions, which reported a 'strong presence' of charlatans:
3. 28 per cent of surgical regions, which reported a weak presence.[47]

As Goubert points out, these answers do *not* provide an accurate record of the numbers of unofficial or 'other' practitioners. What they *do* provide is an illustration of the differing attitudes towards *recognizing* them and *reporting* them, with those reporting a low presence being the most anti-charlatan. Only one *communauté* – Nevers – stated simply that it did not receive charlatans at all.[48] This implies, then, that by the end of the *ancien régime* most areas of France had a large population of unofficial practitioners, working alongside and being accepted by official practitioners (mostly Gelfand's ordinary practitioners, or barber-surgeons), thereby indicating a distinct overlap between *médecine savante* and *médecine populaire*.

If, as seems to be the case, unofficial practitioners were quite openly working alongside official ones, what was the relationship between the two groups? To what extent did they share each other's territory? The evidence of the *enquêtes* of 1786 and 1790 would seem to point to a large 'grey' area in popular medical practice, with what would perhaps appear to modern eyes as a lack of a readily discernible distinction between 'surgeon' and 'charlatan'. In many cases, the standing of the practitioner appears to have been fudged by his activities rather than by his certificates. The Comité de salubrité inquiry reveals the lieutenant at Montdidier reporting 'un charlatan reçu comme chirurgien',[49] whilst the lieutenant at Lyons-la-Forêt complained about two charlatans who were working as officially 'received' surgeons, even though their claim was false.[50] The lieutenant at Domfront noted the presence of many charlatans and empirics, but included some official practitioners in their number, seemingly because of their methods: 'Il y en a beaucoup ... même un médecin et un chirurgien qui jugent l'eau à la vue, et donnent des remèdes à l'arrière des malades.'[51] The records of the *enquête* of 1786 serve only to confuse the matter further, with received surgeons described as empirics. The surgeon Lemaire 'Était empirique, n'a pas la confiance du public à cause de sa passion pour le vin', and the surgeon Lescot, who had been received by the market town of Saint-Georges-de-Ballon, seems to have performed as a mountebank: he was 'un charlatan vendant des drogues sur les traiteaux'.[52] The status of some practitioners appears to have been even more blurred, as exemplified by the surgeon Lamour, branded as an *empirique* who had obtained a diploma to practise but was received without a title.[53] Official approval was not constant, as lieutenants did not always agree with their predecessors. This was demonstrated in Montdidier where a newly appointed lieutenant reported the presence of 'un charlatan dangereux reçu par mon prédécesseur, chirurgien en 1761 ... et trois rebouteurs reçus, sans principe, depuis longtemps'. At Bray-sur-Seine, a shepherd had been received as a *rebouteur* in 1767.[54]

Goubert has shown that evidence provided by surgical *communautés* in the *enquêtes* reveal that the unofficial practitioner had credibility not only with the general population and the 'common swindlers', but also with the official medical profession itself.[55] Physicians stood accused – the lieutenant of Vitry-le-François complained that the physicians would give certificates to those who would pay, thereby misleading the public; the lieutenant of Nuits, however, put it more strongly when he denounced 'tous les charlatans entretenus par le premier médecin du roi qui, pour une certaine somme, leur donnait le pouvoir d'assassiner par toute la France'.[56] Goubert also illustrates how this practice could be condoned at the very top of the French medical tree. Charles Dionis, docteur-regent de la Faculté de Médecine de Paris and grandson of Pierre Dionis, the celebrated surgeon and anatomist, exploited royal privilege in his control of the sales of the cure-all *orviétan* from 1760, the rights to which he had bought. Dionis saw to it that those selling *his* particular *orviétan* would receive a diploma, at the right price.[57]

It is difficult to ascertain what types of treatment the popular practitioners, be they charlatans, empirics or *gens à secret*, offered to their patients. Many of the official surgeons responding to the *enquêtes* of the Comité de salubrité did not describe the occupations of Goubert's 'other practitioners' in their area, nor even distinguish between the three groups, labelling all as one. But the reports of those that *did* classify them (that is, nearly half) reveal that those practitioners regarded as charlatans, whose work included enough treatment of teeth to have them recorded as such, were numerous – second in number only to the *rebouteurs* or bone-setters.[58]

The tooth-drawer and the *expert* – standing beneath the barber-surgeon

So what was the standing of the *expert pour les dents* within the structure of *ancien régime* surgery, and to what extent did the situation in Paris compare with the rest of the country? François Vidal[59] has taken the *expert* to have been a 'major practitioner', neither subject to the control of nor gaining assistance from the master surgeon, with *l'art dentaire* his exclusive business for the rest of the eighteenth century:

> La qualité d'expert pour les dents n'est soumise à aucune condition particulière. Le praticien de l'odontologie est bien, dans l'esprit du texte, un praticien majeur; quelles que soient les difficultés qu'il rencontre, il n'est soumis ni au contrôle, ni à l'assistance d'un Maître en chirurgie. Tout au cours du siècle, l'art dentaire est, et reste, l'affaire exclusive des experts.[60]

He notes that the numbers of *experts* remained low – but as suggested in the introduction to this book, the apparent numbers of practitioners within a particular category will depend both on who is doing the counting, and on who is being counted. With *communautés* throughout France exhibiting different levels of tolerance to *experts* of any colour, the numbers of those reported as having chosen to use the title should be treated with caution. Nevertheless, Vidal's implied view of the *expert* as a practitioner of some status seems to sit uncomfortably with that of Gelfand and Ramsey.

By examining the surgical statutes and their relationship with the models of surgical structure put forward by Gelfand and Ramsey, we can now see that the creation of the official rank of *expert* was a mechanism aimed at the lower reaches of the surgical tree, intended to maintain the status of a particular group of practitioners at a level below that of the surgeon and even the barber-surgeon, the ordinary practitioner of the towns. We have seen that they could hold out no hope whatsoever of assimilation into this body of practitioners of higher standing, with the statutes clearly stating 'qu'il n'est nullement question d'assimiler les futurs experts dans le corps des maîtres en chirurgie'.[61] They were thus being held in their place in this highly structured frame-work, as practitioners who were, for the most part, skilled to a degree (but no high degree, according to contemporaries such as Pierre Fauchard[62]) yet unrefined and of low status.

Who was holding the *expert* 'down' in this way, and why? The statutes of 1699 and 1768, as we have seen, listed those who would decide the professional fate of the applicant: 'le premier chirurgien du Roy ou son lieutenant, et ... les quatre prévots en charge'.[63] Thus control was exerted over this class of practitioner in the same way as it was for all parts of surgery in the *ancien régime*: by the *premier* surgeon in Paris, and by his lieutenants and officers in the provinces. Vidal, in searching for the reasons for the apparent low numbers of *experts pour les dents*, has suggested that demand for their services, limited mostly to the removal of diseased teeth and the removal of scale, was restricted to the wealthy and well-to-do – but we shall see that the wealthy clientele of Paris did not need to consult a practitioner from the lower reaches of the surgical profession in such a socially mismatched manner. Before looking at those they *did* consult, we need to consider the place of the treatment of teeth in the practice of the surgeon.

Notes

1. For a very perceptive refutation of this literature, see Toby Gelfand's argument in 'A "Monarchical Profession" in the Old Regime: Surgeons, Ordinary Practitioners, and Medical Professionalization in Eighteenth-century France', in Gerald L. Geison (ed.), *Professions and the French state, 1700–1900*, Pennsylvania, 1984, pp. 149–80.
2. Toby Gelfand, *Professionalizing modern medicine: Paris surgeons and medical science and institutions in the eighteenth century*, Greenwood, Westport, 1980. Gelfand draws attention to the early modern usage of 'profession' as indicating an organized occupational group, however humble.
3. Laurence Brockliss and Colin Jones, *The Medical World of Early Modern France*, Clarendon Press, Oxford, 1997. See in particular chapter 9, 'The rise of surgery', by Colin Jones.
4. Gelfand, 'A "Monarchical Profession"', p. 150.
5. Gelfand, *Professionalizing modern medicine*, p. 29.
6. In 1681, Jean Biennaise, who had been surgeon to the king's mother, left a sum of 12 000 *livres* to fund a chair of anatomy and one of operations. Ten years later, Louis Roberdeau's legacy paid for a course of osteology and for the construction of the new amphitheatre. Alfred Franklin, *La vie privée d'autrefois: Arts et métiers, modes, mœurs, usages des parisiens du XIIᵉ au XVIIIᵉ siècle d'après des documents originaux ou inédits,* vol. 12, *Les Chirurgiens,* E. Plon, Nourrit et cⁱᵉ, Paris, 1893, p. 145.
7. Gelfand, *Professionalizing modern medicine*, p. 35.
8. Ibid., p. 47.
9. *Mémoire pour les maistres chirurgiens de Paris* (n.d., probably 1700), cited in Gelfand, *Professionalizing modern medicine*, p. 30.
10. *Lettres patentes portant confirmation de l'établissement de l'Académie royale de chirurgie,* Paris, 1748, cited in Franklin, *Les Chirurgiens,* p. 175.
11. Gelfand, *Professionalizing modern medicine*, p. 31.
12. Gelfand, 'A "Monarchical Profession"', p. 166.
13. For the effect this had on the outraged physicians, see Franklin, *Les Chirurgiens,* pp. 170–73.
14. *Statuts et réglements généraux pour les maîtres en chirurgie des provinces du royaume,* 1730 (5th edn, 1772), in Gelfand, 'A "Monarchical Profession"', p. 153.
15. As their letters of reception put it. Matthew Ramsey, *Professional and popular medicine in France, 1770–1830*, Cambridge University Press, Cambridge, 1988, p. 22.
16. *Statuts et réglements*, cited in Gelfand, 'A "Monarchical Profession"', p. 153.
17. Gelfand lists 'naval doctors practising on civilians, occasional artisan healers, parish curés, magical healers, empirics and charlatans'. Ibid., p. 153.
18. Ibid., p. 154.
19. Ibid., p. 152.
20. '*EXPERT* – Depuis le début du XIVᵉ s., il s'applique précisément à une personne qui à acquis par l'expérience une grande habilité; l'adjectif s'emploie en particulier (av. 1613) avec un nom désignant une partie du

corps (oeil expert).' Alain Rey (ed.), *Dictionnaire Historique de la Langue Française*, Dictionnaires Le Robert, Paris, 1992.

21. François Vidal (ed.), *Histoire d'un diplôme*, CDF, Paris, 1993, note to p. 25.
22. Ramsey, *Professional and popular medicine*, p. 24. As with other practitioners of trades within this official category of *expert*, the vast majority remained unlicensed, choosing instead to practise 'unofficially' or illegally.
23. Jean-Pierre Goubert, 'L'art de guérir: Médecine savante et médecine populaire dans la France de 1790', in *Annales Économies, Sociétés, Civilisations*, 5, 1977, 908–26, 919. Here again, the use of the title 'dentist' is the historian's choice, not necessarily the practitioner's.
24. Ramsey, *Professional and popular medicine*, p. 24.
25. Ibid., p. 28. A set of artificial teeth, which was usually made for a complete jaw, was carved from a single piece of ivory.
26. *Statuts et réglemens pour la communauté des Barbiers–Perruquiers–Baigneurs–Étuvistes de la ville, fauxbourgs et banlieuë de Paris*, 1718, article 42, cited in J. Verdier, *La Jurisprudence Particulière de la Chirurgie en France*, d'Houry et Didot, Paris, 1764, vol. I, pp. 91–2.
27. *Statuts et réglemens*, article 55, cited in Alfred Franklin, *La vie privée d'autrefois*, vol. 2, *Les soins de toilette: le savoir-vivre*, Paris, 1887, p. 112.
28. *Statuts et réglemens*, article 60, cited in Verdier, *Jurisprudence*, vol. I, p. 94.
29. See L. B. D'Olblen, *Statuts et Réglemens généraux pour les communautés de Chirurgiens des Provinces, Donnés à Marli [sic] le 24 Février 1730. Enregistrés dans tous les Parlemens du Royaume*. Nouvelle édition, Delaguette, Paris, 1754.
30. 'ceux qui peuvent être agrégés dans la communauté'. *Statuts pour la communauté des maistres chirurgiens jurez de Paris*, Paris, 1701, article 102, cited in Franklin, *Variétés chirurgicales*, p. 207. Royal letters patent approving the statutes were issued in 1699, but they were not registered by Parlement until 1701: I shall refer to them as *Statuts*, 1699.
31. *Statuts*, 1699, article 102, cited in Verdier, *Jurisprudence*, vol. II, pp. 539–40.
32. *Statuts*, 1699, article 102, cited in Vidal, *Histoire d'un diplôme*, p. 26.
33. *Statuts*, 1699, articles 111 and 112, cited in Verdier, *Jurisprudence*, vol. II, p. 547.
34. *Lettres patentes du Roy, en forme d'édit, portant réglement pour le collège de chirurgie*, Paris, 1768, articles 126, 127, 128 and 129, cited in Franklin, *Variétés chirurgicales*, pp. 176–7.
35. Ramsey, *Professional and popular medicine*, p. 23.
36. I am grateful to Dr Andrew Cunningham for pointing out that a Latin-speaking expert is, literally, one 'without knowledge'.
37. see Fauchard, *Le Chirurgien Dentiste*, vol. I, p. xi.
38. François Vidal has suggested that at the start of the eighteenth century the role of those treating teeth had consisted of little more than extraction; but he also notes that regulations drawn up in Bordeaux in 1730 made mention of the cleaning and filling of teeth. See Vidal, *Histoire d'un diplôme*, chapter two.
39. Pierre Dionis, *A Course of Chirurgical operations, Demonstrated in the*

Royal Gardens at Paris. Translated from the Paris edition, 2nd edn, Tonson, London, 1733, preface.

40.   Fauchard, *Le Chirurgien Dentiste*, vol. I, p. xii. Fauchard is claiming here that due to the lack of a skilled and experienced *dentiste* amongst the examiners, the majority of *experts pour les dents* possess a level of knowledge which is 'less than mediocre'. As we shall see later, it is perhaps not surprising that such a remark should come from one closely involved in the creation of a new 'profession' which is claiming a position of high status.

41.   An order by *premier* surgeon Lamartinière prohibited women from treating teeth in 1755, although Franklin provides evidence that this was flouted: see Franklin, *Variétés chirurgicales,* p. 175.

42.   To either a master surgeon or an established *expert* in Paris for a period of two consecutive years, or to master surgeons or *experts* of other towns for a period of three years. See Verdier, *Jurisprudence*, vol. II, pp. 545–6.

43.   Toby Gelfand, 'Medical professionals and charlatans: the *Comité de salubrité enquête* of 1790–91', *Histoire sociale – Social History*, XI (21), 1978, 62–97, 73.

44.   Ibid., p. 81.

45.   Goubert, 'L'art de guérir', p. 923.

46.   Ibid., p. 923.

47.   Ibid., p. 909.

48.   'l'on ne reçoit pas les empiriques'. Ibid., p. 911.

49.   Ibid., p. 910.

50.   Ibid.

51.   Ibid.

52.   'selling drugs from his trestles'. Ibid.

53.   Ibid.

54.   Ibid., p. 911.

55.   Ibid., p. 917.

56.   Ibid.

57.   Ibid.

58.   Ibid., p. 912.

59.   Vidal and his research group are, to the best of my knowledge, the only recent workers to have considered the role of the *expert* in any detail. See Vidal, *Histoire d'un diplôme*, chapter two.

60.   Ibid., p. 26.

61.   *Statuts*, 1699, article 102, cited in ibid., p. 26.

62.   'la plûpart des Experts pour les dents, ne sont munis que d'un sçavoir au-dessous du médiocre'. Fauchard, *Le Chirurgien Dentiste*, vol. I, p. xii.

63.   *Statuts*, 1699, article 111, cited in Verdier, *Jurisprudence*, vol. II, p. 547.

CHAPTER THREE

Teeth as Surgical Practice
in the Seventeenth Century

The practice and, more specifically, the techniques and operations of the officially recognized surgeon of the *ancien régime* are much more clearly visible to modern eyes than are those of the practitioner of popular and traditional folk-medicine. We cannot know what techniques were passed on in the predominantly oral tradition of the seventeenth-century *expert*, for example, no matter what part of surgery he or she was practising – but in the printed books and, later, published lectures of the surgeon we may see what kinds of operations the surgeons offered and what form those operations took. In examining these valuable sources, it can be seen that towards the end of the century the technical part of the surgeon's practice was changing markedly, in two principal ways. The first of these, and perhaps the most readily apparent to us, was the dramatic increase in the number of different operations that could be performed. However, analysis of the methods and techniques employed by the surgeon reveals the second, which is of at least equal significance: an increasing level of complexity and innovation in the way in which tools or instruments could be used – although as we shall see, the surgeon's instruments, for all their cunning design and intricate manufacture, should not be considered as the most important part of his armamentarium. It was the hands, of which the instruments were merely an extension, which were the vital tools of the surgeon.

But before we examine the role of the surgeon and the surgeon's technique in this part of our story, it should be emphasized strongly that the operations for the teeth were an absolutely integral part of standard surgical practice in France before 1700. This point needs particular emphasis, partly because some traditional historians have given the impression that 'dentistry' (as they see it) was a separate entity from surgery which some surgeons would choose to perform alongside, or in addition to, their everyday surgical activities[1] – but, as we shall see, this was emphatically *not* the case. As I have suggested in the Introduction, such attempts to identify 'dentistry in the past' have frequently resulted in the misappropriation of activities that were not dentistry, and as we shall see later, one of the things that was *not* dentistry was what surgeons were doing to teeth before 1700. These activities were *surgery* – an important and integral part of the everyday work of the surgeon.

Examination of the various publications regarding the operations of surgery and the way in which they should be performed reveals that before the start of our period, in the middle of the seventeenth century, the operations on the teeth held a fundamental position in the writings of surgeons. Those parts of books which dealt in detail with the various operations of surgery generally followed a particular pattern which, as we shall see, started with the operations to be performed on the top of the body and worked their way down. The operations for the teeth, therefore, would usually appear as members of that group of operations which could be performed on the head. In analysing these operations, and the ways in which they were performed, it will be necessary to look at them in fine detail and, to some extent, on their own; however, while doing so we must be careful to try to retain them in the context in which they were intended.

But even if we then know *where* these operations for the teeth belong, what questions should we ask about them? Were significant changes in the ways in which teeth were being treated becoming evident in the decades around the beginning of the eighteenth century and, if so, what form did these changes take? If such changes *are* uncovered, we shall need to ask the all-important question of *who* was performing these different operations, as well as what form they took. Were they simply refined versions of the operations performed by established practitioners such as the tooth-drawers or the *experts*, or did they take the form of expensive and exclusive new operations, highly technical in nature and offered by a different group with different aims? Perhaps most important of all, why, if they *were* new, had they appeared now? Why were they being performed *at this time*?

In searching for answers to these questions, we must exercise caution with respect to those that are of a specifically technical nature. Judging an operation to be 'new', or in some way different from what had gone before, will require a thorough understanding of the technical activity performed by the operator, taken in context. Furthermore, in asking *who* was performing these 'new' operations, we shall once again need to take particular care over their identification: we must be able to 'see' practitioners before we can hope to count them. We shall therefore need to be wary of practitioner labels, especially those that have been freely applied retrospectively by later writers. We should also note those labels used by practitioners to describe themselves, and others, in their own writings – again, we shall need to focus most closely on their *activities*. As indicated above, it is these published works which will serve as our principal guides to the operations performed on the teeth, and to the changes and additions which were made to those operations. In examining them, we shall see that the dramatic rise in the number and complexity of such operations which took place in the latter part of the seventeenth century would soon be coupled to a significant change in the kind of practitioner who was both performing and writing about them. As we have seen in the preceding chapters, the vast majority of those offering to treat teeth in *ancien régime* France can be placed well down the ladder of the surgical hierarchy, their work usually restricted to the removal of teeth or the selling of cures for the toothache; but it is in the rarified atmosphere of the higher echelons of this hierarchy (and therefore, initially at least, in Paris) that we shall find descriptions of other, more sophisticated treatments which would form the foundations for the making of the *dentiste*. We should, therefore, first look closely at what was on offer, and by whom, in the surgical practice of the decades before the end of the seventeenth century.

Operations for the teeth: the surgeon's art

Judging by the operations described in books written by surgeons which were intended to provide instruction in their art, by the beginning of the sixteenth century operations for the teeth formed an established integral part of the group of operations which could be performed on the head. The most common of these operations by far was that of tooth removal, but their scope would occasionally reach beyond simple extraction. For example Giovanni da Vigo, in his *Practica* of 1516, had advocated the mechanical removal of the putrid parts of the tooth with small trepans and files,[2] and in the fifth book of *The most excellent workes of Chirurgerye* of 1543 had considered 'the frenche Pockes, of the deade evyl, and scabbe, & of the paynes of the joyntes, & of the tethe'.[3] In this book, he had listed six diseases of the teeth: 'payne, corosion, congelation, dormitation, fylthynes, loosenes'[4] for which he offered various treatments. If these methods failed, the tooth should then be drawn. Da Vigo noted, however, that surgeons 'do remytte this cure to barbours and to vacabounde toothdrawers, howbeit, it is good to have sene and to marke the workynge of such'.[5]

But a marked difference in the way teeth could be treated starts to become apparent in books on the surgeon's art written during the later decades of the sixteenth century. This difference, which took the form of the inclusion of a well-defined set of different operations for the teeth as a distinct part of the operations on the head, would become further established over the next one hundred years. A brief examination of the form such writings took, and of the way in which they developed, will help to provide a clearer image of these techniques.

A detailed section on the operations to be performed on the teeth as part of a wider group of operations had appeared in the writings of Ambroise Paré, who was head surgeon at the Paris Hôtel-Dieu and *premier* surgeon to the king in the second half of the sixteenth century. Paré's description of the various operations and the ways in which they should be performed was first published in 1564, contained within the seventeenth book of his *Oeuvres* which (in the English translation) was entitled 'Of diverse affects of the parts not agreeable to nature, whose cure commonly is performed by the hand'.[6] These operations followed a kind of 'top downwards' pattern: the 'Divers other preternaturall affects, whose cure is commonly performed by surgery'[7] commence with the surgeon's treatment for 'Alopecia, or the falling away of the haires of the head', followed by tinea, vertigo and many chapters on the diseases and operations for the eyes. Chapter twenty-three gives advice on 'the stopping of the passage of the eares, and the falling of things thereinto', and chapter twenty-four instructs the surgeon on the 'getting of little bones and such like things out of the jawes and throate'. After the throat, however, came the teeth: chapter twenty-five is 'Of the Tooth-ache'. Paré described 'La douleur des dents' as ' la plus grand & cruelle qui soit entre toute les douleurs, sans mort'.[8] The suffering patient should not act hastily, however: 'In the bitternesse of paine we must not presently run to Tooth-drawers, or cause them presently to goe in hand to plucke them out.'[9] Having considered toothache, 'Of the other affects of the teeth' follow, and chapter twenty-seven gives details on the ways in which teeth should be drawn, taking care not to shake the patient's head too much and to fill the holes of badly 'eaten' teeth to stop them breaking under the surgeon's forceps.[10]

The extraction of diseased and painful teeth was the most common operation to be performed on the mouth, and was usually achieved by the use of instruments such as the pelican and the forceps. The pelican, supposedly thus named because of its strong resemblance to the beak of the bird, could take many forms and often had many interchangeable parts. It was used to take the tooth out sideways, the claw being engaged over the top of the tooth with the fulcrum applied against the outer gum of the jaw: pressure on the handle would then result in the removal of either all or some of the tooth.[11]

Similarly, several types of forceps had been developed, occasionally with screws to increase or maintain their grip on the tooth – but most simply had two curved jaws, with or without serrations, to grip the tooth to be extracted. Both instruments would have been familiar to the early seventeenth-century surgeon: the first-known reference to the pelican may be found in Guy de Chauliac's *Chirurgia Magna* of 1400,[12]

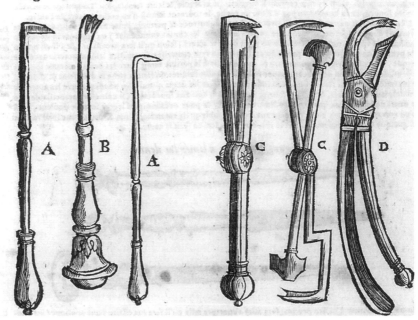

Figure d'vn Pouſſoir , & Déchauſſoir.   Figure d'vn Dauier & Polican.

3.1   Surgeon's instruments for operating on the teeth. Those on the left, the *poussoir* and the *déchaussoir*, are principally used for loosening the teeth prior to their removal with those shown on the right: the *daviet* and the *polican*. (Paré, *Les Oeuvres d'Ambroise Paré*, 11th edn, 1652.)

whilst the forceps have been described as 'probably the oldest of all dental instruments after the fingers'.[13] Some of Paré's instruments for operating on the teeth are shown in Figure 3.1.

Paré's operations for the head included others which were specifically intended for the teeth, in addition to simple extraction. Chapters in this section of his writing gave descriptions of procedures for the fixing of loose teeth, the removal of decay with caustic fluid or the cautery, the filing of teeth to relieve crowding and the breaking off of teeth to allow the application of medicaments to the roots. Following these, Paré turned his attention to the next part of the head, focusing on the operations which the surgeon could perform on the tongue.[14]

The surgical operations of Jacques Guillemeau, Paré's successor at the Hôtel-Dieu, were described in his *Oeuvres de Chirurgie* which was first published in 1597 and translated into English in the same year, as *The French Chirurgerye*.[15] Guillemeau, too, follows the classical descending plan for his operations, commencing with instruction on how to trepan the cranium of the head,[16] followed by the diseases of the nose and mouth.[17] It is within this section, which is divided into seven chapters, that the techniques for treating the teeth may be found:

chapter 1 – of the polipus
chapter 2 – of the Haremouth
chapter 3 – of the ulcerationes, & of the excrescence of the fleshe of the gummes, called *Paroulis*, ende *Epoulis*,
chapter 4 – of the tunge tyinge, or of the shortnes, or brevitye of the tunge, which the Greeckes called *Anciloglossum*, & of the ulceration *Ranula*, which is allsoe called *Batrachos.*
chapter 5 – Howe we ought, to cauterise, and cutt of, the *Uvula*, or pallaet of the mouthe.
chapter 6 – Of the swellinge of the almondes, & of the ulcerations of the same.
chapter 7 – How that we ought to drawe, breake, or cutt of teeth.[18]

According to Guillemeau, there were seven distinct operations which could be practised on the teeth:

There are divers disseases inscidente unto the teeth, which throughe the manuall operation of Chyrurgerye must be cured: as by cauterisinge, of the same, & by dissipation of the gummes from the toeth, by filinge, by cuttinge of, by drawinge by settinge, by cuttinge in thereof, & by allegation & binding together of the teeth.[19]

He also gave descriptions of those instruments which the surgeon might employ to 'drawe, breake, or cutt of teeth'.[20] One had a flat blade for loosening the gums from the teeth, whilst the polycampe, the parrot's bill and the expulser or thruster-out were all intended for the removal of all or part of a tooth; but the author did not recommend immediate recourse to extraction, even for teeth 'that causeth sometimes great doloure, & payne, yet notwithstanding we always endevoure to praeserve him, ether because he is commodius for chawing, or serviceable for the speech, or els is for a decorum or grace unto the mouth'.[21] A white paste was described which was intended primarily for the filling of gaps left by extracted teeth, but which could also be used to fill a hollow tooth. It was made 'from white granulated wax, melted with only a little resin of the olive tree, to which are added mastix powder and finely ground white coral and pearls ... this paste can also serve to fill a hollow tooth, in order to prevent its crumbling'.[22]

Fabricius ab Aquapendente had written of the operations of surgery in his *Opera Chirurgia,* published in Venice in 1619 and later translated into French.[23] Here, the surgeon could find seven distinct types of operation for the mouth, five of which related to the teeth: a method for dealing with lockjaw whereby the sufferer could be fed, cleaning of the mouth and the removal of tartar, the removal of decayed tooth substance with vitriol, application of the cautery (also to remove decay), the removal of protruding teeth, the filing of sharp edges and the extraction of teeth.[24] Fabricius had also described a method of constructing a device to cover defects in the palate, noting that such holes may be either present at birth or caused 'by the French'.[25]

Nearly sixty years later, Johannes Scultetus's published description of the operations of surgery would take the form of a long series of observations of case histories, forming the second part of his book on the use of surgical instruments which was published in English as *The Chyrurgeon's Store-House*.[26] Even in the description of instruments which makes up the first half of the book, it is apparent that treating teeth was not considered as an *adjunct* to the surgeon's art, but as an integral part of it: there is no separate section dealing with the instruments to be used on the teeth. An illustration of forceps for use in tooth removal appears on the same plate as several other types, such as 'an instrument to pull forth small bones in the throat' and 'a pipe of silver' to 'draw out thorns out of the jaws'.[27] The description of one of these figures further emphasizes the surgeon's interest in the teeth:

> Fig. V. is a pair of pincers that represents a Crows bill; with which the roots of teeth are drawn forth: Of which *Cornelius Celsus* (whom, as being admirable in all Chirurgical operations, *Fabritius ab Aquapendente* counsels us to study in both night and day) ... concerning teeth, writes thus; as oft as when a tooth is taken forth, the root is left behind, that must forthwith be drawn out also with a pair of pincers ...[28]

Scultetus describes nine operations for the surgeon to perform on the head and mouth, each one depicted in a figure: the burning out of rottenness in a tooth with red-hot irons, cutting forth a tooth bred out of its place, 'the tunnel applied' for feeding in lockjaw, closing a hole in a palate eaten away with French pox, putting liquors in the ear, the drawing asunder of teeth closed fast together that the sick may be fed, the application of a speculum oris to search for disease in the mouth, the cutting of the string under the tongue and the removal of a fish bone from the throat.[29]

In the second part of the book, entitled *A Century of Chyrurgical Operations*, which the writer described as 'confirming and clearing what hath been briefly mentioned in Description of the foregoing Tables', Scultetus follows the 'top-to-toe' pattern by commencing his accounts with nineteen cases of wounding of the head. Following these, there are two treatments for the eyes and one of the nose, and one 'of a swelling, with a Bag cut out of the upper Jaw'.[30] After describing the removal of an excrescence of flesh on the roof of the mouth, a callous hollowness, and corruption of the palate bone, another tumour in the upper jaw and a gunshot wound in the lower jaw,[31] Scultetus describes

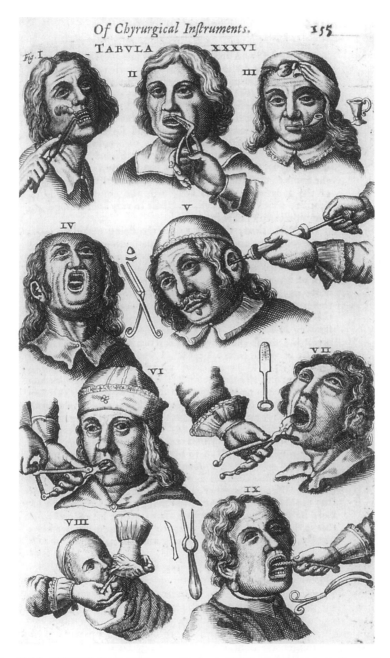

3.2 Table XXXVI from Johannes Scultetus's *The Chyrurgeon's Store-House* (1674). There is no specific caption to this plate, but Scultetus refers to it in his text to illustrate the various instruments which the surgeon may use in operations on the head.

his treatment for 'a Periodical Pain of the Teeth, most happily Cured', and how he dealt with 'a strong Apoplexy, upon breeding Teeth'.[32] Following these are accounts of treatments for the diseases of the tongue, the king's evil (scrofula) affecting the neck, swallowing problems, diseases affecting the face and so on.

Thus the possession of instruments and the knowledge of how to use them for the removal and, to some extent, the repair of diseased or damaged teeth was an important and basic part of the seventeenth-century surgeon's armamentarium for treating the head. The operations which he would employ in this treatment had changed little from those described in the 1560s by Paré. But in the second half of this century the structure of French surgery would change dramatically and, as a direct result of these changes, the way in which surgery was practised and the way in which its practitioners would be perceived would also change spectacularly. Whereas surgery had previously been firmly placed in the sphere of the trade guilds and companies, with all the implications of relatively low prestige that would accompany the practice of a manual occupation, it would now gain rapidly in status and standing. By the early decades of the eighteenth century many more operations of increasing complexity would be on offer, performed by surgeons who had attained high standing both at court and within academic medicine. Thus the period from around 1660 would see the beginnings of a 'making' of the surgeon, built by the surgeons themselves on technical invention and social advancement – and we shall see that it would be on the back of this 'making' of the surgeon that the *dentiste* would, in turn, 'make' himself. Therefore, before we examine the mechanisms and methods by which the practice and title of the *dentiste* were constructed, we need to ask what changes were taking place in the structure and practice of surgery in the *ancien régime* and, more importantly, how these changes were achieved, and on what foundations they were built.

Notes

1. Many writers have 'lifted' the operations for the teeth out of their rightful context within complete works on surgery in this way. Malvin Ring, for example, writes that 'There is an extensive discussion of the surgical treatment of dental problems in the work of Johannes Scultetus' (Ring, *Dentistry*, p. 149); but for Scultetus, these would very much have been straightforward instances of *surgical* problems. Ring also states that 'Paré also had an extensive dental practice' (Ring, *Dentistry*, p. 129). In fact, Paré treated teeth in the course of his work as a surgeon.

    The dental historian's picking of 'dental' cherries from surgical writings is clearly demonstrated in Walter Hoffmann-Axthelm's reading of Fabricius

Hildanus's *Observationes et curationes* (as Hoffmann-Axthelm calls it) of 1606, from which he extracts the thirty-eighth observation of the first hundred (observations) and the tenth and twenty-second of the second hundred, places them together, and views them as representative of Hildanus's approach to the treatment of teeth. But these observations belong properly where Hildanus placed them. Reading them thus shows instead that the first concerns the removal of tumours, the second the cure of headaches and the third the cure and repair of a perforated sore on the palate. Hildanus's full title reveals the full surgical nature of his writing – *Observationum et curationum chirurgicarum centuriae. In qua inclusae sunt viginti et quinque, antea seorsim aeditae: reliquae nunc cum nonnullis instrumentorum, ab autore inventorum delineationibus, in gratiam & utilitatem artis chirurgicae in lucem prodeunt* (Guilielmi Fabricii Hildani, 1606). As we shall see later, Hoffmann-Axthelm also misappropriates the French surgeon Garengeot's detailed description of the instruments for use on the teeth as 'dentistry'.

2. 'we may remove the said corrosion with trepans, files or other convenient instruments'. Cited in Bennion, *Antique Dental Instruments,* p. 65.
3. Giovanni da Vigo, *The most excellent workes of Chirurgerye, made and set forth by maister John Vigon, heed Chirurgien of our tyme in Italie, translated into english,* Edward Whytchurch, 1543, boke v, fol. clx. Facsimile reprint published by Da Capo Press, Amsterdam and New York, 1968.
4. Ibid., fol. clxx.
5. Ibid., fol. clxxii.
6. See Ambroise Paré, *Les Oeuvres d'Ambroise Paré, conseiller et premier chirurgien du roy,* Nicolas Buon, Paris, 8th edn, 1628. For clarity, I have drawn some references from *The Workes of that famous Chirurgion Ambrose Parey, translated out of Latine and compared with the French by Thomas Johnson,* Cotes and Young, London, 1634.
7. Paré, *Workes,* p. 637 ff.
8. Paré, *Les Oeuvres,* p. 609.
9. Paré, *Workes,* p. 656.
10. Ibid., p. 659.
11. Bennion, *Antique Dental Instruments,* p. 31.
12. See Hoffmann-Axthelm, *History of Dentistry,* p. 129 for a discussion of the first writer to describe the pelican.
13. Bennion, *Antique Dental Instruments,* p. 50. It may be of interest to note that the jaws of modern dental forceps are still referred to as 'beaks'.
14. Paré, *Les Oeuvres,* p. 609 ff.
15. Jacques Guillemeau, *The Frenche Chirurgerye, or all the manualle operations of Chirurgerye, with divers, & sundrye Figures, and amongst the rest, certayne nuefownde Instrumentes, verye necessarye to all the operations of Chirurgerye,* trans. from the Dutch by A.M., 1597.
16. Ibid., second treatise.
17. Ibid., fifth treatise.
18. Ibid., chapter headings for the fifth treatise.
19. Ibid., fifth treatise, chapter 7, p. 27.
20. Ibid., p. 26.
21. Ibid., p. 27.
22. Ibid.

23. And Italian and German amongst others. W. Hoffmann-Axthelm, *History of Dentistry,* Quintessence, Chicago, 1981, p. 142.
24. Fabricius ab Aquapendente, *Opera Chirurgica,* Venice, 1619, p. 32. Translation in Hoffmann-Axthelm, *History of Dentistry,* p. 142.
25. Also called syphilis. Frankfurt edition of 1684, II, p. 85, cited in Hoffmann-Axthelm, *History of Dentistry,* p. 142.
26. Johannes Scultetus, *The Chyrurgeon's Store-House. Furnished with Forty three tables cut in Brass, in which Are all sorts of* INSTRUMENTS, *both Ancient and Modern; useful to the performance of all Manual Opperations, with an exact Description of every* INSTRUMENT ((by Johannes Scultetus, a famous Physitian, and Chyrurgeon of Ulme in Suevia. Faithfully Englished by E. B). Starkey, London, 1674.
27. Ibid., plate x, p. 24.
28. Ibid., p. 25.
29. Ibid., p. 154.
30. Ibid., pp. 259–70, observations 20–23.
31. Ibid., pp. 270–78, observations 24–7.
32. Ibid., pp. 278–80, observations 28 and 29.

CHAPTER FOUR

The Fall and Rise of Academic Surgery in the *Ancien Régime*, and the Appearance of a Surgical *Science* for the Teeth

Shortly after the middle of the seventeenth century, the status of the Paris surgeon appeared to have reached such a low level that one hundred years later Antoine Louis, the secretary of the Paris Académie de chirurgie, would reflect woefully that 'the beautiful century of Louis XIV was an iron age for our art'.[1] Yet at the time of Louis's writing, surgeons were enjoying what Toby Gelfand has described as 'undeniable success in terms of their own objectives and public recognition'.[2] How could such a spectacular change have taken place in the accepted medical hierarchy of the *ancien régime*, and why? Gelfand's work on the turbulent shifts of power within and between the various members of this structure has already been of great value in providing a picture of those on the lower rungs of the surgical ladder. It will also serve now as a platform from which to view the rise of French surgery in the late seventeenth and early eighteenth centuries, helping, in the process, to show how that rise was achieved and how it would affect the standing of the academic surgeon. With his help, and by looking at the teachings and writings of some contemporary surgeons and the actions of others, we shall be able to travel one step further towards an understanding of the part played by technique and theoretical knowledge in this rise – and, as a result, we shall see that surgeons no longer saw their activity purely as an 'opération manuelle' as had been the case in Paré's time.[3] Knowing *how* to cure would no longer be enough – the surgeon would now need to know *why* to cure *in that particular way*. By the first decade of the eighteenth century, the practice of surgery would demand the possession of a full and detailed body of theoretical knowledge founded on principles and precepts, essential for the successful invention and performance of operations: a *science* for the surgeon.[4] It should be noted that the word *science* will be italicized to indicate the use of the French term, and not as an indication of emphasis. But what circumstances would encourage such a demand for theoretical knowledge, and how would it be created?

The rise of the *premier* surgeon

The union of the small group of surgeons of the community of Saint-Côme (known as the surgeons of the long gown), who had enjoyed academic privilege for more than two hundred years, with the much larger and wealthier guild of barber-surgeons (surgeons of the short gown) which took place from 1655 to 1660 signified a failure on the part of the academic surgeons. Their argument that surgery was a liberal art requiring the pursuit of academic studies rather than the simple apprenticeship of the *métier* was rapidly becoming less audible. Any kind of formal teaching or liberal education, such as that enjoyed by the physicians, seemed to be unnecessary as the great majority of surgery was performed quite adequately by the practically trained members of the barber-surgeons' guild. The physicians favoured this practice, over which the Faculté exercised great control: for them, surgery was performed with the hands, not the head. This had been stated clearly in 1607 when a Parisian surgeon had offered to lecture to the barber-surgeons, but parliament had intervened ruling that 'science [that is, theoretical knowledge] is not for those who work only with their hands'.[5] The new company was dominated by the barber-surgeons, who would 'cast a very thick shadow through which the College of Saint-Côme could scarcely be perceived'[6] – and by a court decree of 1660, all signs of the academic status of the long gown would disappear. The titles 'bachelor', 'licentiate', 'doctor' and 'college' were forbidden, along with public teaching and the defence of surgical theses by surgical students.[7] The physician Gui Patin could urge his colleagues of the Faculté, with their influence over the barber-surgeons, to 'Behold how the surgeons of Saint-Côme have been crushed, and their house delivered to our barber-surgeons who are completely subordinate to us.'[8] The ruling of 1660 had granted the union the legal status of the old barber-surgeons' guild, and leadership of the new community passed automatically into the hands of the king's *premier* barber. Thus the practice of surgery appears to have been placed firmly within the hierarchy of the guild system, to be considered only as a *métier*, the province of the craftsman barber-surgeon and, as a result, firmly under the control of the physicians.[9]

But despite this apparent crushing of academic surgery and its absorption into the larger, wealthier yet less prestigious barber-surgeons' company, the remainder of the seventeenth century would see a strengthening of the surgical guild which, coupled with a marked increase in prestige, would lead to the rise of the 'monarchical profession'[10] of surgery which we have already observed in our analysis of the practice of the *expert*. The spectacular success of this rise would eventually place the king's *premier* surgeon in a position of great power and influence, and over the next few decades surgery would continue to gain in power and status in moving towards acceptance as a liberal art requiring an academic education. Early steps in this direction soon became apparent. Only eight years after the *premier* barber had taken control over the newly formed company, the king's council ordered him to sell his rights and privileges over the art of barber-surgery to the *premier* surgeon, François Félix. This order would be reported in 1764 as having been made specifically at the king's request;[11] however, it could not be seen as a complete victory for the surgeons of the long gown as Félix had risen from the ranks of the barber-surgeons.[12]

The teaching of surgery would enjoy a great resurgence in the latter decades of the seventeenth century, in particular with the lectures presented by the surgeon Pierre Dionis at the Jardin des Plantes which, as we shall see when we consider Dionis's work in more detail, were central to the rise of theoretical surgery. Toby Gelfand has described these courses as 'completely overshadow[ing] those of the physician-professors who nominally had responsibility for teaching anatomy and surgery at the *Jardin du Roi*'.[13] Crowds of four or five hundred would attend Dionis's courses; but surgical teaching would be offered to even greater audiences at the École de Chirurgie in the next few years. With the aid of a 12 000-*livres* legacy from the surgeon Jean Biennaise,[14] public demonstrations would resume at Saint-Côme in 1681 to which even the humblest *serviteurs* were to be admitted.[15] Ten years later a further bequest by the Paris surgeon, Louis Roberdeau, would endow more courses and provide funds towards the construction of a new amphitheatre, which would be completed in 1695 and would allow seven hundred and fifty persons to attend demonstrations.[16]

The surgical statutes of 1699 would further reinforce the structure of the hierarchical framework of surgery, as we have already seen in Chapter Two with regard to the work of the *experts*, and would also confer upon the master surgeon important status and respectability. These statutes were drawn up by the *premier* surgeon, Charles-François Félix, who had succeeded his father to the post in 1676,[17] and René d'Argenson, the lieutenant-general of Paris police: thus it was Félix *fils*, exercising his influence with the king, who would lay the foundations for a unified surgical profession in France.[18] The statutes would ensure that power would now be centralized in the office of the king's surgeon and in an élite group of surgeons picked by him – real control was now confirmed in the hands of royal officials, not with the master surgeons themselves. Total control, therefore, now lay with the *premier chirurgien du roi*, who was

> chef et garde des chartes et privilèges de la chirurgie et barberie du royaume, a toute juridiction sur les maîtres chirurgiens jurez de

Paris, barbiers, perruquiers, sages-femmes, et tous autres exerçans l'art et profession de la chirurgie ou partie d'icelle.[19]

The *premier* surgeon now had great power, receiving revenue from each surgical *communauté* and from every new master admitted to them. On assuming office, his privilege of *joyeux avènement* (or joyous accession) entitled him to a sum from each member of each *communauté*. The official structure of the *communauté* would now have the *premier* surgeon at its head, his *lieutenant*, four *prévôts*, a *greffier* and the body of master surgeons, who were under the direct control of the *prévôts*.[20] But of paramount importance to those who occupied the higher reaches of the surgical framework was the fact that the statutes confirmed that the master surgeon could now look upon himself officially as the practitioner of a liberal art, thereby enjoying all the privilege this would attract: 'Ceux qui exerceront purement et simplement l'art de la chirurgie seront réputez exercer un art libéral, et jouïront de tous les privilèges attribuez à tous les arts libéraux.'[21] Viewed in conjunction with the articles of the same statute which were intended to govern the practice of the *experts*, it is clear that only the master surgeon could claim the practice of a liberal art in this way. As we have seen, the operations for the teeth (and others, such as the delivery of children and the operations for the eyes) were an integral part of this practice; but the *experts* and *sage-femmes* who were prohibited in law from practising any part of surgery other than that which they had been accepted for were, as we have also seen, forbidden to take the title of surgeon. They were therefore specifically *not* surgeons at all – and unable to make any such claims to the liberal nature of their art.

Surgeons would continue to encroach upon territory previously occupied by physicians alone. For example, 1714 would see the publication of a Liste de Messieurs les Chirurgiens de Paris for the first time in *L'Almanach Royal*,[22] accompanying the list of physicians which had appeared annually since at least 1566.[23] Ten years later Louis XV would create five chairs at Saint-Côme as proposed by his *premier* surgeon, and would grant further prestige to the academic surgeons in the establishment of the Académie de chirurgie in 1731. As Toby Gelfand has pointed out, *académies* were 'tangible expressions of the king's patronage of a group of *savants* [which] epitomized the organization of learned knowledge in eighteenth century France'.[24] Whilst the physicians of the Paris Faculté, one of the last strongholds of orthodox Galenism, had defied royal orders for the establishment of an academy in the late 1720s (and would continue to do so),[25] surgeons had no such theoretical commitment and the establishment of the Académie de chirurgie would thus help to legitimize their move towards a learned culture. This learned status would be cemented in place by a royal declaration of 1743, which ordered a strict separation of surgery from barbery and required future master surgeons to obtain 'le grade de maître ès arts dans quelqu'une des universités approuvées de notre royaume'.[26] However, forces other than those of academic status also had their part to play in the rise in royal patronage of the surgeons.

The rise of the standing army and the military surgeon

During the latter half of the seventeenth century, Louis XIV's imposition of central control over the military would result in the building of what had become by 1689 the largest standing army in Europe: an army which would require the services of many surgeons to maintain its manpower in good fighting condition. The degree of medical support required was significant, and the king's establishing of the Corps de Santé militaire coupled with an edict of 1708 would set up military hospitals in fifty-one French cities. In the process, a hierarchy of medical personnel would be put in place under the supervision of the *premier* physician, the *premier* surgeon and the minister of war.[27] The Act of 1708 specified that sick and wounded soldiers would be treated by qualified physicians and surgeons, and as a result posts were created for surgeon-majors in each of the military hospitals, along with a further 159 in the regiments. In typically hierarchical manner, a framework composed of a large number of military surgeons of lower rank reached down to form the base of this structure, and throughout the eighteenth century surgeons would remain of principal importance to the medical care of the army. The surgeon Pierre Dionis saw the battlefield as a clear advertisement for his art, claiming that 'it is in the armies and sieges that surgery triumphs, it is there that everyone recognizes its empire and its necessity, it is there that its actions rather than its words make their own eulogy'.[28] Forty years later, during the War of the Austrian Succession, roughly one-third of the Northern armies under the command of Maréchal Maurice de Saxe used the services of surgeons only, and it would not be until the Seven Years' War of 1756–63 that substantial numbers of physicians would start to take up military duties.[29] Military service also played a significant part in providing valuable experience for the increasing numbers of would-be surgeons. This was recognized in the statutes of 1699, which would allow the equivalent of one year's apprenticeship to those who had served in a military campaign.[30] Thus the importance attached to the part played by the surgeons in maintaining the health of the standing army would both enhance their prestige and encourage further royal patronage over a long period.

It would appear, then, that in the space of eighty years surgery would enjoy a spectacular rise in status and prestige, gaining the high ground in *ancien régime* medicine and standing alongside, if not above, the physicians of the Faculté. But we need to look more closely at how this was achieved before we can ask how it may have influenced the treatment of teeth by surgeons in the decades around the beginning of the eighteenth century. In looking for reasons for the rapid rise in the standing of surgery, we shall find on the one hand a picture of changing techniques and the use of new, innovative operations built on improved method and theoretical knowledge, and on the other a social history of rising status coupled with social emulation. As we shall see later, in the narrower view afforded by the practice of the *dentiste*, both of these factors are central to this picture of rising respectability.

The rise of the court surgeon: Félix and the fistula

A spectacular gain in respectability and status for the king's surgeon was demonstrated in the granting of *lettres d'anoblissement* to the *premier* surgeon Félix in 1690. To earn this reward, Félix had fulfilled an important set of criteria: in particular, he had performed a great personal service for the king. Four years earlier, Louis had been suffering with an anal fistula. Various remedies had been tried for ten months, but Louis remained in excruciating pain. Meanwhile, Félix had practised his operation on patients at the Hôtel-Dieu. After both surgeon and patient eventually submitted to the ordeal of the knife, Louis was completely healed within two months and had no apparent recurrence. As a result, Félix received an extremely generous financial reward coupled with ennoblement, which was granted under the express understanding that he would continue to serve the king's person whilst running no risk of *dérogeance*, or losing his noble status for doing so.[31] We shall examine the mechanism by which such rewards were earned and attained in greater detail in a later chapter, along with the problems raised by performing a 'noble' duty with one's hands – but the effect on the court of the highly successful performance of this operation was immense. The year 1686 became *l'année de la fistule*, in which it was a great privilege to have the same affliction as the king. The French historian Alfred Franklin noted that

> Tout le monde se flattait d'en avoir, et les gens assez heureux pour en posséder réellement une, laissaient éclater leur orgueil et leur joie. Ils couraient chez les chirurgiens, demandant avec hauteur qu'on leur fit *la même opération qu'au roi*.[32]

The surgeon Pierre Dionis would remark later in the lectures that accompanied his course of demonstrations at the Jardin Royal that many had 'turned up their posteriors to a surgeon' when they had had no need whatsoever of an operation. Many had even been angry when he, Dionis, had refused to cut them:

> This disease seems at present to be more rife than formerly; we every Day hear of Operations performed on such Persons as did not before seem afflicted with it; 'tis a Distemper grown in fashion since that which the King had, and on which the Chirurgeons were forced to perform the Operation in order to its Cure. Several of those who before that Time carefully conceal'd their having it, are not now asham'd to publish it, and some Courtiers have even chosen *Versailles* for the Place where they will undergo this Operation, because the King should be informed of all the Circumstances of their Indisposition. Those who have only a small draining run immediately and turn up their Posteriors to a Chirurgeon, for him to make Incision; I have seen above thirty who desir'd to have the Operation perform'd, and whose Folly was so great, that they seem'd angry when they were assured that they did not at all want it.[33]

Thus, to have need of an operation for a fistula would now exceed mere social acceptance – for a while, at least, it would come close to being socially *essential*, real or not.

The successful cure of the king's fistula could only have helped to further Félix's rise to power via Louis's endorsement of the surgical statutes, which were drawn up in the years after the surgeon's ennoblement; but perhaps somewhat paradoxically the social standing at court of the *premier* surgeon would be raised higher still, displacing the *premier* physician in the process, on Louis XIV's death in 1715. Georges Mareschal, Félix's successor, had detected the king's illness at an early stage and had recommended urgent treatment;[34] however, Gui-Crescent Fagon, the *premier* physician, had rejected this advice and stubbornly insisted that the king's health was not in danger, even when it was clear that he was dying.[35] When the king did so, of severe gangrene, Fagon was dismissed. Gelfand notes that

> Prior to 1715, the royal surgeon had been distinctly subordinate to the royal physician, a subordination clearly revealed in Mareschal's deference to Fagon. After Fagon's ignominious departure, the chief physician never again dominated their surgical counterparts. If anything, the king's surgeons tended to assume the first rank.[36]

Presumably partly as a result of this shift in hierarchy, from 1715 Mareschal and his colleague and successor François de la Peyronie would secure rulings from the Crown which were very favourable to the surgeons and which would greatly enhance their power. The most important of these would be the establishment of teaching at Saint-Côme in 1724 and of the Académie de chirurgie in 1731.[37]

Official French surgery was clearly on the rising path to high status and respectability, aided by those surgeons who were climbing the social ladder. In looking at the picture presented by the surgeons at court, we have seen some of the strong social and political influences – but was there also a 'technical' side to it? If so, what form would such technical change take? Was this rise in prestige built in conjunction with changes in the types of operations performed, and the *way* in which they were performed? In asking what part both technique and the theory on which it was based would play in this spectacular rise, we first need to ask how this technique was perceived, and what effect this perception would have on the surgeon's status.

Surgical training in Paris in the early eighteenth century: 'the best in the World'[38]

From the latter part of the seventeenth century to the middle of the eighteenth, French surgery came to be considered as the foremost in Europe. There were a few well-respected surgeons in other countries, perhaps most notably William Cheselden in London who had developed a highly successful operation 'for the stone' and had performed many operations on the eye. But even Cheselden acknowledged the superiority which had been enjoyed by French surgery at the turn of the century, citing hospital training as the key:

> It must be confessed, that both anatomy and surgery flourished much later in England than in France, where all possible encouragements were given to both: while, in London, the governors of the two hospitals [St Bartholomew's and St Thomas's], being mostly citizens, out of a false policy, entirely refused the education of pupils in one hospital, and allowed of but nine at a time in the other.[39]

In France, the surgeon Pierre Dionis focused his discussion of what constituted a good surgeon on the school at Saint-Côme:

> By good Chirurgeons I don't mean those who pretend to that Character, because they have learn'd to spread a Plaister, and to Bleed; nor those, who, influenced by no other Ends than those mean ones of Interest, have intruded into that illustrious body: But I would be understood to speak of those, who, after a commendable Education, have imbib'd the precepts of Chirurgery from good Masters, and have afterwards practis'd in the Hospitals and Armies, conform to those Lights and the sound Method which they learn'd at the School of *St. Côme*, undoubtedly the place where the most able Chirurgeons of *Europe* are form'd.[40]

Having praised the wisdom of the *premier* surgeons Félix and Mareschal, both of whom had sent their sons to be accepted at Saint-Côme, Dionis reveals that his own two sons, on wishing to become surgeons, had also submitted to the Society's rigorous examinations for the mastership. But he sounded a warning that the lesser examinations such as those of the *expert* could, if allowed to flourish, diminish the reputation of the college and therefore, by implication, the standing of academic surgery:

> As soon as they [his sons] determin'd to be Chirurgeons, I exposed them to this trial; they performed their twenty five Acts with the utmost Vigour, and learnt in that Society what they could not meet with elsewhere. God grant that the easy and conniving Admissions and superficial Examinations which have Introduced into that Society several who thought themselves not able to incorporate themselves by the Master-proof, don't diminish its ancient Splendor, and bring it to relax the Regularity of its Acts, by prodigally allowing to be Masters, Persons unworthy of that Title, and that the School at *Paris*, may keep up its former Reputation of being the best in the World.[41]

It was not merely loyalty to his countrymen that led Dionis to consider French surgeons as the best in Europe, if not the world. Toby Gelfand, in his discussion of hospital teaching as private enterprise in London, has also noted that 'In the allied fields of surgery and midwifery,[42] ... Parisian superiority had been taken for granted till about 1750'.[43] He goes on to state elsewhere that

> From a technical standpoint, French surgery assumed a position of European leadership in the late seventeenth century and the first half of the eighteenth. French or, to be more precise, Paris surgeons built this reputation on major operations, new instruments, and anatomical work for which cadavers were in plentiful supply. Their publications dominated the literature, and Paris became the outstanding center for learning anatomy and surgery.[44]

French publications on surgery were indeed numerous. In the period from 1690 to 1746 seventy-one writers published surgical books in France, of which fifty-five were from Paris – yet in the same period, only nineteen were produced in Britain (all of them in London).[45] Of these French publications Pierre Dionis's *Cours d'opérations de Chirurgie*, based on the lectures presented at the Jardin des Plantes in the 1670s and running to several editions throughout the eighteenth century, would assume great prominence. Dionis's remarks have already helped to illustrate the prominent role which French surgery was assuming in this period; an examination of his teaching at the Jardin and the publications that followed will help to uncover what it was that made this teaching so important.[46]

Pierre Dionis at the Jardin des Plantes: the *Cours d'opérations de chirurgie*

In January of 1626 a royal edict had marked the formal foundation of the Jardin des Plantes Médicinales, to be under the *surintendance* of the king's *premier* physician, Jean Héroard.[47] Nine years later, in June 1635, another edict had signalled the official establishment of the Jardin in the faubourg Saint-Victor, followed by the appointment of three demonstrators: Jacques Cousinot, 'démonstrateur et opérateur pharmaceutique pour faire la démonstration de l'intérieur des plantes'; Urbain Baudinot, 'démonstrateur et opérateur pharmaceutique'; and Marin Cureau de la Chambre, 'démonstrateur et opérateur des opérations pharmaceutiques'.[48] Just one month later, a further *ordonnance* stipulated that this last demonstrator should also 'faire la démonstration oculaire et manuelle de toutes et chacunes des opérations de chirurgie, de quelque nature qu'elles puissent estre'.[49] Unfortunately little seems to be known about the content of this early surgical teaching, or what form it took: despite writing fifteen books, Marin Cureau de la Chambre never alluded either to his teaching or his demonstrations.[50] He held the post for a long time, however, until in 1671 he was succeeded by his son François, who was a *médecin ordinaire du roi* and the queen's *premier* physician, holding many important posts at court.

Whatever form Marin Cureau de la Chambre's teaching of anatomy at the Jardin des Plantes may have taken, he appears to have neglected it somewhat, particularly towards the end of his time as *démonstrateur*. His son, however, reinstated it in 1672; but apparently unable to fulfil all his many commitments, he appointed the physician Pierre Cressé to perform 'les discours anatomiques'[51] and the young surgeon Pierre Dionis to perform the dissections and demonstrations. Dionis sets out the details of the arrangement in the preface to his *L'anatomie de l'homme*, which was based on the dissections he performed at the Jardin:[52]

> These Anatomical Exercises were reviv'd in the Royal Garden, in the Year 1672; after a discontinuation of several Years. Mr. *de la Chambre* the Anatomy Professor, being the Queen's First Physician, was diverted from attending these Lectures: and therefore commission'd Dr. *Cresse* a member of the Faculty of *Paris* to pronounce the Anatomical Discourses, and nominated me for making the Dissections and Demonstrations.[53]

It seems, however, that Cressé also found himself too busy to perform his duties at the Jardin Royal,[54] and despite holding the official title of *démonstrateur,* which reflected the regulations in force in the 1670s forbidding surgeons from lecturing in public, it was Dionis who addressed the audience during the dissections.

The physicians of the Paris Faculté de Médecine objected vociferously to the demonstrations presented at the Jardin under the *surintendance* of the *premier* physician, now Antoine d'Aquin, claiming that only they had the right to dissect and to present anatomical lectures. Their attacks were effectively crushed, however, when Louis XIV in person placed his support firmly behind his court surgeons. Dionis noted of the dissections performed at the Jardin that

> Tho' this establishment was of singular use to the Publick, yet it met with opposition from some, who pretended that the right of Dissecting and making Anatomical Lectures was lodg'd in them only. But his Majesty stiffled [*sic*] the opposition by a particular Declaration, which was ratify'd and recorded in the Parliament of Paris, 1673. his Majesty himself being present. In this Declaration, his Majesty ordered that Anatomical dissections and Chirurgical Operations should be performed *gratis* and with open doors, in the Amphitheatre that he had built for that purpose in the Royal Garden; and that his Professors should have the preference of all others in being serv'd such Corps or Subjects as were necessary for carrying on these Exercises.
>
> Pursuant to his Majesty's commands, I Dissected publickly for eight Years together, that is, from the Year 1673 to the Year 1680, at which time his Majesty did me the honour to nominate me for being First Surgeon to the Dauphiness of France; and my Accession to this honourable Post oblig'd me to discontinue the publick dissections.[55]

Dionis's courses of demonstrations were therefore presented in the right place, with the professors of the Jardin Royal having first call on corpses from 1673 on the king's authority and, as Laurence Brockliss has pointed out, the use of an amphitheatre which was the best equipped in France, even having rooms where students could perform dissections themselves.[56] As a result, the courses rapidly proved to be immensely popular, a typical audience numbering from four to five hundred. It soon became necessary to restrict entry to surgeons' apprentices only, thus providing a useful means by which barbers' apprentices, with their 'short gown' connotations, could be excluded. Dionis claimed

> For the space of eight Years I have performed those [demonstrations] in the Royal Garden, to which the Concourse of Students was so great, that the largest Hall destin'd for them would not hold one half of the Auditors; which oblig'd us to prepare seal'd Tickets, which we distributed to Chirurgeons Apprentices, that they alone might enter, and to avoid Confusion by the exclusion of those who were plac'd to serve their time in Barber Shops, and of those whose bare Curiosity drove them thither.[57]

Although tickets were issued, no charge could be made for, as Dionis would note in the preface to *L'anatomie de l'homme*, the king had declared that the demonstrations be *gratis*.

As we shall see later, in an analysis of the content of the lectures which accompanied Dionis's demonstrations, they would be absolutely central to the building of a theoretical foundation for the practice of surgery. The full courses extended over a period of twenty-eight days, with the first eight given to osteology, the following ten to anatomical dissection of the body and the final ten to demonstrations of the operations of surgery. In 1691, the first two parts of the course were published as *L'anatomie de l'homme*, followed in 1708 by the final part, published as the *Cours d'opérations de Chirurgie*. Both books would prove popular: *L'anatomie* would run to eight editions, including one in Latin and one in English, while the *Cours d'opérations* would make a great impact on the teaching of surgery in France, its tenth edition (including two in English) appearing as late as 1777. The entry for Dionis in Michaud's *Biographie Universelle* of 1852 would describe this work as 'le premier bon ouvrage composé sur cette matière ... il a été, pendant un siècle, le guide des professeurs et des élèves'.[58]

L'anatomie de l'homme as the basis for the *Cours d'opérations*

For Pierre Dionis, these courses on anatomy and operations were powerfully and inextricably linked together. He did not consider surgery to be built purely on manual dexterity and practical skill, but also on sound knowledge of the body in its perfect, or complete, state. He made this clear to his audience at the start of his very first lecture on anatomy:

> You know, Gentlemen, that Surgery is an Operation of the Understanding, which considers the Maladies of a Humane Body; and that it is likewise an Operation of the Hand, which manages the Instruments and Remedies that are requisite to cure them: insomuch that for the better performing what is required, not only the knowledge of a sound state ought to precede that of an infirm, but the Surgeon ought to know Man in his perfect state, and the good conformation of all Parts of his Body, that he may be the better able to re-establish his Health, when it comes to be altered or destroyed, by some Disease, or ill Accident. It is by Anatomy, Gentlemen, that he must acquire this Knowledge, seeing it is the *basis* and foundation of surgery; it is by this, that he unravels and dissects the most minute Parts, of which this admirable Structure is composed, that he searches into all the springs and motions, and finds out whatever is curious or secret in Nature.
>
> And here would be a fair opportunity to praise and extol Anatomy, and to let you know at the same time the indispensable necessity of understanding it, if a Man would ever become an expert Surgeon.[59]

Thus the surgeon must know man in his complete state, and the only way he could acquire this knowledge was through a thorough knowledge of anatomy which, for Dionis, formed the basis and the foundation of surgery – and without this knowledge, the prospective surgeon could not hope to succeed.

We may see through Dionis's published *Cours d'opérations* that the demonstrations on which they were based were not built on *cases*, that is, sufferers with particular diseases, used to demonstrate and explain the operations in the manner of the master and his apprentice; they were built on *cadavers* – subject material with no particular disease or injury. On these, therefore, he could perform a whole series of operations based on a complete and thorough knowledge of anatomy, which he had taught in the eighteen preceding demonstrations: in this way his surgery could *only* be built on anatomy, following the order of the dissection.[60] From the body of anatomical theory thus gained, a series of principles, or fundamental elements of knowledge, could be constructed for the operations which were to be performed on the human body. Such a principle would not be presented simply as 'general advice'; it would both form the *starting-point* of the theory and be the *last* thing taught, deduced from the theory itself.

Looking more closely at Dionis's writings, and the way in which he constructed his demonstrations, will help to reveal the way in which the foundations for technical change in surgery were laid. In doing this, we shall see that in addition to the social influences and factors discussed earlier, the rise of surgery would be built on the construction of a body of theoretical knowledge, a *science*, the possession of which surgeons such as Dionis would now argue for strongly as forming a central focus for the hitherto purely manual trade of surgery. Examination of the writings of surgeons who would follow Dionis, such as René Garengeot, will reveal that by the 1720s the practice of the surgeon would stand firmly on such a *science*. It would now demand the performance of a wide range of technically complicated operations, all of which were governed by a body of precepts, or practical rules for their performance. These precepts would be founded on a series of fundamental principles which, in turn, had been built quite literally on a body: a body of theoretical knowledge of anatomy.

The surgeon as natural philosopher: Dionis's 'absolute necessity' of a *science* for surgery

As we have already seen, the first eighteen of Dionis's demonstrations at the Jardin des Plantes concerned the skeleton and anatomy. At the beginning of the final group of ten, which taught the operations of surgery as they would later be published in the *Cours d'opérations*,

Dionis returned to the theme of his original introduction, stressing to his audience the need for a thorough understanding of '*Theoretical Chirurgery*, on which ought to be founded the second part, which is called the *Practick*'.[61] He supposed that his audience had attended his earlier demonstrations, and that as a result 'all here present are instructed in the *Theory* of *Chirurgery*; ... in this Course I confine my self to entertain you with nothing extraneous to what all Men understand by *Chirurgical Operations*; all which I pretend to demonstrate to you, which will abundantly fill up the time usually allow'd to publick Lectures'[62] – these demonstrations focused therefore on the second, practical part of surgery. But Dionis never let his audience lose sight of the importance of firm theoretical principles for surgery, founded on anatomy. In the preface to his book, he argues strongly that the practice of the surgeon should not be considered purely as a mechanical art – because it is founded on theoretical knowledge it should also deserve the name of *science*. He points to the importance of theoretical knowledge of anatomy and its contribution even to the *science* of physics:

> All Philosophers are agreed on the Importance of *Physics*, which science, in order to instruct us in the History of Nature, does not content itself with mounting up to the Heavens, examining what passes in the Air, descending to the Bottom of the Sea, and raking into the Entrails of the Earth, but penetrating into every Being in particular, acquaints us with all the Parts which compose and form the Ornament of the Universe.
>   This Science could not discover the Springs which actuate all the Bodies we see, without the Assistance of Anatomy, by whose means dissecting and separating all the Parts, even to the minutest Particles which compose the whole, it lays open all the Secrets of Nature; and a Course of Philosophy would be imperfect, if depriv'd of the Lights which Anatomical Demonstrations afford it.
>   If the Natural Philosopher is indispensibly obliged to have recourse to Anatomy, to discover the internal Part of each Being; how much is the Chirurgeon oblig'd to apply to it, considering his Object is the Body of Man.[63]

If the *science* of anatomy is, therefore, so essential to the natural philosopher, how much more essential is it to the surgeon – whose practice is firmly based on it? The surgeon, by etymological definition, works with his hands. But this does *not* mean that surgery may not enjoy the name of a *science*. For Dionis, the two cannot be divorced: for as the mathematician uses instruments in his practice (which indisputably deserves the name of *science*), so the surgeon uses instruments in the practice of his – and those instruments are his hands.

> I call Chirurgery an Art, in order to confine myself within the Bounds of its Etymology, which derives it from the two *Greek* words, *Keir*, which signifies a Hand, and *Ergon*, which imparts

operation; so that the Chirurgeon and Manual Operator are Synonymous Terms, common to all who work with the Hand. Tho' by this Etymology the Chirurgeon seems to be confounded with all other Artists, 'tis thence redounds his greatest Glory; since it distinguishes him from, and places him above, all the rest. The Ancients, who gave Names to all Arts, call'd him a Painter who painted Pictures, Sculptor him who carv'd images & c. But by way of Excellence have left that of Chirurgeon to him who operating on Human Bodies, has for his Object the noblest of Beings.

We might indeed somewhat justly bestow on Chirurgery the Name of a Science, contrary to the Opinion of some who will have it to be barely a Mechanic Art; 'tis true, it Operates with the Hand; but its Performances being only such as Reason dictates, it does not less deserve the Name of Science than the Mathematics, which trace out on Paper those Figures and Demonstrations which the Mind suggests: Both these Sciences equally require their proper instruments; and as the use of the Mathematical ones belongs only to the Mathematician, so the Chirurgical are peculiar to the Chirurgeon; for the Separation of the Theory from the Practice is equally impossible in both these Sciences: And as we should think him an ignorant Mathematician who could neither delineate his Figures, nor frame his Demonstrations; we ought also to believe him uncapable of helping those who require his Assistance, who stands in need of any Hand besides his own to cure the Diseases of which he boasts the Discovery.[64]

Whilst the practice of surgery cannot succeed without the use of the hands, for Dionis it also demands the use of the mind. In building a comparison with mathematics, he is taking surgery out of its traditional place amongst the base, manual occupations and placing it on a higher level, taking as its basis learned theoretical knowledge alongside acquired manual skill. Thus, although its practice must necessarily involve the use of the hands, such manual practice *cannot*, for Dionis, be separated from theoretical knowledge.

But in the object of his activities the surgeon has been granted the gift of serving the body of man, the 'noblest of beings'. The theory of surgery should, therefore, be considered as an essential *science*; but Dionis argues that it is not *a science* – it is *the science*.

We may, if we please, not only rank Chirurgery amongst the Sciences; but look on it as one of the noblest, most certain, and most necessary of them all. That which enobles a Science is the Dignity of its Object. That of Chirurgery is the same which God had of his Omnipotence, and on which he was pleased to work with his own Hand; for in the Creation of other Beings, Holy Writ informs us, that God only spake, and they were made: And when this Science directs any Performance by the Suggestion of a Train of Consequences which it deduces from its Principles, 'tis certainly the same Body to which it is to be apply'd. Can the Chirurgeon alledge any thing more glorious for himself, than that God, after having made

Man, and given a Form and Figure to all the Parts of his Body perfectly proper and suitable to the Actions to which they were destin'd, left him in the Chirurgeon's Hands to take care of his Preservation, and keep up the Symmetry of all the Parts which he receiv'd from the Creator. God, when on Earth, practis'd this Art, exercising on all Occasions that perfect Chirurgery in all its Parts, which at the same time as it knows the Indisposition, applies the Hand and Remedy to cure it; and the Apostles, the Successors of his Charity as well as his Power, did not disdain the Application of their Hands to the Infirmities of Patients, and by their charitable Assistance converted an infinite Number of People, who seeing them perform extraordinary Cures, were convinc'd of the Truth of their Doctrine. Kings and Princes made Dressing the Patients, which implor'd their help, their principal Occupation, not thinking it below their Dignity to apply their Royal Hands to the curing and relieving of the same Subject which God himself had formed with his sacred Hands; and without ransacking Antiquity for instances, we have seen our own Sovereign cause to be prepar'd in his Presence, and charitably distributed to all who ask'd it, a Remedy which he receiv'd from the Prior of *Cabrieres*; so that in all Ages Chirurgery has not been thought unworthy the Practice of the greatest on Earth.[65]

In having as its object the human body, the body of the *only* being God chose to make with his own hands, the *science* of surgery is thus ennobled to the highest degree possible: God, his Apostles, and even the king himself had, by Dionis's analysis, all practiced surgery. Thus the *science* of surgery was of paramount importance – it was an 'absolute necessity', without which man may not even survive:

To prove the absolute necessity of Chirurgery, we need only consider, that all other Arts and Sciences are no farther necessary to Man, than as they contribute to his commodious Living; but that Chirurgery is absolutely necessary, even in order to his very Living; for at the moment of his Birth he implores its help to make the Ligature of the Navel, or to cut the String under the Tongue, (which frequently he brings into the World at his Birth), without which he would perish as soon as born. We may add, that without this Science the Earth would be almost depopulated by reason that there are few People in the course of their Lives, on which Chirurgeons have not perform'd some Operation, to save them from Death.[66]

For Dionis, therefore, the absolute necessity of the *science* of surgery, ennobled by the dignity of its object, cannot be overestimated. All other arts and *sciences* make man's existence more comfortable, and contribute to his endowment with convenience; but the *science* of surgery, the theoretical knowledge upon which the practice of the surgeon is built, is *absolutely necessary* to his very existence.

Dionis's strong argument for a *science* of surgery is, therefore, that surgery is built on precepts and principles which form the bases of the various types of operations, built in turn on a thorough understanding of the *science* of anatomy. In the *Cours d'opérations*, built firmly on this *science*, these general principles may clearly be seen. The operations are divided into four principal categories: *synthesis*, which 'rejoins what was separated'; *diæresis*, which 'separates those parts whose Union is inconsistent with Health'; *exæresis*, which 'removes whatever is super-fluous'; and *prosthesis*, which 'adds what is deficient'.[67] The principles which apply to each type accompany their description: synthesis, for example, is 'an Operation which dextrously re-unites and replaces those parts of our Bodies, which are separated, or displaced contrary to the common Course of Nature'; and is either general or particular in na-ture. General synthesis is common to all operations – it will require the application of '*Splents* or *Ferula*'s, *Plegets* or *Bolsters, Bandages*'.[68] It will also require the proper situation of the parts affected, and use of the instruments and methods which may contribute to the restoration or re-establishment of the parts in their rightful place. The second type, the particular synthesis, is for either soft, fleshy parts or for hard and bony parts. Each of these can take two forms: for soft parts, either reduction or suturing, and for bony parts either the reuniting of broken bones or the resetting of luxated or dislocated ones.[69] Later in this chapter, we shall see how Dionis applied such elements of theoretical knowledge as these to the performance of particular operations, when we watch him in action via his detailed descriptions of the operations to be performed on the teeth.

A *théorie* for surgery: Garengeot's *preceptes*

The generation of surgeons who would follow Dionis would build their practice on the firm basis gained by the construction of theoretical knowledge in addition to practical skill. When René Garengeot pub-lished his book on the operations of surgery in 1720, the need for a body of theoretical knowledge was implicit in his title: *Traité des opera-tions de Chirurgie, suivant la Méchanique des Parties du Corps Humain, la Théorie & la Pratique des Chirurgiens de Paris les plus sçavans & les plus experimentés*.[70] For Garengeot, it was in Paris, where surgeons could become *les plus experimentés* by the use of corpses, that this knowledge of theory could best be gained – and without it, it was not possible to become a good surgeon. At the start of his treatise, he emphasizes the importance of both theory and practice: 'we shall lay down these rules; that all chirurgical Operations ought to be performed *speedily*, *safely*, and *dexterously*. But to make Use of those Precepts, a Surgeon ought to know that the Operations consist of two Parts; the

one concerns the Theory, and the other concerns the Practice.'[71] A
sound understanding of both these parts was required, but an accurate
knowledge of anatomy was absolutely essential:

> The first [viz. theory] takes in the Knowledge of the Disease, its
> Course, Beginning, Progress, State, and End, and of some other
> Circumstances, which ought to be known before one goes about
> the Operation, that one may judge the Necessity of its Perform-
> ance, and what Remedies are proper for the Disease: This is to be
> learned by the reading of good Books, and by an Accurate Knowl-
> edge of Anatomy, without which 'tis impossible to be a good
> Surgeon.
> The Practice consists in the Method of preparing the *Apparatus*,
> in the Knowledge of Instruments, the manner of operating, and
> other Particulars to be learned only by frequenting good Surgeons,
> by reading the Observations of able Practitioners, and by a con-
> stant attendance in Hospitals.[72]

Thus, in order to become a good surgeon, good manual ability and a
thorough knowledge of instruments must be underpinned by an equally
thorough understanding of the theoretical knowledge on which that
operation was constructed.

The way in which Garengeot used principles of theoretical knowledge
to form the building blocks of the operations of the surgeon becomes
more apparent if we examine details of this construction more closely.
For example, in looking at his 'precepts necessary for the well dressing
of Wounds',[73] in which he describes seventeen practical rules by which
this part of surgery should be performed, it becomes apparent that these
rules have a firm theoretical basis. They are built on a sound knowledge
of both the structures involved and of the healing processes of the body:

> I. *Precept.* One must avoid the Method of some Surgeons, who
> probe Wounds at every Dressing, and thereby make small Wounds
> every time they use a Probe, by tearing or compressing the Ex-
> tremities of the small Tubes, which are very soft and tender.
> II. *Precept.* Great Incisions ought not to be made without Neces-
> sity, for fear of encreasing the Wound. The Surgeon ought to make
> them only, when 'tis necessary to evacuate the purulent Matter, or
> to take out some extraneous Bodies, or some fragments of Bones
> broken or carious.
> III. *Precept.* The Operator must dress the Wound softly, and with-
> out exciting any Pain, forbearing to introduce into the Wound
> Dozels, Tents, and other dilating Bodies, which stopping the small
> Tubes occasion Inflammations. It plainly appears that all those
> things are contrary to Nature; for when a Wound thus filled is
> uncovered, the Dozels and Tents come out of it all at once.
> IV. *Precept.* A Tent is absolutely necessary after the *Gastroraphia*,
> when the Surgeon has made the Ligature of the *Epiploon*, or the
> Suture of the Intestin, or the Operation of the *Bubonocele*, or in

the dressing of a *Fistula*: But Tents ought not to be used, when they appear needless, especially in the Wounds of the Joints.

I shall shew in the next Chapter, that this Precept ought to be observed only in some *Fistula's*, and that the use of Tents is repugnant to Nature and the Design of the Surgeon.

V. *Precept*. The Dressings ought to be speedy, in order to avoid the Impression of the Air, which coagulates the Juices and the Blood of the Extremities of the Fibers, and of the small vessels, and thereby occasion general Obstruction attended with Inflammations, and consequently with great Pain, and even with a Fever.

VI. *Precept*. Wounds ought to be dressed but seldom, that Nature may have Time to produce the small, fleshy, bony, or tendinous *Papillæ*, which ought to fill up the Wound. One must dress at least twice a day those Wounds, that suppurate much, especially in Summer, to avoid the Corruption, & *Gangrene*, & c.

VII. *Precept*. The Wound ought to be gently wiped, for fear of taking away the nutritive Juice, which must repair the lost Substance, and occasioning a Pain, by irritating the nervous Fibers of the Wound.

VIII. *Precept*. Rottening Ointments ought to be used as little as possible.

IX. *Precept*. Fat and oily Remedies ought not to be used in those Wounds, wherein there is an Inflammation or an Erysipelas, because locking up the Pores, they prevent Transpiration, and encrease the Disease.

X. *Precept*. Spirituous Remedies ought to be laid aside, when the Suppuration is in a good way, because they harden the Extremities of the small Vessels, and occasion a reflux of Matter. On the contrary, gentle and balsamick Remedies ought to be used, such as the Balsam of *Fioraventi*, and *Copahu*, *the Essence of Terebenthine*, & c.

XI. *Precept*. One ought to prevent or destroy the Callosity, which shuts up the Extremities of the Tubes, and keeps them from pouring the nutritive Juice to repair the lost Substance.

XIII. *Precept*. A *Seton* ought to be used, when the Wound is quite thorough, to convey the Remedy within the Wound, and hinder the Lips from being re-united sooner than the Bottom.

XIV. *Precept*. The Compresses ought to be imbibed with some warm Liquor, such as Wine, or some Fomentation, when the Dressing is to be taken off, that they may easily be loosened, and no Divulsion be made in the Fibers of the Wound.

XV. *Precept*. Plaisters ought to be used as little as possible, because they close the Lips of the Wound, and hinder Transpiration.

XVI. *Precept*. Wounds ought not to be rolled strait, since the Bandage is only designed to keep on the Remedies, (excepting however longitudinal Wounds, to bring remote Lips together;) for Compression hinders the Circulation.

XVII. *Precept*. Lastly, the Surgeon ought to use evacuating, and lenitive Remedies, such as Phlebotomy, Glisters, Diet-Drinks, Evulsions, *&c.* Vulneraries are proper, when the Blood is thick and clogged with a Chyle of the same Nature; but then there ought to be no Inflammation in the Wound. They are also proper in the Wounds of the Viscera. The best way of giving them is to make a thin Decoction of vulnerary Plants, and to put a spoonful in each Glass of the Patient's usual Drink.

Studying these precepts reveals that the theoretical knowledge on which they were built could extend even to the invisible level of the small vessels and nervous fibres of the wound – and that they required a sound theoretical understanding of the healing process, such as the need to retain the 'nutritive juice, which must repair the lost substance' of precept VII.

The performance of each operation in particular should also follow a series of general precepts. When amputating a leg, for example,

> For the right performing of that Operation, the Surgeon ought to mind four essential Things: The first consists in preventing an Effusion of Blood during the Operation: The second, in preserving the Skin as much as possible: The third, in extirpating the Limb: The fourth, in searing the Blood after the Operation.[74]

Garengeot's writing then gives the reader a series of rules which should be adhered to for each one of these four 'essential things'. However, despite providing this detailed account of the many precepts and principles for the surgeon, Garengeot, like Dionis before him, assumed that they were already well known by his readers:

> If I have not enlarged upon the general Precepts, which concern Operations, 'tis not because I believe they are useless, but because they have been treated of in Chirurgical Introductions; and therefore I supposed that those, for whom I write, are sufficiently acquainted with them.[75]

The importance placed upon a theoretical basis for the practice of the surgeon, founded on general principles, would increase throughout the early decades of the eighteenth century. Guillaume Mauquest, Sieur de la Motte, would 'parle succinctement des principes de Chirurgie' in his *Traité complet de Chirurgie* of 1722,[76] placing *science* alongside manual skill:

> L'on apprend la Chirurgie par l'étude des principes de cet art, & par celles du corps humain & des maladies qui demandent pour leur guérison l'opération chirurgicale. Elle est partagée en théorie ou science, & en Chirurgie-pratique qui est un art de plus utiles; la premier consiste à sçavoir les causes, les signes, le prognostic, & la cure des maladies chirurgicales entreprise sur de bonnes indications, & le seconde dépend de la parfaite dextérité à mettre en execution ce que les preceptes enseignent, appellée Chirurgie-pratique, dans laquelle on ne peut exceller qu'après avoir travaillé sous de bons Maîtres, dans les hôpitaux des plus grosses villes, & dans ceux des armées pendant un long-tems …[77]

M. De la Faye would publish his *Principes de Chirurgie* in 1738, a short book which contained the principal elements of surgery, and the precepts which were based on them: 'Cet ouvrage n'est qu'un très-petit abrégé des Elémens de Chirurgie, dont il contient les principales définitions & les préceptes généraux.'[78] By the 1740s, the surgical writer would no longer need to dispute the need for a *science*, only its content.

We now have a picture of a wide-ranging body of theoretical knowledge, the possession of which would be a prerequisite for the successful practice of surgery by the third decade of the eighteenth century. But how would the operations for the teeth, as an important part of this practice, fit into such a picture? Would these operations too become more complex and innovative, and grow with the practice of the surgeon – or would their performance become somehow divorced from his 'everyday' work? To answer these questions, we first need to look more closely at the part played by the operations for the teeth in the practice of the surgeon in the early decades of the eighteenth century, as the *science* for surgery was under construction, and at how he would view those operations.

Pierre Dionis and the operations for the teeth: a new type of practitioner

If we continue to look at the *science* for surgery, the necessity of which was argued for so strongly by Dionis, through his *Cours d'opérations de Chirurgie*, we can see that the operations for the teeth have a significant role to play. By focusing on them in particular, we can also see that the practice of the surgeon has grown still further – with, in the case of the operations for the teeth, a dramatic outcome. Whilst they are still, for Dionis, part of this practice, they no longer simply belong with the treatments for the head, as they had for surgeons such as Paré and Scultetus. The expanding nature of the surgeon's practice now demanded that the operations for the face be considered separately. Thus, whilst Dionis's demonstration six (of ten) dealt with the operations for the head and eyes, he accorded the operations for the teeth a central position in his seventh 'demonstration of Chirurgical operations – Of those which are practised on the FACE'.[79] These comprised the operations of the polypus, the ozœna (a fetid polypus in the nose), wounds in the nose, bleeding in the head, the hare-lip, operations on the gums, the teeth, the tongue, of the uvula, the almonds, sore throats, operations practised on the ears, the parotids, the goitre and the king's evil. Within this demonstration, Dionis lists seven categories of operations for the teeth:

seven sorts of Operations are practis'd. The first is the opening or
widening the Teeth when they are set too close together; the second, to cleanse them when they are foul; the third, to hinder their
rotting; the fourth, to stop the Holes which grow in them; the fifth,
is to file them when they are too long and jagged; the sixth, to pull
them out when rotten; and the seventh, to substitute artificial ones
in the place of the natural.[80]

Each one of these operations was then performed as a demonstration
on the cadaver, with direct reference to possible causes of disease and
the explanations and demonstrations of the appropriate instruments –
and all was founded on the anatomical structure on view. For the first
operation, Dionis noted that 'Sometimes the Teeth so close themselves,
that 'tis impossible to open them to take in Food.'[81] There were four
likely causes: accident, 'Abscess on the Parotides, suffer'd to scarify,
without having put a small Gag betwixt the upper and lower Teeth, to
keep them at a sufficient Distance from one another: Obstinacy of a
melancholy child which will not open its mouth', and convulsion of the
muscles which move the jaw.[82] To treat such a problem, the surgeon
should use a levitor[83] to separate the teeth, the action of which forces
the jaw open. He should turn the screw of the levitor slowly, 'lest he
offer thereby too much Violence to the Parts'.[84] Once open, food should
be given. The dilator should be removed, and the surgeon should 'introduce in its place a Gag, which we leave there, that they [the teeth] may
not return to their former posture'.[85] However, a more drastic cure
could also be demonstrated:'If 'tis impossible to open the Teeth, we
ought to break one of them, in order to get in the End of the little Horn,
by the interposition of which we give him his Nourishment, and prevent
his dying of Hunger'.[86]

The second operation, the cleaning of teeth, may be considered by
some surgeons to be beneath them (''Tis so common to clean the Teeth,
that it seems not to deserve the particular Application of a Chirurgeon');[87]
but this was nevertheless an important operation. Despite careful use of
toothpicks and sponges, crusts would still form on the gum which
would 'require strong Instruments to disengage them from the Teeth'.
The surgeon should take care:

> wherefore the Left-hand, with which we depress the under Lip or
> raise the upper, is to be wrapp'd in a fine clean piece of Linen: If
> the Instrument which we are to use is of Iron, 'tis also to be
> covered with Linen for neatness: Then the Operator having plac'd
> the Patient with her Face turn'd towards the Light, and seated her
> on a proper Seat, he places himself on one side of the Patient, and
> kneeling on the Ground on one Knee ... when he thinks he hath
> taken off all the Crusts and Scales, he makes use of an Opiate ...
> He immediately causes the Patient to wash her Mouth several times
> with water.[88]

Having thus cleaned the teeth, Dionis demonstrated the different methods used in removing the carious parts of the tooth, depending on where the decay is:

> If the *Caries* is visible, we are to scrape it off with the Scraper T, and if betwixt two Teeth, we may make use of the File V, to clear it of its Blackness: If the hollow place be at the top of the Tooth it is to be cauteris'd with Oil of Sulphur or Vitriol, a little drop of which we convey into the rotten Tooth, with one of the little Pincers used in Miniature; and if the Rottenness augments, the Operator tries to stop it by cauterising it with the little actual Cautery X, which being heated with it, he touches the whole Cavity of the Tooth; ...[89]

Holes in the teeth required stopping up. It frequently happened 'that by a Settlement of Serosities in a Tooth, it grows hollow, and that the Hole ceases to augment after the Flux is over'.[90] The best way to stop up such a hole, and the materials which should be used, formed the basis for discussion.

> To remedy all these Incommodities, the Operators hunt after ways of stopping the Hole of the Tooth: Some affirm, that it may be filled with Leaf Gold and Silver; but these leaves, being subject to break, cannot long stay in: wherefore we should rather make use of a bit of beaten Gold or Silver, to which we have given the form of the Hole which 'tis to stop. Some prefer Lead, because that being more pliable, we force it in, and fill the Cavity easier than with any other Metal, making no more Alteration in the part than Gold itself would. Others, without taking so much pains, stop these Holes with Wax, which answers the same end, preventing the Meat and Drink from entring [sic] and excavating it more.[91]

Filing of the teeth, according to Dionis, was practised in three particular cases: '*viz.* to separate them when they grow towards one another; to level them when some of them grow too long; to even and polish them when their Points turn inwards, and grate against the Tongue, or grow jagged outwards, and prick the Cheeks'.[92] When performing this operation, the surgeon should take particular care to support the teeth, to prevent breaking or splintering them, and should take care to file evenly. Pointed or broken molar teeth should likewise have their jagged edges removed.

The sixth operation for the teeth consisted of their removal. This operation was the most common, and, according to Dionis, was perceived by the public to be the usual work of the tooth-drawer.

> The sixth Operation which the Teeth require, is the drawing of them, and is the most common of them all, being what we see daily practis'd. There are very few Persons who have not one pulled out; and some are so impatient, that on the least Pain they feel, they

cause their Teeth to be pull'd out; but 'tis a pernicious Custom to
post so hastily to the Tooth-drawer. It frequently happens, that the
Pain goes off in a small Time, and that the Patient repents that such
a light Uneasiness has cost him a Tooth; we are not then to proceed
to this Operation before the Tooth is so putrified, that there are no
means left to save it, or the Pain which it excites in the Gum is
become continual and unsupportable; but those who draw their
Teeth as often as they feel any Pain, soon unfurnish their Mouths,
and afterwards find themselves at leisure to repent their Rash-
ness.[93]

There was, however, a sound theoretical basis to what Dionis described
as

five or six Cases, in which we cannot dispense with this Operation:
First, In Children, when their first Teeth, which are called their
Milk-Teeth, are inclin'd to fall out, when as soon as they are loose,
we are immediately to draw them, which is done with an end of
Thread wound about the Tooth, with which, after the Knot is
fixed, we pull it out. Pursuant to the popular notion, the sooner we
pull out this Tooth, the straighter its Successor grows; this Opinion
is not too well grounded, but yet these Teeth should always be
pull'd out, because they must fall of themselves, and if the
Chirurgeon opposes it, and the second Tooth grows amiss or awry,
the Mother is sure to lay the Blame on him, and never forgive him;
so much are Women prejudic'd in favour of vulgar Errors.[94]

The second instance in which the surgeon should extract a tooth arises
when it has become very loose in the gum. If this has arisen due to
biting something too hard, or by a blow to the tooth, it should first be
tied to encourage it to tighten again. If this is unsuccessful, despite the
surgeon's instructions not to use it for eating, the loose tooth will need
to be removed. Similarly, if a tooth is very rotten it will require removal.
This could be extremely difficult, if it was too decayed for the easy
application of an instrument: the surgeon should try 'Pelicans, and
other Tooth-drawing Instruments, which I [Dionis] shall presently shew
you'.[95] Fourth, extraction should be attempted when the tooth has
broken and only the root remains. This was difficult: 'the Chirurgeon is
then to apply his whole Industry to get out the rest of the Tooth, and to
make use of a Punch if the fragment jets out a point above the Gum'.[96]
The fifth and sixth occasions when the surgeon would need to remove
teeth both relate to the removal of those that are misplaced or un-
wanted.

Fifthly, when the Teeth grow outwards, they are to be drawn out;
for the Tooth which thus grows out of its Rank, very much incom-
modes the Person to whom this Misfortune happens, and occasions
a Deformity which shocks all who look at him ... Sixthly, when
there grows a Supernumerary Tooth ...[97]

The growth of a supernumerary, or extra, tooth[98] had befallen the Duc de Berri, at the age of eight. Dionis described the way in which this tooth had been removed – a tooth which the Duke 'did not need, to proclaim his Happiness, being the son of the greatest King in the Universe'.[99]

But the surgeon following Dionis's advice should be wary of offering *all* of these operations freely if he intends to practice surgery in general, and that of tooth removal in particular. The successful performance of this operation frequently required the exertion of much force, especially if the tooth was fixed very firmly in its socket. Such exertion may readily cause an unsteady hand and consequent difficulties for phlebotomies performed soon afterwards:[100]

> This Operation consists barely in an Effort of the Wrist, in order to pull out the Tooth; this Effort is to be redoubled when the Tooth resists it, and the Operator is not to give over 'till the Tooth is out; for which Reason those Chirurgeons who are daily very much engaged in the Practice of Bleeding, and are willing to preserve a steddy Hand, never ought to meddle with Tooth-drawing, lest the straining Efforts which that Practice obliges them to, should make their Hands shake …[101]

But there were other reasons besides the maintenance of a steady hand for avoiding the removal of teeth. Performing this operation could, for the surgeon, carry with it the danger of confusion in the eyes of the public with the charlatan and the street entertainer – those whose intention, as we have seen earlier, was to deceive.

> If I advise the Chirurgeon to abandon this, 'tis not only by reason of the Prejudice which may accrue to his Hand by it, but also, that it seems to favour of the Buffoon and Mountebank ['du charlatan & du bâteleur' (literally, street entertainer) in the original French]. Most of these Tooth-drawers, abusing their Talent to impose on the Publick, pretend that they want nothing besides their Fingers, or the End of a Sword to pull out the deepest rooted Teeth; but the Chirurgeon is to scorn these Feats of Activity, and as Probity ought to be the Rule of his Actions, he must distinguish himself from those whose Aim is to deceive others.[102]

The extraction of teeth was therefore, for Dionis, lecturing in the decades before the beginning of the eighteenth century, too open to abuse to occupy a comfortable position in the respectable practice of the master surgeon.

But whilst this demonstration was unequivocally still addressed to the surgeon, Dionis's writings reveal the early signs of a change which was taking place in the treatment of teeth: a change which will prove to be of the highest significance to our story. According to Dionis, *three* distinct groups were now involved in this treatment in some way:

surgeons, tooth-drawers and what he describes as a new group, working on the teeth only. Whereas Ambroise Paré, in dealing with the
operations for the teeth, had simply described how the surgeon alone
should treat them and had mentioned no other types of practitioners
(by either title or activity),[103] at the start of his section on teeth Dionis
refers to 'several persons' for whom the treatment of teeth represented
their whole employment – they made their living *solely* by the performance of such operations.

> The teeth alone at present furnish the whole Employment of sev-
> eral Persons call'd Operators for the Teeth. It must be own'd that
> these Gentlemen, the sole Object of whose Labour are these Parts
> only, may excel in their Art, rather than the Chirurgeon, whose
> Science is of an infinite Extent: But yet he is not to neglect this Part
> of Chirurgery ...[104]

Dionis's description of the activities of this new group provides further
evidence that to attempt to practise the whole of surgery was becoming
increasingly difficult as the number and complexity of surgical operations grew ever greater. The narrow field of practice of a small, particular
group, focusing its attention on one specific area in this way would
therefore (according to Dionis) allow its members to perform its operations more effectively than the surgeon, whose knowledge and abilities
were of necessity more widely spread – but nevertheless, their performance was still a part of surgery. These 'persons' are referred to in both
French and English editions as *opérateurs*[105] – but again, we should
exercise caution in our interpretation of the use of this word. Dionis
uses *opérateur* as a descriptive term, not as a title: it is used throughout
his writing to indicate a person performing an operation, of any kind.
Thus little or no distinction is made between the words *opérateur* and
chirurgien, the first indicating that a person is performing a 'surgical'
activity and the second as a title to bestow upon that person because
their activity *is* surgical. Thus the two words are, in this context, to
some extent interchangeable, and can even on occasion be applied to
the same person: for example, Dionis recommends the services of the
chirurgien M. Carmeline, a 'fort habile Opérateur pour les dents'[106] –
we shall see that M. Carmeline would later become well known in Paris
as a *dentiste*.[107] In similar fashion, the compilers of the *Encyclopédie* of
1751 would take an *opérateur* to be no more or less than one who
works on the human body with his hands, to preserve or to restore
health.[108]

We have now surveyed a series of operations to be performed on the
teeth which are described in detail in books on surgery and have
become an established part of the surgeon's art, requiring skill
and experience for their successful performance. Where the modern

historian may have expected the surgeon to continue to perform little more than the simple operations of extraction and cleaning, we now find *seven groups* of operations which appear to have gradually gained in complexity and which have become an integral part of the *science* of surgery. Thus the surgeon following Dionis's writings can now widen or regulate crowded teeth, clean those that are foul, delay their decay, fill their holes, file them when too long, remove them when rotten and replace them when lost – all actions which now have their basis in theoretical principles.

But a significant change in the content of books written on surgery starts to become apparent in the early decades of the eighteenth century. As we have seen, Dionis advised against the frequent extraction of teeth by the surgeon, suggesting instead that it be left to 'those operators who make it their daily Practice, and have no other Trade to get their living';[109] yet of far greater significance is that within a very short space of time books on the art and *science* of surgery would no longer contain a section on the teeth and their treatments. Garengeot's *Traité des Opérations de Chirurgie*, published only ten years after the first imprint of Dionis's book, would, as we have seen, cover the theory and practice of every operation of surgery in fine detail. Yet the writer makes no mention of the operations for the teeth *at all* – even in the final section of the book, in which he provides details of the instruments which would be used by the surgeon in these operations,[110] the instruments for the teeth make no appearance whatsoever.[111] Similarly, neither Mauquest, Sieur de la Motte's *Traité complet de Chirurgie* of 1722 nor de la Faye's *Principes de Chirurgie* of 1738 make mention of the teeth. Henry-François Le Dran's *Traité des opérations de Chirurgie*, published in 1742, provides a most comprehensive description of all those operations which the surgeon may be expected to perform, but again there is no mention at all of the teeth, their diseases or the instruments which would be used to treat them.[112] Similarly Arnaud's *Memoires de Chirurgie*, published in the same year, contains no references to the teeth,[113] and when Xavier Bichat published P.-J. Desault's *Oeuvres Chirurgicales* after his teacher's death in 1795 the only *maladies de la bouche* which were mentioned were diseases of the lower jaw and of the salivary glands and tongue.[114] It would appear, therefore, that surgeons had indeed come to regard the operations for the teeth as the province of a different type of practitioner, as Dionis had recommended that they should – and that as a result the body of knowledge regarding the teeth had itself been extracted from the whole practice of surgery. As we have seen via the writings of Dionis, in the decades around the beginning of the eighteenth century senior surgeons of high standing, while acknowledging the number and variation of the operations for the teeth within the *science* of the surgeon, were advising *against* their performance because of the 'infinite extent' of that *science*.[115] The implication was that the field of surgery was now so large that the operator attempting to practise every aspect of it would be in danger of spreading his abilities *and his theoretical knowledge* too thinly – yet *at the same time* the same surgeons could observe that there was, for the surgical treatment of teeth, a number of 'Gentlemen, the sole Object of whose Labour are these Parts only, [who] excel[led] in their Art'.[116] It seems unlikely, then, that the 'gentlemen' thus praised would have been practitioners at the very bottom of the hierarchical ladder, forbidden even to take the title of surgeon. In this statement, Dionis is implying that it was precisely because a particular group of surgeons had chosen to work within a field that was relatively narrow and well defined that they could perform its operations with such great success. Who were these gentlemen, and why would they choose to limit their practice to the operations for the teeth?

Notes

1. Antoine Louis, *Histoire de l'Académie royale de chirurgie*, 1768; cited in Toby Gelfand, *Professionalizing modern medicine: Paris surgeons and medical science and institutions in the 18th century*. Greenwood, Westport, 1980, p. 21. It should be noted that Louis, like many eighteenth-century surgeons, was looking to glorify the surgical tradition.
2. Gelfand, *Professionalizing modern medicine*, p. 8. A long and detailed account of the standing of surgery in this period and beyond, and of the surgeons' struggle with the physicians, would be outside the scope of the present work. An excellent account may be found in part I of Gelfand's book, on which much of the following argument will be built.
3. Paré, *Les Oeuvres*, p. 1.
4. For a discussion of the way in which I use the term *science* (and science), see the Introduction.
5. *Recherches critiques et historiques sur l'origine, sur les diverses états et sur les progrès de la chirurgie en France*, Paris, 1744, p. 133; cited in Gelfand, *Professionalizing modern medicine*, p. 26. As we shall see in a later chapter, the implications of the practice of a manual occupation were not favourable for those seeking status and respectability in the *ancien régime*. The perception of surgery as a manual trade would endure, especially (and perhaps not surprisingly) amongst physicians. In 1701, the *premier* surgeon Georges Mareschal operated on Fagon, the *premier* physician, for the stone: when Mareschal offered advice after the operation, Fagon refused it, saying 'I needed your hand, but I do not need your head.' Georges Mareschal de Bièvre, *Georges Mareschal, seigneur de Bièvre, chirurgien et confident de Louis XIV (1668–1736)*, Paris, Plon-Nourrit et c^{ie}, 1906: cited in Gelfand, *Professionalizing modern medicine*, p. 42.

6. Verdier, *La Jurisprudence particulière de la Chirurgie en France*, vol.1, p. 209; cited in Gelfand, *Professionalizing modern medicine*, p. 24.
7. Gelfand, *Professionalizing modern medicine*, p. 28.
8. Gui Patin, *Lettres*, ed. J.-H. Reveillé-Parise, Paris, 1846, vol. 3, p. 175, cited in Gelfand, *Professionalizing modern medicine*, p. 29.
9. I shall not, for the most part, consider the role of the physicians at court. For an account of their activities in this period, see Laurence Brockliss and Colin Jones, *The Medical World of Early Modern France*, chapter 5: 'The sick and their practitioners'. For the rivalry between court doctors (of Paris) and the school of Montpellier, see Colin Jones, 'The Médecins du Roi at the End of the Ancien Régime and in the French Revolution', in Vivian Nutton (ed.), *Medicine at the courts of Europe, 1500–1837*, Routledge, London, 1990, pp. 209–61. See also Laurence Brockliss, 'The Literary Image of the *Médecins du Roi* in the Literature of the *Grand Siècle*' in the same volume, pp. 117–54.
10. See Gelfand, *Professionalizing modern medicine*, p. 6.
11. 'Le roi Louis XIV trouva cette jurisdiction du premier barbier extraordinaire et peu sortable avec les fonctions de son office'. Verdier, *Jurisprudence*, vol. 1, p. 12, in Gelfand, *Professionalizing modern medicine*, p. 30. It is not clear why the king should choose to make such an order: I can find no evidence of Louis having undergone any treatment at this time which would have been likely to have raised Félix's standing in royal eyes. However, the great increase in popularity of wigs allied to the strong connections between the barber-surgeons and the new *barbier-perruquiers'* guild may have played a part.
12. Gelfand, *Professionalizing modern medicine*, p. 30.
13. Ibid., p. 34.
14. Surgeon to Anne d'Autriche, Louis XIV's mother.
15. Gelfand, *Professionalizing modern medicine*, p. 32.
16. Ibid., p. 33.
17. Franklin, *La vie privée d'autrefois*, vol. 12 (1893), *Les Chirurgiens*, p. 136.
18. See Gelfand, *Professionalizing modern medicine*, pp. 31ff.
19. *Statuts pour la communauté des maîtres chirurgiens jurez de Paris*, Paris, 1701, article 1, cited in Franklin, *Les Chirurgiens*, p. 153. The statutes were granted in September 1699, but not registered until February 1701.
20. *Statuts*, 1699, article 5, cited in Franklin, *Les Chirurgiens*, p. 153.
21. *Statuts*, 1699, article 24, cited in ibid., p. 150.
22. Ibid., note to p. 169.
23. Franklin, *La vie privée d'autrefois*, vol. 11 (1892), *Les Médecins*, p. 123.
24. Gelfand, *Professionalizing modern medicine*, p. 11.
25. Ibid., p. 10.
26. *Déclaration du roy, qui rétablit les chirurgiens de Paris dans l'état où ils étaient avant l'année 1655 et ordonne que le premier chirurgien du roy en demeura le chef ainsi que par le passé ...* , article 1: cited in Franklin, *Les Chirurgiens*, p. 177.
27. *Edit du roi, portant création d'Offices de Conseillers de Sa Majesté, Médecins et Chirurgiens Inspecteurs Généraux, et Majors à la suite des armées, dans tous les Hôpitaux, Villes Frontières, et ancien Régiments,*

Paris, 1708, pp. 1–4, cited in David Vess, *Medical revolution in France, 1789–1796,* Florida State University, Gainesville, 1975, p. 24.

28. J. Guillermaud (ed.), *Histoire de la médecine aux armées,* i. *De l'Antiquité à la Révolution,* Paris, 1982, cited in Laurence Brockliss and Colin Jones, *The Medical World of Early Modern France,* Clarendon Press, Oxford, 1997, p. 691.

29. J. Colin, *Les Campagnes du Maréchal de Saxe,* Chapelot, Paris, 1901, vol. I, pp. 220–23 and Jean Colombier, *Code de médecine militaire,* Paris, 1772, vol. 2, pp. 49–51, cited in Gelfand, *Professionalizing modern medicine,* p. 44.

30. *Statuts,* article 42. Cited in Gelfand, *Professionalizing modern medicine,* p. 45.

31. 'à la charge de vivre noblement, sans néanmoins que l'exercice de notre premier chirurgien que nous voulons être continué par ledit sieur Félix, lui puisse être imputé à dérogeance'. Jean Devaux, *Index funereus* (1714), p. 100; cited in Franklin, *Les Chirurgiens,* p. 143.

32. Franklin, *Les Chirurgiens,* pp. 140–41.

33. Pierre Dionis, *A Course of Chirurgical operations, Demonstrated in the Royal Gardens at Paris.* Translated from the Paris edition, 2nd edn, Tonson, London, 1733, p. 222. For reasons of clarity I shall generally refer to this English translation of the 1710 French edition, which I have checked for accuracy, additions and omissions.

34. See Gelfand, *Professionalizing modern medicine,* pp. 58–9.

35. Fagon, however, wielded much power at court. For a full account of the way in which he did so (which Laurence Brockliss has called the 'Fagonization' of the court), see Brockliss, 'The Literary Image', in Nutton, *Medicine at the courts of Europe,* pp. 117–54.

36. Gelfand, *Professionalizing modern medicine,* p. 59. Laurence Brockliss, however, has noted that whilst physicians attending the king usually remained in office when there was a change of monarch, 'Only the *premier médecin du roi* was definitely required to resign his position.' Brockliss, 'The Literary Image', p. 122. Despite the implication that Fagon would therefore have gone anyway, Gelfand's argument that Fagon's failure to treat the king appropriately was paramount is a very strong one.

37. Gelfand, *Professionalizing modern medicine,* p. 60.

38. Taken from Dionis, *A Course of Chirurgical operations,* preface: see below.

39. Le Dran, *The Operations in Surgery of Mons. Le Dran, Senior Surgeon of the Hospital of La Charité, Consultant Surgeon to the Army, Member of the Academy of Surgery at* PARIS, *and Fellow of the Royal Society at* LONDON. 4th edn, Hawes Clarke and Collins, London, 1768: Cheselden's editorial to Gataker's translation.

40. Dionis, *A Course of Chirurgical Operations,* p. 2 (first demonstration).

41. Ibid., preface.

42. To which, as we shall see, should also be added 'dentistry'. I shall consider some of the implications for midwifery (or more specifically, man-midwifery) later.

43. Toby Gelfand, 'Invite the philosopher, as well as the charitable: hospital teaching as private enterprise in Hunterian London', in Bynum, W. F.

and Porter, R. (eds), *William Hunter and the eighteenth century medical world*, CUP, Cambridge, 1985, pp. 129–51, 129.

44. Gelfand, *Professionalizing modern medicine*, p. 9.
45. Robert James, *Dictionnaire universel de Médecine*, 6 vols, Paris, 1746–48, III, 444–7; cited by Gelfand in Bynum and Porter, *William Hunter*, note to p. 138.
46. For a clear account of the teaching of anatomy in Paris in this period, and the role of dissection in that teaching, see Toby Gelfand, 'The "Paris Manner" of dissection: student anatomical dissection in early eighteenth-century Paris', *Bulletin of the History of Medicine*, XLVI, (2), 1972, 99–130.
47. Yves Laissus, 'Le Jardin du Roi', in René Taton (ed.), *Enseignement et diffusion des sciences en France au XVIIIᵉ siècle*, Hermann, Paris, 1964, pp. 287–341, 287.
48. Ibid., pp. 324–8.
49. Ibid., p. 313.
50. E. T. Hamy, 'Recherches sur les origines de l'enseignement de l'anatomie humaine et de l'anthropologie au jardin des plantes', *Nouvelles Archives du Muséum d'Histoire Naturelle*, 3rd series, 1895, vol. III, 1–30, 7.
51. Laissus, 'Le Jardin du Roi', p. 329.
52. Pierre Dionis, *L'anatomie de l'homme, siuvant la circulation du sang, et le dernieres decouvertes, demontree au Jardin Royal*, d'Houry, Paris, 1691.
53. Pierre Dionis, *The Anatomy of Humane Bodies*, translated from the 3rd edn, Bonwick, London, 1703, preface (not paginated).
54. For a discussion of this failure to lecture on the part of Cressé, see Guy Meynell, 'Surgical Teaching at the Jardin des Plantes During the Seventeenth Century', *Gesnerus*, 51, 1994, parts 1 & 2, 101–8, 102.
55. Dionis, *The Anatomy of Humane Bodies*, preface. Dionis was successively 'premier chirurgien de la reine, de la dauphine, du dauphin et des enfants de France'. M. Michaud (ed.), *Biographie Universelle*, Thoisnier Desplaces, Paris, 1852. I have as yet been unsuccessful in my search for a biography of Dionis.
56. Laurence Brockliss, *French Higher Education in the Seventeenth and Eighteenth Centuries: A Cultural History*, Clarendon Press, Oxford, 1987, p. 399. It may be that Cheselden's comment regarding 'all possible encouragement' for French surgery, quoted above, perhaps referred to more than hospital training.
57. Dionis, *A Course of Chirurgical operations*, preface.
58. Michaud, *Biographie Universelle*, entry for Pierre Dionis.
59. Dionis, *The Anatomy of Humane Bodies*, pp. 1–2.
60. In his introduction, Dionis notes that what I have referred to as the 'top-to-toe' approach to teaching was used by many surgeons 'amongst whom is *Fabricius* of *Aquapendente*, [who] have plac'd those Operations perform'd on the Head before all the rest; from them they proceed to those of the Breast, and descend to those of the Belly, and end with those of the extreme Parts: And, lastly, others assert, that in order to keep the Subject long enough, we ought to follow the most usual Order of *Anatomy*; and to that end begin with the lower Venter, in order to empty it immediately after the finishing of the Operations practis'd in that Region; from whence we should ascend to the Breast, and then to

the Head, reserving the extreme Parts for the last. Which Method we shall observe, as the most commodious for the Preservation of our Subject, and most follow'd in publick Demonstrations.' Dionis, *A Course of Chirurgical operations*, p. 2.

61. Ibid., p. 3.
62. Ibid.
63. Ibid., preface.
64. Ibid.
65. Ibid. The Prior of Cabrieres entrusted his secret remedy for the hernia to the king in 1680. The king made it up himself, so as to maintain the secrecy, and it was distributed to those in need of it by his *premier valet de chambre* until the Prior's death, when its recipe was published.
66. Ibid.
67. Ibid., p. 3.
68. Ibid., p. 4.
69. Ibid., pp. 4 ff.
70. Cavelier, Paris, 1720. With the English reader in mind, I shall refer mostly to the English translation which was published three years later (see following note), which I have checked for accuracy of translation.
71. Renatus James Croissant Garengeot, *A Treatise of Chirurgical Operations, according to the mechanism of the parts of the humane body, and the theory and practice of the most learned Surgeons in Paris*. Revis'd and corrected by Mr St Andre, Woodward, London, 1723, p. 2.
72. Ibid., pp. 2–3. It should be noted that this book was written in France: the Englishman of this period wishing to learn from hospital experience would not find it so easy. See Gelfand, *Professionalizing modern medicine*, and Robert Kilpatrick's 'Nature's Schools: The Hunterian revolution in London hospital medicine 1780–1825' (unpublished Ph.D. thesis, University of Cambridge, 1989) for excellent descriptions of the picture of surgical teaching in both French and English hospitals in this period.
73. Garengeot, *A Treatise of Chirurgical Operations*, pp. 42–6.
74. Ibid., p. 487.
75. Ibid., preface.
76. Guillaume Mauquest, Sieur de la Motte, *Traité complet de Chirurgie, contenant des observations & des refexions sur toutes les Maladies Chirurgicales, & sur la maniere de les traiter*, Huart, Paris, 1722, preface.
77. Mauquest, *Traité complet de Chirurgie*, p. 3.
78. M. *** (de la Faye), *Principes de Chirurgie*, Paris, 1738, avis. In the first part of this book, which dealt with 'la Cure des Maladies en général', de la Faye claimed to 'exposerons ensuite les moyens généraux de guérir des Maladies Chirurgicales. Enfin nous donnerons les regles générales qu'il faut suivre dans la pratique de chacun de ces moyens' (de la Faye, *Principes*, p. 165). In deciding on which type of operation should be employed, a new vocabulary would help: the surgeon should consider *co-indication* (the same means of operating as considered in other cases), *contre-indication* (the rejection of means suggested in other cases), *contre-co-indication* or *correpugnance* (the rejection of means that the *contre-indication* has already rejected).
79. Dionis, *A Course of Chirurgical operations*, seventh demonstration.
80. Ibid., p. 334.

81. Ibid.
82. Ibid.
83. After each instrument is mentioned, a reference letter is placed in the text. This is by no means unique to Dionis's writing: such letters were frequently inserted to refer the reader to an engraving, as was also the case with the published *Cours d'opérations*. However, the narrative style of Dionis's accounts, which accompany a demonstration, should perhaps allow the reader to hear the accompanying words 'like so ...'.
84. Dionis, *A Course of Chirurgical operations*, p. 334.
85. Ibid.
86. Ibid., pp. 334–5.
87. Ibid., p. 335.
88. Ibid. It is not immediately apparent in comparisons between the French original and the contemporary English translation why the translator has chosen to make the subject female.
89. Ibid., p. 336.
90. Ibid.
91. Ibid., p. 337.
92. Ibid.
93. Ibid.
94. Ibid., p. 338.
95. Ibid., p. 339.
96. Ibid.
97. Ibid.
98. Typically, a supernumerary tooth will appear between the two upper central incisors, causing them to grow apart, or at the side of the jaw, in the premolar region. If the Duc de Berri's tooth had indeed appeared at the age of eight, it is most likely to have been in the front of his mouth.
99. Dionis, *A Course of Chirurgical operations*, p. 339.
100. The significance of Dionis's warning should not be underestimated. For the vast majority of trained surgeons, phlebotomy was far and away the most commonly performed operation. Brockliss and Jones note that 'In 1697 the Carpentras surgeon P.-A. Barjavel performed over 400 surgical operations but they were nearly all phlebotomies, thirty-four of the thirty-six in the month of May, for instance.' Brockliss and Jones, *The Medical World of Early Modern France*, p. 318.
101. Dionis, *A Course of Chirurgical operations*, p. 341. It may be noted from the present writer's own experience that the modern dentist can, on occasion, find it extremely difficult to write legibly or perform intricate work immediately after extracting a particularly firm tooth, typically, perhaps, a sound lower molar in a densely boned male.
102. Dionis, *A Course of Chirurgical operations*, p. 341.
103. See, for example, Paré, *Les Oeuvres*, p. 611.
104. Dionis, *A Course of Chirurgical operations*, p. 334.
105. Pierre Dionis, *Cours d'opérations de Chirurgie, de'montre'es au Jardin Royal*. 4th edn, d'Houry, Paris, 1740, p. 608, and *A Course of Chirurgical operations*, p. 334.
106. Dionis, *Cours d'opérations de Chirurgie*, p. 623.
107. Carmeline would be described in 1728 as 'Maitre Chirurgien à Paris, & célèbre Dentiste'. Fauchard, *Le Chirurgien Dentiste*, vol. II, p. 189.
108. 'Opérateur, – f. m. (*chirurgie*) celui qui opere de la main sur le corps de

l'homme, pour lui conserver ou lui rétablir la santé.' *Encyclopédie*, 1751 edn, vol. 11.

109.   Dionis, *A Course of Chirurgical operations*, p. 341.

110.   Garengeot, *A Treatise of Chirurgical Operations*, pp. 527–81.

111.   However, Walter Hoffmann-Axthelm, in his *History of Dentistry*, 'picks up' a section on the instruments for the teeth which Garengeot included in his *Nouveau Traité des instrumens de chirurgie les plus utiles, et de plusieurs nouvelles machines propres pour les maladies des Os*, published five years later, and identifies this as 'dentistry'. But a careful reading of Garengeot's title, and even a cursory glance at his writing, shows that this book has very little to do with either the theory or practice of surgery. It is purely intended to describe the instruments used by surgeons, particularly those used for treating bones; and, as we shall see, the instruments for the teeth *would* still be used by a surgeon, albeit now of a particular kind – one who would 'specialize' in the treatment of a particular type of bone.

112.   H. F. Le Dran, *Traité des opérations de chirurgie*, Charles Osmont, Paris, 1742.

113.   George Arnaud, *Memoires de Chirurgie*, J. Nourse, London, 1768.

114.   P.-J. Desault, *Oeuvres Chirurgicales, ou exposé de la doctrine et de la pratique de P.-J. Desault*, compiled by Xavier Bichat, Méquignon, Paris, 1812, pp. 210–16.

115.   Garengeot, writing in 1725, noted that surgery was now composed of many different *sciences*: 'La Chirurgie, cet Art si estimable non-seulement par rapport au corps humain qui est son sujet, mais encore à cause de tant de differentes sciences, dont le Chirurgien doit être instruit'. Garengeot, *Nouveau Traité des instrumens*, p. 33.

116.   Dionis, *A Course of Chirurgical operations*, p. 334.

CHAPTER FIVE

The Making of the *Dentiste* Technically: Pierre Fauchard and the Work of the *Chirurgien Dentiste*

We can see that the picture of the theory and practice of surgery, as viewed through publications and lectures, is starting to change as we look at the early decades of the eighteenth century, with the image of the surgical treatment of teeth fading from our view of the activities of the 'general' surgeon. We shall find that an examination of those books which would *now* deal with the treatment of the mouth and teeth will reveal a new type of surgeon, choosing to treat teeth alone, whose presence we have begun to perceive on the margins of this picture. Thus, while the operations for the teeth and the methods of treating their diseases were indeed disappearing from the 'general' surgical book, the first of what would become a large number of publications on this particular aspect of surgery *alone* was now emerging. We shall see that such books were not written by *experts* or *arracheurs* who were climbing up the hierarchical ladder in an attempt to align themselves with surgeons, as the traditional story implies. They were written by members of a new group of 'particular' surgeons[1] who, while retaining the implications of their surgical title, would declare their particular interest in the teeth, and the celebration of that interest, by assuming the new title of *chirurgien dentiste*[2] – in other words, the appropriated word in this title was *dentiste* and not *chirurgien*. But who were these new, 'particular' surgeons? Who was writing about teeth in this way, and why were they doing so? The first, and most visible to the modern historian, was the Parisian surgeon Pierre Fauchard whose book, entitled *Le Chirurgien Dentiste, ou Traité des Dents*, was first published in 1728.[3]

Fauchard's *Le Chirurgien Dentiste* is an extremely full and detailed account of the practice of a Parisian surgeon who chose to focus on the treatment of teeth at the beginning of the eighteenth century. As we shall see, his writing reveals a wide-ranging vision of the treatment of teeth, built on a broad theoretical base and wide personal experience. While many writers of traditional dental history have looked closely at the way in which Fauchard treated teeth, his writing has not hitherto been used as a resource for an analysis of technical innovation. Rather, it has been taken by such writers to be a resource for the study of the origins of 'scientific dentistry'[4] and, as I shall show in this chapter, such a statement is intrinsically accurate; but not as such people mean, for the meaning of the words has changed. Rather than the implied application of modern science (as deduction from experimentation) to something that was already being done (dentistry), we shall see that analysis of this extremely valuable resource will help to reveal the practice of the *dentiste* as having been built on a *science*, a body of theoretical knowledge founded on fundamental principles, and to reveal the way in which that building was effected. We shall also see that it was the first book of *any* kind on dentistry.

Pierre Fauchard

Pierre Fauchard was born in Brittany, in the area around Vannes, in 1678.[5] He had never lost sight of his early wish to practise surgery, to which he had been destined since youth – but it had been the particular interest of his master, a naval surgeon, in the diseases of the mouth which had first sparked his special interest in this part of surgery.

> Destiné dès ma jeunesse à la Chirurgie, les autres Arts que j'ai pratiquez, ne me l'ont jamais fait perdre de vûe. Je fus l'Eléve de M. Alexandre Poteleret, Chirurgien Major des Vaisseaux du Roi, très expérimenté dans les maladies de la bouche: Je lui dois les premiéres teintures des connoissances que j'ai acquises dans la Chirurgie que j'exerce; ...[6]

The progress he made with this able man had encouraged an emulation which took him along a path towards a highly successful practice in the treatment of teeth, and on the way Fauchard would collect and record his many discoveries and experiences. His writings drew on the successes he had enjoyed in the practice of 'la bonne Chirurgie',[7] since the last years of the seventeenth century: it was 'le fruit d'une étude assiduë & d'une experience de trente années'.[8] His wide experience in treating teeth would lead him to much new knowledge, and to the invention of new instruments and the perfection of established ones. He became highly skilled in the construction of artificial teeth, and experimented with the application of enamel to improve their appearance; he also invented a number of machines designed specifically to close holes in the diseased palate which, if left open, could cause great discomfort and embarrassment on eating and drinking. After more than twenty years of experience in practising this particular part of surgery he had been ready to publish his writings on the teeth in 1723; however, 'les occupations continuelles que me donne ma profession' would cause its delay for a further five years.[9]

Fauchard's particular abilities and skills were well recognized, and his standing in society was good. He appears to have been held in high regard by his 'medical' contemporaries, receiving many referrals of patients from them and a number of plaudits in the form of approbations for his book. He became an established member of Parisian society – in 1740 the chronicler Barbier would describe him as 'le premier homme de Paris pour dents', with 'beaucoup d'amis dans les gens de considération'.[10] Barbier's opinion will, however, serve to remind us that despite the reliance which I shall place upon Fauchard's book in particular, he was not the only *chirurgien dentiste* in Paris in this period. This is also supported by the frequent references which may be found to Fauchard's *confrères* and to other *dentistes* in the narratives of his case histories and technical discussions,[11] but nevertheless he appears to the modern historian as the most visible member of this group of particular surgeons who had chosen to focus on the treatment of the teeth.

The success of Fauchard's practice as a *dentiste* would allow him to lead the life of a wealthy bourgeois. He had chosen to make his city dwelling in the Rue des Cordeliers, on the other side of which stood the new École de chirurgie and the amphitheatre of Saint-Côme.[12] In 1734, he purchased 'a vast estate, with the chateau called "de Grand Mesnil" near Orsay',[13] and he would die a wealthy man on 21 March 1761. He would be buried at his parish church which, appropriately enough, was dedicated to the patron saint(s) of the surgeon, Saint-Côme: the notice of interrement would describe him as 'Pierre Fauchard, ancien Maître Chirurgien-Dentiste'.[14]

Throughout a long practising life, which continued for at least forty years, Fauchard had profited from the counsel and knowledge of his medical friends, amongst whom he could count some of the most able physicians and surgeons of Paris. As we shall see later, he would (quite literally) work alongside some of the most respected and well known, including the physicians de Jussieu[15] and Winslow[16] and many of the senior *chirurgiens-jurez* of Paris. The latter would include, in 1727, no less a personage than the king's *premier* surgeon François de la Peyronie[17] who, as we have seen, was arguably the most important 'medical' person in the kingdom. Many of these prominent men would provide *approbations* for Fauchard's writing on the teeth and, as we shall see later, his working relationship with both them and with his clientele will be of great assistance in the uncovering of the way in which the *dentiste* was made. This may best be seen through Fauchard's writing in *Le Chirurgien Dentiste*.

Le Chirurgien Dentiste, ou Traité des Dents

Fauchard's view of surgery for the teeth, as gleaned from his writings, represents a profound departure from the way in which surgeons had previously written on this particular part of their practice. *Le Chirurgien Dentiste* provides its reader with a very full and highly detailed anatomy of the teeth, describing their structure, function and use, a comprehensive and extended classification of all those diseases which may affect the teeth throughout life, together with the operations which should be performed to treat them, careful descriptions of the instruments which should be used in the performance of those operations, and many very full accounts of case histories and of the writer's reflections upon them. These case histories reveal that Fauchard was developing a series of what he called *faits*,[18] or *principes*: fundamental elements of knowledge concerning the teeth, and that at the same time he was establishing them he was also building on them. Many of the case histories are presented as part of a series, illustrating the same point, rather than singly: the *principes* founded on them, and put forward in the *réflexions* which accompanied most of them, will prove to be of great value in providing us with a view of the construction of the theoretical foundations on which the *dentiste* was made. The writing and production of such a work would have been no light undertaking for one engaged in the daily treatment of patients, and Fauchard himself was highly unlikely to have written it for purposes of self-advertisement and possible financial gain. At the time of its first publication he was already around fifty years old and, to judge by the evidence provided by the case histories contained within it, suffering from no shortage of well-to-do patients – we have already noted his wealth and the many signs of a successful *bourgeois*. The answers to these questions concerning Fauchard's motives for writing will be central to our understanding of how the *dentiste* was made; however, before we search for them, we first need to look in detail at how this body of theoretical knowledge for the teeth and their treatment was created.

Fauchard's writing concerns one particular part of the body *only* – a part whose operations had typically, as we have seen, occupied just a part of one chapter in the typical surgical publication of the seventeenth century. In this focus on the mouth and teeth, Fauchard makes no discussion at all of any other parts of the body except in consideration of those symptomatic diseases which are caused by the teeth. But this does not make for a short book: there are fifty pages on the anatomy of the teeth alone, and *one hundred and three* diseases of the teeth are listed in total, which the writer divides into three classes, and describes in highly theoretical terms. The first is composed of those diseases whose causes are external; the second, those with hidden causes, i.e. that attack the parts of the teeth held in the alveolus or covered by the gum; and the third, the symptomatic diseases (i.e. those affecting other parts of the body) which are caused by the teeth.[19] The first class of external diseases numbers forty-five, listing those caused by scale, dirt, erosion of the enamel, decay, fractures of the body of the tooth and looseness of the tooth; the seventeen diseases of the second class include caries of the roots, neck and internal cavity of the tooth, fracture of the roots, phlegmatic inflammation of the membrane lining the cavity of the tooth, abscess, loss of the tooth germ (from which a new tooth grows), inflammation of the membrane which covers the roots, diseases of the dental vessels and atrophy of the gums. The third class, the symptomatic diseases, number forty-one and include diseases of the alveoli, haemorrhage caused by extraction or the rupture of vessels, ulcers and fistulae of the gums, tongue, chin and palate caused by the teeth and sickness, diarrhoea and inflammation of the eyes, also caused by the teeth. This great number of diseases was by no means definitive: Fauchard remarked that the experience gained in future practice would perhaps reveal even more.[20] Noting that other writers on the diseases of the teeth had neglected to identify such a wide range of diseases, or to describe the differences between them, he stated that this was 'sans doute parce qu'on n'a point observé réguliérement tout ce qui concerne les dents dans l'état contre nature'.[21]

The *science* of the *parfait dentiste*

Having thus listed the great number of diseases which could affect the teeth, even though they constituted such a small proportion of the skeleton, Fauchard turned his attention to the operations to be performed for their cure. The way in which these should be performed was of particular importance: by considering each one in detail, he would thus enable the operator to avoid prejudicing both his patient's health and the reputation of the art, noting 'toutes les circonstances ausquelles il faut faire attention, pour ne rien entreprendre au préjudice de la santé du malade, & de la réputation de l'art'.[22] The 'réputation de l'art' was all-important, and formed the focus of a highly sensitive issue: with surgeons as respected and powerful as Dionis pointing to a new group treating the teeth alone, yet with the image of the charlatan and the *arracheur* large in the public view, the new *chirurgien dentiste* would perhaps occupy a precarious position in the surgical hierarchy of the *ancien régime*.[23] In Fauchard's opinion, such a practitioner had only begun to appear around 1700, after the most famous surgeons had abandoned such treatment, leaving the mouths of the people of Paris wide open to abuse from those whose practice was based neither on theory nor experience, having neither principles nor method:

> Les plus célébres Chirurgiens ayant abandonné cette partie de l'art, ou du moins l'ayant peu cultivée, leur négligence a été cause que des gens sans théorie & sans expérience, s'en sont emparez, & la pratiquent au hazard, n'ayant ni principes, ni méthode. Ce n'est que depuis environ 1700. que dans la Ville de Paris on a ouvert les yeux sur cet abus.[24]

What sort of operations were now on offer from this new type of practitioner? Perhaps unsurprisingly, given the broad picture of the diseases of the teeth presented in Fauchard's book, the number of operations with which the *chirurgien dentiste* should be acquainted has swollen dramatically compared with those of the surgeon of twenty years before. Fauchard gives a broad description of the categories into which he suggests these operations should fall: in an introductory chapter entitled 'L'idée générale de la pratique contenuë dans les Chapitres suivans',[25] he outlines fourteen, as opposed to Dionis's seven, main operations. These are: the cleaning of teeth, the separation of teeth, their reduction, the removal of caries, cauterizing, filling, straightening, arranging, strengthening (firming), trepanning, removing teeth from their alveoli, replacing them in the same alveoli, removing them for replacement in different alveoli (that is, in another mouth) and the substitution of artificial teeth in place of those that are lacking.[26] These operations should not on any account be entered into lightly – their understanding would require 'une connoissance aussi parfaite, qu'elle est rare',[27] which would ensure that the *chirurgien dentiste* would know when to operate, when to defer, and when even to abandon his performance of an operation. Thus the possession of a sound understanding of an operation did not necessarily mean that it should always be performed.

Each of these operations would demand of those who chose to perform it a light hand which was both sure and skilful; but, for Fauchard, it would also demand the use of the mind: 'Toutes ces opérations demandent dans celui qui les exerce, une main légére, sûre, adroite & une parfaite theorie'.[28] He argued that the possession of theoretical knowledge – a *science* – was an essential adjunct to the *dentiste*'s possession of a skill: according to him, errors would only arise through either a lack of knowledge of the true cause of the disease, or of the true means of arriving at its treatment.[29] Possession of this complete, perfected body of knowledge – this 'parfaite théorie' – would therefore produce a new type of practitioner, the *parfait dentiste*.[30] But without it, only ignorance and imprudence would reign:

> De là il faut conclure que la science requise, pour être un parfait
> Dentiste, n'est pas si bornée que plusieurs se l'imaginent, & qu'il
> n'y a pas moins d'imprudence & de danger à se mettre entre les
> mains d'un ignorant, que de témérité & de présomption dans la
> plûpart de ceux qui entreprennent l'exercice d'une profession si
> délicate, sans en sçavoir à peine les premiers élémens.[31]

Fauchard placed himself firmly at the centre of the creation of this
science, claiming to have established the principles upon which it was
built: he had 'établi les principes sur lesquels la pratique dont il s'agit,
doit être fondée'.[32]

So, according to Fauchard, by the third decade of the eighteenth
century there could be found a *parfait dentiste* – not a 'perfect' dentist
in the modern, qualitative sense of the word, but a complete, 'perfected'
and thoroughly learned practitioner who was in possession of a wide-
ranging body of theoretical and technical knowledge: a *science* for the
teeth. The foundations of this knowledge were firmly set in a thorough
understanding of the anatomy of the mouth and teeth, which would in
turn allow him to focus on the treatment of those parts *only*.

Fauchard's wide-ranging body of operations for the teeth is built on a
comprehensive structure of 'precepts', or practical rules, which should
be followed for their successful performance. These precepts are, in
turn, constructed on a broad foundation composed of 'principles', or
primary elements of knowledge of the teeth and their diseases. To gain a
clearer understanding of the precepts we should, therefore, examine the
principles on which they are founded. However, for the purposes of this
analysis, these terms should be retained in their strict technical usage. In
the interests of clarity, therefore, in this particular context I shall refer
to them as *principes* and *préceptes*.

Principes and *préceptes* for the operations for caries of the teeth

An analysis of Fauchard's approach to caries, or tooth decay, will
provide us with an example of the construction and application of a
series of *principes* to a disease to which the teeth were particularly
susceptible, often with disastrous consequences – as Fauchard put it,
'La carie est une des plus funestes maladies qui puissent arriver aux
dents: Son progrès les détruit & les consume'.[33] The following examination of this disease draws heavily on Fauchard's writing; and in order to
gain a context, these accounts of his work will, of necessity, be full.

According to Fauchard, caries was the cause of pain. While noting
that some argued that the teeth were as other bones, and were therefore
insensibles, it was clear to him that if the anatomy of the tooth were

considered carefully, then the teeth must be as 'capable de sentiment'[34]
as any other part of the body.

> Il est vrai qu'à ne considérer les dents simplement que comme des
> os, on peut dire qu'elles sont insensibles; mais si on les considére
> comme des parties munies, recouvertes & tapissées de membranes,
> de vaisseaux & de nerfs, on ne doit pas leur refuser la qualité d'être
> sensibles, ainsi que toutes les autres parties du corps.[35]

Fauchard subscribed to the latter view; and in order to understand this
pain, therefore, his reader would need a thorough understanding of the
anatomy of the teeth, which Fauchard had already established at the
beginning of the book: 'Pour mieux concevoir la sensibilité des dents, il
faut se rappeller ce que j'ai établi au commencement de ce Traité touchant
les différentes parties qui composent les dents.'[36]

The kind of pain which was caused by caries was of a fixed and
permanent type, 'ce que l'on exprime ordinairement, lorsque l'on dit
que l'on a mal aux dents',[37] and it was produced in various ways.
Caries, when allowing the air to dry or shrivel the nervous fibres and
the walls of the small vessels of the tooth, made them tense and unyield-
ing. The fluid trying to enter them would then distend the walls of those
vessels, thereby causing 'cette espéce de douleur appellée distensive'.[38]
Alternatively, if there were some small vessels which had ruptured or
burst, the fluid thus discharged would change, become corrupt and
produce a sharp pain – 'la douleur nommée poignante'.[39]

For Fauchard, these extremely likely explanations[40] of the *causes* of
pain in carious teeth, built on a detailed knowledge of their anatomy,
would serve well for those who intended to work on the teeth. They
would act as fundamental bases of knowledge, on which further elements could be built regarding the way in which the disease should be
treated. They 'faciliteront les moyens de trouver les remédes propres à
réussir dans certaines conjonctures, soit pour emporter radicalement le
mal, soit pour appaiser la douleur, la calmer, ou du moins la rendre plus
supportable'.[41]

Having considered how caries caused toothache, Fauchard builds up
a picture of the disease and the operations which should be employed to
cure it. First, he considers how the tooth is destroyed:

> This disease is produced by a humour which insinuates itself be-
> tween the bony fibres of the tooth, which decays only because
> these fibres are destroyed; the fibres are destroyed, only because
> the little parts of which they are composed are displaced; and these
> parts are displaced only because they are weakened [*ébranlées*].[42]
> That which most ordinarily destroys the texture of the tooth, is
> the humour which stops and encircles it [*arrêtée autour d'elle*], of
> which each particle communicates to the tooth its particular im-
> pulse, which finally separates the particles from each other, and

forms cavities which make the whole extent of the surface appear blackish. With regard to the detached parts, they may be so crumpled [*froissées*] and so much reduced in their mass, that they follow the movement of the humour, and escape with it.[43]

Fauchard was well acquainted with both the natural state and the non-natural state of the bony fibres of the tooth, repeating the extensive description of them gained from observations under the microscope by the *mathématicien* M. de la Hire.[44] He had also acquired such knowledge at first hand, having used the 'excellens microscopes' of the surgeon de Manteville himself many times in his examinations of carious teeth.[45]

The causes of the disease caries could be either external or internal:

External causes are blows, violent shocks, the use of the file practised imprudently on the teeth, the application of certain bodies, the air, altered saliva, the impression of hot and of cold and certain foods. Interior causes are those which are found in the mass of the blood or in a particular fault of the lymph.[46]

For Fauchard, it was not difficult to see how these various causes, either external or internal, could produce caries. Blows and violent shocks could

cause the outpouring of the fluid contained in the vessels, or by the shaking of the whole tooth, when the little parts become compressed, pulled or torn from the vessels, or because they act immediately on the linings [*tuniques*] of these same vessels. Caries can also be caused by the action of the file, when it uncovers the cavity of the tooth, or when it gets too close to it. Corrupted saliva, acrid foods, certain corrosives [*corps rongeans*] applied to the teeth, to deaden pain, or to whiten them, &c. may also cause caries, by their particles insinuating themselves with saliva the length of the roots of the teeth in the interstices of the membraneous filaments, which may weaken, or corrode the vessels ...

The causes contained in the mass of blood produce caries only when they render the blood less fluid, and disposed to forming obstructions in those vessels of very small diameter, which do not have sufficient space, yielding to the liquid which forces them to dilate.[47]

With the various causes of caries explained, the different types which may affect the teeth are then identified and classified. Fauchard had identified many:

Caries of the teeth can be ordered under many species. If we consider the different parts, and the different causes which produce it, we will establish many types of caries, which demand different consideration in the manner of their operation and in all their treatments.

Scorbutic caries, caries of the pox [*la carie vérolique*], scrofulous caries &c.

Soft caries, or putrescent, & dry caries.

Superficial caries, and that which is the least incommodious & the least dangerous, and that of which one can most easily stop the progress.

Deep caries [*la carie profond*], on the contrary, is that which causes the greatest pain, & which often involves the removal of teeth, above all when it has penetrated the cavity of the body of the tooth, or of that of the root.

Dry caries resembles mastic, & causes no pain, unless it degenerates into a different species of caries.[48]

From both this understanding of the disease and from his knowledge of the anatomy of the tooth, Fauchard could create a series of *principes*, or primary elements of knowledge concerning the nature of each different type of caries and the way in which it would attack the teeth.[49] Thus caries which was dependent on internal causes would usually attack the roots of the teeth, either externally or internally (that is, in the cavity of the tooth root). Caries from external causes generally attacked the exterior part, either the enamelled body of the tooth or the neck of the tooth, but rarely the root, unless the tooth was loose in its socket and thus separated from the gum. Internal caries was more difficult to recognize than external, particularly when it attacked the roots or the neck of the tooth, because it would remain hidden by the gums and the alveoli. It could therefore only be discovered by informed inference, built on the violence and nature of the pain, or by the swellings, tumours or abscesses which usually accompanied it. External caries was both easier to recognize and to cure, because it could be removed more easily and remedied by such means as filing, scraping, cauterizing or filling (*plomber*) the carious part of the tooth. Particular *principes* may be applied to the treatment of each type of caries: that which gnaws as if a worm is eating the tooth, which Fauchard attributed to 'un virus vérolique, scrofuleux, scorbutique, &c.'[50] is that which advances rapidly: it is the most to be feared, and the most difficult to cure. Soft or putrescent caries, however, is usually easier to stop. That which should be feared the least is dry caries, as it can be filled, filed, or cauterized: it is slow growing, and does not necessarily require removal.

Principes for the techniques of treating carious teeth

The causes of the particular types of this disease, as described in Fauchard's writing, could now be used as the building blocks on which to construct a series of *principes* on which should be founded the techniques to be used in its treatment. If the caries had not progressed too far, it might be possible to arrest the decay, and in order to do this the *chirurgien dentiste* should follow the methods and techniques described in Fauchard's book. In considering such cases, Fauchard would also indicate those instances when it may be possible to cure the caries altogether. But if the disease had become well established, and had caused much damage, there would often be little choice remaining but to extract the tooth:

> Once it happens that the cavity situated in the middle of the body of each tooth, is uncovered by caries, or otherwise; we can ordinarily hope to treat such a disease, only with the help of divers operations, and by those remedies which are the most specific; still there is great risk, when by methods practised methodically and thoroughly, we address ourselves to treat a caries which has made much progress.[51]

Despite such extensive damage, there could sometimes, however, still be hope for the tooth: 'Ce qui peut arriver de plus heureux dans ces occasions'[52] was when the filaments of the nerves which enter the tooth are not near the carious part, or the vessels which go to the carious tooth are not dried out, or consumed by some cause, or have not been weakened to the point at which they are no longer capable of *sensibilité*.[53] This was established knowledge, a *fait*, from which conclusions about the unsuccessful nature of some types of treatment could be drawn: 'De ce fait bien établi, nous devons conclurre que les remédes particuliers, dont une infinité de gens se vantent d'avoir le secret, n'ont paru réussir'.[54] Such remedies could only succeed, according to Fauchard, when the vessels of the tooth have already been weakened or dried out with the effect of the same humour which had caused the disease, or when at last this 'humeur rongeante'[55] had become so reduced as to make the inflammation and pain cease – in other words, when the tooth would have ceased to give trouble anyway. Fauchard noted that in such cases the seller of the remedy would not fail to claim success for his drug, without the public perceiving its uselessness. There were many variations: some claimed to cure toothache with special elixirs, some by prayer and signs of the cross; others by giving specifics intended to kill the worms which they claimed caused the caries.[56] Some pretended to be so skilled that, if one believed them, they could treat the strongest toothache by touching with fingers dipped or washed in a rare and mysterious liquor, a popular method which, as we have already seen, had 'fait assez de bruit en Paris'.[57] There was an infinity of other remedies for the toothache 'dont la plûpart sont si ridicules & si extravagans, que le détail en seroit inutile & ennuyeux'.[58] Even respectable authorities had made such suggestions as scarifying the ears with a lancet. The *célébre* Italian physician Valsalva had advised application of the cautery to the ear, giving full details of its size and the exact place of application but, while acknowledging his authority, Fauchard (some-what diplomatically) could not believe that the *common* type of toothache could be cured by such a method.[59] The respected surgeon Dionis had suggested the use of 'l'huile de souffre, ou de vitriol',[60] of which a small drop should be placed in the damaged tooth: if the caries continued, Dionis advised the application of the actual cautery. However, 'sans vouloir attaquer le mérite d'un aussi habile Chirurgien',[61] Fauchard then did so by claiming that such treatment was dangerous and could do great harm. According to him, these oils were very corrosive and could excite or increase the pain, gnawing and tearing the tissue of the tooth. Their slow action would render the pain more powerful and longer lasting, the effects impossible to limit: they would become insinuated throughout the carious cavity, and would attack healthy parts as much as diseased. The saliva would mix with them, bringing them into contact with the gums, thereby producing further disorder. Clearly the *science* of the particular surgeon could at times exceed that of the (general) surgeon when applied to his particular part of surgery.

For Fauchard, the *principes* of theoretical knowledge regarding this disease would dictate four principal means by which it could be cured, if it had not yet reached the internal cavity of the tooth. The first was with files or rasps; the second, the application of lead; the third, the use of oils, or essence of cinnamon and cloves either mixed together or employed separately; and the fourth, the application of the actual cautery.[62]

> When a tooth is only slightly carious, it will suffice to remove the caries, using the instruments of which I shall speak later, and to refill the carious cavity with lead. If the caries has penetrated a little further, and is causing pain, it will be necessary, after having removed it, to place a piece of cotton, rolled and soaked in oil of Cinnamon, or of Cloves, in it every day. This practice should be continued for a sufficient period, taking care to arrange and press the cotton by degrees, until the sensitive parts are accustomed to the pressure: four or five days later, one removes afresh the matters which remain in the carious cavity: this precaution sometimes prevents the pain from returning: it produces in the osseous fibres of the tooth sufficient small exfoliation: it prevents the continuation and the progress of the caries, and of the pain. If, after having continued this method for a long time, the pain does not cease, it will be necessary to apply the actual cautery, and some months after to fill the tooth, if the disposition of the carious cavity permits it; because one encounters sometimes carious cavities arranged in a way, that it is not possible to place lead in them.[63]

If, however, the caries had progressed too far and had reached the cavity of the tooth, a completely different course of action based on knowledge of what was *now* happening in the tooth, and, therefore, on different *principes*, was called for on the part of the *chirurgien dentiste*.

> If the caries has penetrated just to the cavity of the tooth, it will create an abscess; as I have often observed in many people, in whom caries of the *incisives & canines* caused much pain. I then introduced the tip of my probe just into the cavity of the tooth, to ease the evacuation of the matter: as soon as the pus was evacuated, the pain ceased. I left these persons rested in this way for two or three months: at the end of which time, I filled their carious teeth, to prevent them from further damage.[64]

Fauchard referred to this operation as 'trepanning' of the teeth, and gave a full description of the *préceptes* which should be observed in its performance.[65] The pain caused by the *dents incisives & canines*, when they were worn down or carious, would cease nearly every time when the affected teeth were trepanned. If the caries was to be found in between, or at the sides of the teeth, the *dentiste* should commence by separating them as much as necessary, and widening this separation at the carious part, which should be done with small half-round files. Following this, he should remove all the carious matter from the tooth, with the rasps of the *bec de perroquet* and the awl. This done, he should open and enlarge the canal, or the internal cavity of the tooth, with *un équarissoir*,[66] or a perforator of the same size as the canal. He should then take a long, fine needle, such as an embroiderer would use, and, holding the large end in his fingers, or in a clock-maker's tweezers, introduce the point of the needle as far as possible into the depth of the cavity of the tooth. This should be done two or three times, after which the cavity should be successfully opened up and its interior membrane pierced. By this means, the abscess that had been forming, or the humours which had collected inside, may leave the cavity of the tooth with ease. The pain would stop immediately, or very soon afterwards.

The *préceptes*, or practical rules, by which the *dentiste* should perform this operation are many, and Fauchard deals with each one in great detail. For example, he advises that particular caution should be exercised with the needle, which should be made flexible before insertion into the canal: it should therefore be annealed in the flame of a candle. This means there is less risk of its breaking, and staying in the cavity of the tooth, from where it could not be removed – such an accident would prevent any cure. With the temper removed, the needle will follow the direction of the canal of the tooth, and adjust itself to any variations. But there were also rules which should be observed for the safety of the patient: the needle must be threaded, so that the patient is at no risk of swallowing it if it should slip from either hands or tweezers. If, however, the canal is so fine that a needle will not pass down it, then a suitable drill must be used, mounted on a stand held in the left hand. As with several other of the instruments described in his text, Fauchard provided his reader with an illustration of a bow drill

5.1 A reconstruction of a bow drill following Fauchard's design. Although described in his text as for use in trepanning teeth, the caption to Fauchard's illustration describes the drill as 'an instrument used in the manufacture of artificial teeth'. (Fauchard, *Le Chirurgien Dentiste*, 1746, plate 30.) Facsimile made by the author.

(Figure 5.1), which appears similar in design to that used by the watch-maker. With the bow held in the right hand, the *dentiste* can pierce the canal with the drill and open the tooth as required.[67] After the canal is opened it must be dressed with cotton containing drops of oil, as already described; but care must be taken in the way this is done. Any matter which has been left in the tooth must be able to escape through the cotton, which must therefore not be packed in too tightly.

Principes for the design of the instruments used in the removal of caries, and the *préceptes* governing their use

While noting the practical rules which should be observed in performing the operations for the treatment of caries, Fauchard makes frequent reference to the instruments which should be used in those operations. In the chapter of *Le Chirurgien Dentiste* in which these instruments are described, he lays down a series of important *principes* governing their design, and the *préceptes* for their use. He places each instrument in one of four distinct categories, distinguished by the design of their cutting ends. In the first group are all those which have four faces, ending in a sharp point, which he calls 'forets à ébiseler' (drills for chiselling). In the second are those whose point is formed by three faces, called 'rugines pointuës en bec de perroquet' (parrot's beak with pointed rasp), and in the third the 'rugine mousse en bec de perroquet' (parrot's beak with blunt rasp). The fourth group is composed of instruments whose cutting end is formed of two faces, which are called 'rugines en alêne' (awl rasps).[68]

The design and construction of each of these types of instrument is described in fine detail. The first, the drills, have a round shaft and are about two and a half thumbs long from the handle to the beginning of the point, which should be about two lines long. The second are curved excavators, the pointed ends of which are formed by two little bevels strengthened by a ridge, which forms the upper angle of the curved part. This instrument resembles the parrot's beak used to clean teeth. The third is the same design as the second, but with a blunt point, and the fourth are little awls from which the point has been broken, and then the end reheated to remove the temper. On their concave side they are rounded, on the convex flat: this surface, ending in a kind of chisel edge, forms the cutting point. Given a moderate temper, and finished on the grindstone, this type of instrument should be eight lines long for the shortest and a thumb and a half for the longest.[69] A diagram illustrates the construction of each (see Figure 5.2).

Fauchard provides his reader with a detailed description of the way in which each of these instruments should be used in treating specific types of caries. If, for example, the surface of the tooth has carious holes, but they are too small to clean and fill, then these holes should be

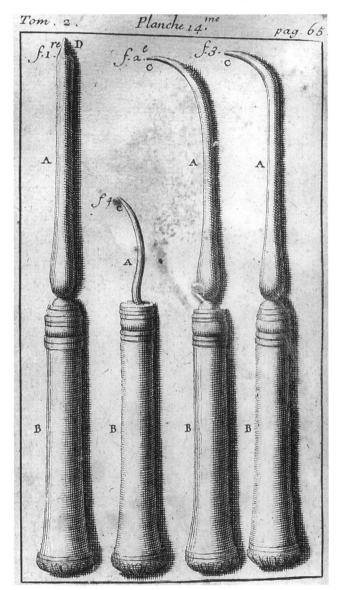

'Planche XIV. qui contient la figure de quatre Instrumens qui servent à ruginer la carie des Dents.

La Figure I. représente le foret à ébiseler, vû dans son étenduë.

La Figure II. représente la rugine en bec de perroquet pointuë, vûë latéralement.

La Figure III. représente la rugine en bec de perroquet mousse, vûë de même.

La Figure IV. représente la rugine en alêne, vûë latéralement.'

5.2 Fauchard's instruments for the removal of caries. (Fauchard, *Le Chirurgien Dentiste*, 1746.)

enlarged or excavated with the chisel drill (figure I in plate XIV, Figure 5.2), taking particular care to choose one of the right size. In using this instrument, the *dentiste* should observe the following rules: the subject who is to be operated on must be seated on 'un fauteuil convenable',[70] his head leaning against its back. The *dentiste* should place himself on the right side, or at the front, whichever is necessary. Without moving from this position, and with the patient remaining in the position as placed, it will be possible to work on each part of the teeth equally well, whether the caries is situated on the surfaces, or at the extremities of the crowns; whether it is found on the lateral surfaces, or on the external and internal surfaces. For the internal surfaces of the teeth on the right side, and the external surfaces of the teeth on the left, however, the *dentiste* will need to pass from the right to the left side of the patient. If the *foret à ébiseler* is to be used on the upper surfaces or the lateral surfaces of the teeth in the lower jaw, the *dentiste*, still positioned on the right, must pass his left arm over the patient's head. He must cover the commissure of the lips with a piece of fine linen, and should part the lower lip from the teeth with the index finger of his left hand, the thumb parting the upper lip. The instrument, held in the right hand, is placed on the carious part of the tooth. It should be turned between the thumb and index finger, from left to right and right to left: by this means the carious hole in the tooth will be enlarged. If, however, the caries is situated on the external surfaces of the teeth on the right side of the jaw, the *dentiste* must stand in the same place, pass his left arm over the head of the patient, place the thumb on the incisors of the same jaw and the index finger on the gum, to depress the lower lip. The other fingers should be placed under the chin to steady it. To enlarge carious holes on the external surfaces of the teeth on the left side, the *dentiste* must move around to the patient's left, hold the lower lip with the first finger and thumb of the left hand and place the instrument on the caries with his right: while standing in this way, he can also attend to caries on the internal surfaces of the teeth of the right jaw.

If, however, the *dentiste* intends to operate on carious holes in the upper teeth, he must stand on the right or in front of the patient, with a knee on the ground. He should raise the upper lip with the middle finger of the left hand, depress the lower with the first finger of the same hand, and hold the instrument in his right, protecting the lips as he does so. For the external surfaces of the teeth on the right side, he must stand on the right and, holding the instrument in the right hand he should hold back the upper lip with the thumb of the left hand, and the lower lip with the first finger of the same hand. To reach the carious holes of the external surfaces of the left side, he must stand on the left, separate the upper lip with the middle finger of the left hand, part the lips (duly protected with linen) with the first finger of the same hand while holding the instrument in the right. In this position, the operation is the same for the internal surfaces of the teeth on the right side of the upper jaw.

This complicated and highly involved series of *préceptes* relates simply to the use of *one* particular instrument, used in the operation to remove *one* particular type of caries; and by looking at just one operation in this detail we have gained a clearer picture of the way in which Fauchard's wide-ranging body of knowledge of the operations was applied to each of the particular diseases of the teeth. He presents a large number of similarly complex and detailed rules for the use of all the many other instruments, with each set of *préceptes* upon which their use is based derived from the *science* required of the *parfait dentiste*.

But how had this *science* been gained? How could a particular surgeon such as Fauchard, focusing his attention on one part of the body only, have built up a broad body of theoretical knowledge which would act as a foundation upon which he could construct a complex and wide-ranging series of operations? We have already seen how knowledge of both the disease and its causes was built on theory in our analysis of Fauchard's writings on caries, and the technical basis on which the operations for that disease, and the design of the instruments used to treat it, should be founded. We now need to examine the practical rules which should be applied to the choice of operation, and to the way in which it should be performed – and we shall see that the large number of case histories recorded by Fauchard as *observations* and *réflexions* will allow us to understand how he and his *confrères* would apply these *préceptes* to their patients' mouths.

Making a *science* for the teeth: Fauchard's *observations* and *réflexions*

If we look at the operations for the teeth in action, through the great narrative detail provided in *Le Chirurgien Dentiste*, we may start to see both the way in which Fauchard constructed these operations on fundamental elements of theoretical knowledge and how, once constructed, they could be used in turn to extend the *science* of the teeth further. These stories of specific instances of disease are presented as *observations*, which are accompanied either individually or in groups by a *réflexion*. In the *observation*, Fauchard presents a detailed account of the case under examination. This typically follows a pattern: first, the reason for the patient's consultation, and then a description of what the *dentiste* found on examination. After this comes a highly detailed account of the operation performed and, importantly, who it was performed by; finally Fauchard describes the outcome of the operation. Built on the *observations* are the *réflexions*, in which each case, or series of cases, is analysed with regard to the nature of the disease encountered and the way in which it has been treated. This analysis also follows a general pattern, containing two important elements: first, what has been learnt from his experience of the patient's disease, and second, *how* what has been learnt should be applied to similar cases. In this way, Fauchard uses the *observations* and *réflexions* to construct and establish his *principes*, the fundamental elements of theoretical knowledge concerning both how the body works and the scope of the operations for the teeth – which he will use to establish the perfected practice of the *dentiste*.

The *observations* and *réflexions* recorded in Le Chirurgien Dentiste show that Fauchard was demonstrating the acquisition and possession of a particular body of theoretical knowledge from about 1700, and adding to it and developing it markedly from the early 1720s. Thus the majority of the *observations* relate to consultations made between 1721 and 1727, and here the possession and application of a *science* by the *chirurgien dentiste* may clearly be seen – often standing, sometimes literally, alongside that of the surgeon. These records present a broad picture of the practice of the *dentiste*, ranging from remarks made to Fauchard concerning the succession of teeth (that is, the growth of new teeth to replace others) to detailed accounts of highly complex operations requiring the services of many practitioners.

In most of these cases the patient has sought treatment from a surgeon; usually a 'general' surgeon accustomed to performing operations on the whole body, but in a few instances a *dentiste*, usually Fauchard, has been consulted from the outset. Sometimes the *science* possessed by the 'general' surgeon has allowed him to complete the cure successfully, as we shall see in the highly unpleasant experiences of the Compagnon Maçon François le Blanc; but more commonly the surgeon, be he *chirurgien ordinaire* or *maître*, has not had sufficient knowledge of this particular part of surgery to effect a cure without the assistance of a *dentiste*. As we shall see later in the case of the Comte de Corneillan, by the late 1720s there could also be particular cases in which the *dentiste* would be involved in a joint consultation of medical men, each using his particular knowledge to perform a part of the cure, and consulting together in order to achieve the best outcome for their patient. This kind of consultation was generally only necessary in very complicated and involved operations; but before looking at these, and at the implications of the *dentiste*'s involvement in them, we shall examine some *observations* of a more straightforward nature. As we are now familiar with Fauchard's understanding of the causes of caries, and with the theoretical knowledge governing the methods which should be used to treat it, we shall see how, for Fauchard, the *principes* for performing its operations could be both applied and extended in curing both the disease and its effects.

Performing the operations for caries

We have already examined the theoretical basis and practical rules on which Fauchard's operations to treat caries were founded; and as we shall see, the consequences of *not* possessing such knowledge could be extremely serious. Although pain was usually the first concern of the sufferer with caries, Fauchard lamented that this disease could on occasion cause grave damage – if neglected it could cause tumours or abscesses, the matter from which could find its way not only between the gums and the alveoli, but even between the muscles of the face and between the periosteum (the membrane covering the bone) and the bone. These abcesses could extend along the side of the jaw, forming fistulae as high as the zygoma (the bridge of bone at the top of the cheek, in front of the ear) or into the sinuses of the cheekbones[71] or, as we shall see, even reaching up to the base of the skull and beyond. In the lower jaw, its ravages were no less troublesome, even leading to possible loss of life: 'Elle a causé plus d'une fois la perte d'une grande partie de cette machoire. Ce qui est encore pire, c'est qu'il en a coûté la vie à quelques-uns, qui n'ont péri que par des maladies semblables.'[72] What could the *dentiste* do to prevent such disaster, and how could he gain understanding of the disease through its treatment to extend his ability to prevent it further?

The problems caused by caries, and the way in which such problems should be addressed, are well illustrated in Fauchard's *observation* regarding the case of Madame la Marquise de Trans, from Bretagne.[73] This lady had suffered with a severe headache for a long time, which several experienced physicians and surgeons had assured her was caused by rheumatism. After undergoing varied treatments over a period of many years, all without success, her medical advisers had suggested that this 'situation fâcheuse'[74] might be resolved by a trip to take the waters at Bourbon. Before undertaking this journey, the *marquise* found herself in Paris, where she consulted *un médecin célébre* who, in similar fashion to her previous advisers, treated her ailment as rheumatism and gave her remedies which proved useless. However, as she had always insisted that the pain was in both her head and her teeth, the physician eventually came to believe that her problems could indeed be caused by the teeth; and he therefore suggested that she might gain some benefit from consulting a *dentiste*. As Fauchard had had the honour of being known to her for many years, he was summoned to see her.

Having examined her teeth, Fauchard found that the *marquise* had considerable caries in her *grosse molaire du côté gauche* of the lower jaw and in two teeth on the right side of her upper jaw, and that the gum around all three was swollen and inflamed. After examining the teeth with his probe, he told his patient that the caries had reached an extent which made it impossible to save the teeth, and that as he did not doubt for a moment that they were the sole cause of her headaches, he believed the teeth should be removed. She at first rejected his advice; but realizing that it concurred with that of the physician, she finally agreed to the removal of two, which operation Fauchard duly performed. As the pain was not completely relieved by the extraction of these teeth, five days later she called the *dentiste* again to extract the third: this was the last *grosse molaire* of the upper jaw. Her pain disappeared promptly, and from then on the *marquise* would have no more, either in her head or in her teeth.

In his *réflexion* on the *marquise*'s case Fauchard states that her headache was symptomatic of, and entirely caused by, the caries in her teeth, and not rheumatism: this was proven when the pain ceased on their extraction. Successful treatment required identification of the cause of the disease, which was why the remedies administered previously had had no effect at all on the headache which had continued to torment her: it had done so because her pain was not the product of a general cause but a local one, and her treatment should have recognized this – 'Il ne s'agissoit pas de combattre une cause universelle, mais une cause locale qui consistoit en la carie de ces trois dents.'[75] However, without having the experience of such *observations*, it would be difficult to imagine that caries of the teeth was capable of causing a headache of such apparently indeterminate origin that it had deceived many *habiles* physicians and surgeons, who had therefore unwittingly allowed their patient to languish in pain for so long. Fauchard, as a direct result of the knowledge he had gained and upon which his practice was founded, had performed an operation which had freed her completely from her supposed rheumatism. In doing so, he had also saved her the trouble and expense of a long journey, and spared her the risk of the dangerous effects resulting from the inappropriate taking of the waters of Bourbon.

Violent pains in the head and jaws were frequently attributed to rheumatism by well-respected physicians and surgeons. In 1727, Mademoiselle Chabot of Orléans, aged twenty-seven, was attacked by very violent pains in the head and the teeth, and consulted the 'habile

Médecin'[76] M. Eustache and the master surgeon M. Noël. These gentle-men believed that her pain could only come from rheumatism, as the pain was no worse in any one tooth than in all the rest on that side, and there were no swellings or inflammations evident. She duly underwent a course of bleedings, enemas, purges and *cataplâmes*:[77] she was bled twice in the arms and twice in the feet, received many more enemas, was purged twice, and continued the *cataplâmes* for some time with no relief from her pain. During this treatment, she herself noticed that 'la deuxième petite dent molaire du côté gauche de la machoire supérieure'[78] was carious, which tooth M. Noël's apprentice duly removed for her. The pain ceased, and it was believed that the cause of her problems had been found and removed; but one hour later, it returned with renewed vigour, causing as much discomfort as before. It stayed for several months before disappearing spontaneously. But at the beginning of 1728, the young lady was visiting Paris, when she was again struck by the pain, with still no indication as to what might be causing it. She consulted the surgeon M. Petit, who suggested she consult Fauchard as he recognized that the pains could be caused by teeth that had become carious: he was also of the opinion that to return to the remedies which had been prescribed before could do her more harm than good. Fauchard was duly sent for and, having heard all the details of the problem from the patient, carried out his examination. He found the second *grosse dent molaire* in the lower left jaw to be carious enough to be causing her pain, and recognized that the only cure was its extraction. The patient consented, and the tooth was no sooner removed than the pain stopped immediately, never to return.

Fauchard noted in his *réflexion* that it was not usual to encounter pains like these, equivocal in origin and complicated in nature, which were caused by the teeth. Such cases did, however, provide evidence that the teeth could cause such pains, of which no one could be sure of the outcome: 'on ne voit encore que trop fréquemment de ces sortes de cas, & personne ne peut être sûr de n'y pas tomber'.[79] Had Mlle Chabot placed herself in the hands of an experienced *dentiste* from the start, she would have avoided both the continuation of her pain and the complex treatments she had received, which may have done her harm. Neverthe-less, from this and several other similar cases, it should be concluded that the *dentiste* should always be ready to learn from his practice, regarding both the treatment and prevention of disease; but problems could occur in any part of the body, and only by consulting those with experience of that part could understanding be gained.

Curing toothache by extraction and replacement

The simple extraction of the offending tooth was not, however, the only operation which Fauchard could perform to relieve the pain caused by caries: others could be devised, built on his knowledge of the disease. As we have seen, he had reasoned on the means by which this pain was produced. According to him, caries would allow air to reach the nerve fibres and small vessels of the tooth, which would then dry out and become tense. Pain would ensue when fluid distended these vessels as it entered them; alternatively, if some of the small vessels inside the tooth ruptured or burst, the fluid thus discharged would become corrupt and, by irritation of the parts they touched, produce pain.[80] The pain therefore came from the nerves and vessels *within* the tooth, and extraction of that tooth, which would necessarily involve the removal of those nerves and vessels, would cure it – but Fauchard could go further than this. His understanding of the way in which such pain was produced, coupled with his knowledge of the structure of the tooth, would allow him to invent a more complex cure which, for some patients, was far more satisfactory.

Fauchard recounts a number of successful treatments in which the painful carious tooth was first extracted and then immediately replaced in the socket from which it had been drawn. In 1725, for example, the eldest daughter of M. Tribuot, 'Facteur d'Orgues du Roi',[81] went to see him, racked with great pain from the *premiere petite dent molaire* of the upper right jaw, which was carious. This young lady was unsure of what to do: she was keen to have the tooth drawn to relieve the pain, but she was equally concerned about the deformity which would be left after its removal. She asked if it could be drawn and then replaced, as Fauchard had done for her younger sister. He replied that this could indeed be done easily – but only if the tooth did not break on removal, the alveolus did not split and there was no significant damage to the gum. The patient decided on this course of action, and Fauchard, taking every care, managed to remove the tooth without trouble. He duly replaced it immediately in the alveolus, ensuring that it was in exactly the same position that it had occupied previously, and held it in position with thread for several days. After a short period of pain, the tooth was filled with lead in order to preserve it from further caries.

Extraction followed by immediate replacement was also the treatment proposed by Fauchard for the thirty-year-old Mademoiselle de la Roche, governess of the children of M. de Lamoignon de Blanc-Mesnil[82] She consulted Fauchard to seek relief from the pain caused by the first *petite dent molaire* in her upper right jaw, which was carious both on its 'partie latérale & postérieure'.[83] Having examined this caries, the *dentiste* told his patient that there was no other cure but to have the tooth drawn; but she was concerned about her appearance, and as all her other teeth were 'fort belles & fort saines, & qu'il lui étoit fâcheux de perdre celle-ci, par la difformité que son extraction auroit faire à sa bouche',[84] he said that if it could be removed with no damage to tooth, alveolus or gum, he would replace it and re-tighten it in the jaw. This he did, tying it to the adjacent teeth with thread and prescribing suitable mouthwashes of a pint of red iron wine, honey of roses and 'une bonne cueillerée de mon styptique astringent'.[85] Twelve days later, the thread was removed and the tooth found to be firm. Sometime after this, Fauchard cleaned the carious hole with his instruments, and filled it: from then on, the patient would feel no further pain, the tooth serving her as well as her others.

These cases, and others like them, helped Fauchard to establish and to illustrate the successful application of important *principes* concerning the removal and replacement of teeth in their own alveoli, founded on anatomical knowledge of the parts involved. As we have seen, he knew how the caries caused the tooth to be painful, and that its removal would cure that pain. But by combining this understanding with sound anatomical knowledge of the size of the canal at the tip of the tooth root ('On dira sans doute que les canaux des dents, & les vaisseaux qui y entrent, sont très-fins'),[86] Fauchard could further build the theoretical foundations of his practice. Removal of the tooth would sever the painful nerve fibres, and release the corrosive fluid within the tooth; but he could deduce that if the tooth were replaced quickly, union would occur between the healthy vessels of the tooth and those of the alveolus, despite their small size. The fluids which come from the socket could circulate to the tooth, and vice versa, almost as if they had never been divided. For Fauchard, the certainty of this was clearly demonstrated by the tooth's continued sensitivity to the action of the file after replacement: 'La réunion & la distribution des nerfs dans une telle dent paroît très-certaine; puisqu'on remarque qu'une dent sortie de son alvéole, qu'on y remet, ou qu'on transplante sur le champ, est quelquefois aussi sensible à l'action de la lime, après qu'elle est reprise & raffermie, que celles qui sont toujours restées dans leur place naturelle.'[87]

Fauchard's understanding of the way in which carious teeth could cause pain, and the theoretical foundations upon which he based their replacement, were further reinforced by the initial failure of his treatment of M. Capitaine de Romatet[88] who had had a carious canine removed from his mouth and replaced with one from a soldier of his own Company. In performing this operation, Fauchard had been obliged to file the soldier's (much larger) tooth to make it fit the officer's mouth, to such an extent that the cavity of the tooth had been exposed: two weeks later he had filled the resulting hole with lead. Severe pain had ensued almost immediately, and the *dentiste* was forced to remove the lead again two days later, after which the pain receded. From this, there was something to be learnt: Fauchard reasoned that in the action of filling the tooth with lead, some of it must have entered the cavity of the tooth, thereby preventing the fluid from the ruptured vessels from escaping: this fluid would have been responsible for the *capitaine*'s pain. Removing the lead had allowed the release of the fluid to resume, thereby effecting a cure.

Curing toothache with the *trépan*

As we have seen previously, Fauchard considered dry caries to be the least dangerous variety, as it could cause little harm unless it changed its character to a different form of the disease.[89] This unfortunate state of affairs struck M. le Marquis de Parabére, a noble *de l'epée*,[90] in July 1724. The *marquis* had had 'depuis nombre d'années la premiére grosse dent molaire du côté gauche de la machoire inférieure, cariée d'une carie séche',[91] which had caused him no pain. But the character of this caries changed, and the *marquis* called Fauchard to extract the tooth which was now causing him 'beaucoup de douleur' when the air was allowed to strike it.[92] On his arrival, the *dentiste* examined the patient's mouth with great care; but the caries in the tooth indicated was so small and hard to see that he could not persuade himself that it was the cause of so much pain. The tooth was a particularly useful one for chewing, so despite the patient's determination to have it removed Fauchard refused. Considering the case carefully, he drew upon his knowledge of anatomy in order to deduce a method by which it could be cured. After careful thought about the distinctive nature of this case, he judged that although the caries appeared slight it could, by means of fine canals linking the cavity of the tooth and the air outside, have penetrated the membraneous parts and nerves within that cavity, irritating and inflaming them.[93] Fauchard reasoned therefore that opening up the cavity would allow the abscess which had formed and the matter contained therein to be released, thus curing the patient while retaining his tooth.

Having considered carefully the technique he should use, Fauchard inserted the point of a small, curved probe into the carious part of the *marquis*'s tooth. The instrument acted as a trepan, penetrating easily right into the cavity in the centre, and he had barely withdrawn it when blood and pus issued from the hole just as his reasoning had predicted it would.[94] Fauchard said to the sufferer, and to the large number of 'personnes de distinction qui se trouvérent présentes',[95] that he was convinced that the pain would now be completely gone, and that the tooth would be conserved. But having great difficulty in believing him, they wished the tooth drawn without delay. To calm them, win their confidence and lend support to his prognosis, the *dentiste* told them that he had had much experience of several similar cases in which this treatment had succeeded. Nevertheless, if the pain had not gone by evening he promised that he would extract the tooth anyway. It was not necessary – the pain went, never to return, and the *marquis* could soon use his tooth again as well as any of his others.

This case clearly illustrates the way in which Fauchard could use theoretical knowledge, and reasoning based on that knowledge, to develop the *science* of the *dentiste* further, applying it to the successful performance of operations on his patients. He had *not seen* any of the elements of this disease with his eyes – he had *deduced by reasoning* from a number of cases that there were fine canals, which on this occasion had communicated the caries to the cavity of the tooth, thereby forming an abscess. He had followed his reasoning, and had treated this tooth as if there *were* such an abscess, even though he had seen neither it nor the fine canals which were responsible for its formation; and he had been successful. Therefore, by taking an element of fundamental knowledge, reasoning upon it, building upon that reasoning and applying the new knowledge thus gained, he had extended the foundations of his practice still further.

Principes and *préceptes* for the performance of operations by the *chirurgien dentiste*

Some of the other types of operations recorded in the *observations* show how a set of particular *principes* governed the way in which the *dentiste* should perform his operations. In deciding whether to operate or not, the *dentiste* needed to recognize that there were some operations which should always be performed. This is demonstrated in the earliest of Fauchard's *observations*, which dates from 1696, and illustrates an important *principe* regarding the removal of first teeth which have failed to be shed naturally. M. de Crespy de la Mabilière had refused to have some stubborn milk teeth removed when young and, as a result, these teeth had stayed in place for too long, forcing his *secondes dents incisives* and his *canines* to grow 'hors de rang'.[96] After pressure from parents and friends, he eventually decided to have something done about it at the age of twenty-two and, as Fauchard was a long-standing friend of the family, he was duly consulted. He examined the state of the greatly deranged teeth carefully, and realized that he would need to remove some to make room. Thus three canines were extracted (each, of necessity, from a different quadrant), and the patient's front teeth rearranged 'dans le même ordre qu'elles doivent être naturellement'[97] with the aid of the pelican. These teeth, now loose, were fixed in place with waxed thread, which was left in place for fifteen days, 'après lequel tems, ayant ôte ce fil, ces dents se trouvèrent si bien raffermies & si bien arrangées, qu'il ne paroît pas aujourd'hui que les dents en question ayent jamais été difformes'.[98]

This young man's treatment was based on an important *principe* concerning the removal of first teeth, the application of which helped to establish that *principe*. One should always, according to Fauchard, take precautions to prevent derangement caused by the first teeth not giving way to the second. This was based on the knowledge that if the first teeth were not lost naturally, the second teeth would not be able to find room in the jaw and would, as a result, move across the gum as they came through it: 'C'est dans ce tems-là qu'il ne faut pas manquer d'ôter les premiéres dents, pour leur faire céder la place'.[99] In such a case as this, therefore, the *dentiste* should take care not to ignore this operation. He *must not fail* to remove the stubborn first teeth: if he does, he will 'rendra le bouche difforme ... On n'ignore plus à présent la possibilité de cette opération, ni le bon succès qui l'accompagne.'[100]

Having decided whether or not an operation should be performed, either routinely or in a particular case, the *dentiste* should base his decision regarding *when* it should be done on firm theoretical grounds. The timing of an operation could make a great difference to its outcome, and to the discomfort suffered by the patient. This was demonstrated in the case of the wife of the banker M. Begon of Paris, who in 1721 had consulted Fauchard regarding a 'tumeur excroissante qui lui étoit survenuë à la gencive du côté droit de la machoire inférieure'.[101] This growth was hard, mushroom-shaped and about the size of a nut. Not knowing a *médicament* which would destroy such a growth, the *dentiste* offered to remove it for her, favouring the use of an instrument to cut its attachment which would result in the least bleeding. But Mme Begon, fearful of an operation, chose not to take Fauchard's advice and resolved to leave things as they were. One year later, however, the swelling had grown to such a size that she returned, having resolved to have it removed. She was duly astonished when it was done immediately, and with very little pain: it bled only slightly, and healing was prompt. Fauchard, building on his knowledge, examined the lump carefully. He noted that it was hard, 'comme osseuse, ou pierreuse',[102] and similar in solidity to one removed from a patient by the late 'M. Carmeline Chirurgien Dentiste'[103] which he had described in an earlier *observation*.[104] After a thorough discussion of the likely cause of such a swelling, Fauchard noted that any delay in operating should be avoided in cases such as this: as soon as such tumours were discovered, 'il faut tâcher de les résoudre, ou de les faire suppurer le plus promtement qu'il est possible'.[105] If such methods did not succeed, he must operate immediately: 'il faut sans hésiter en venir à l'extirpation'.[106]

Once the *dentiste* has decided that an operation is necessary, and the patient is ready and willing to undergo it, he must know which *type* of operation should be performed – and this decision, too, should be based on sound theoretical knowledge. In 1725, M. Bretonnier, Avocat consultant au Parlement de Paris, had noticed that a *grande dent incisive* in his upper jaw and a *petite incisive* in his lower jaw were 'si chancelantes qu'elles ne tenoient presque plus dans leurs alvéoles, [and] surpassant les autres de beaucoup en longueur'.[107] These teeth had become so loose that they were knocking together on eating and speaking, and causing great discomfort. M. Bretonnier consulted Fauchard in the hope that they could be treated rather than removed, which the *chirurgien dentiste* achieved successfully by cleaning and fixing with gold wire. The diseased gum around them was cut back with scissors, but it took longer than expected to stop the bleeding which resulted from this operation. The patient returned to Fauchard the next day, with the gum still bleeding slightly: the *dentiste* assured him there was nothing to fear, and that if he rested and avoided getting too hot the problem should resolve itself. But although the patient followed this advice, the bleeding continued for four more days and nights. Fauchard was called again to the patient, who was now very weak. He proposed the use of the actual cautery, the wisdom of which was confirmed by the physician M. de Jussieu, 'qui s'y trouva present',[108] and the bleeding was eventually stopped.

This *observation* showed that sometimes the *dentiste* could encounter new cases, in the treatment of which he must proceed in a particular manner. He had treated this haemorrhage as a trifle, a 'bagatelle',[109] because he had seen so many other, similar, cases which had not caused such trouble – but in this case, the patient had nearly succumbed. Fauchard stated that M. Bretonnier's bleeding had been caused by both a systemic and a local factor. The blood was scorbutic, too fluid and diffuse, and the vessels of the gum had become varicose. Nevertheless, such a state of affairs should not affect the choice of operation: in mouths with similar problems, it was *absolutely necessary* to remove the diseased gum. This was a *principe* to which the *dentiste* should firmly adhere:

> il est absolument nécessaire en pareil cas d'emporter les mauvaises gencives, lorsqu'elles sont, comme celles-ci l'étoient, livides, gonflées, molles, prolongées considérablement, presque toutes détachées des

dents, & sujettes à saigner d'elles-mêmes; c'est pourquoi lorsque l'on sçait remédier à des hémorragies semblables, & que les gencives se trouvent en pareil état, il ne faut jamais négliger de les couper & de les dégorger ...[110]

Thus, for Fauchard, in every case where the gum is livid, swollen, flabby, detached from the teeth and bleeding easily, it *must* be removed: in such instances, the *dentiste* must not neglect this course of action. One special case, such as this, does not argue against the general case.

Once the *dentiste* had come to a decision regarding the need for an operation, its timing and its type, he would be ready to proceed to its performance, guided by his theoretical knowledge of how this should be done. But apart from that body of knowledge which was particular to each different type of treatment, there was also that which applied to the performance of operations in general. The *dentiste* should bear in mind that problems may arise of which he has no experience; but in solving them, he could then establish further *principes* which, according to Fauchard, he could use to his advantage, thus building on his knowledge. A clear example of this is the case presented by a Maître Cordonnier of Nantes, who in 1711 had requested that Fauchard remove the *premiere petite dent molaire* in his upper right jaw, which was causing him 'une douleur insupportable'.[111] Although it looked as if it would not be an easy tooth to extract, the *dentiste* nevertheless undertook the operation but, in the process, he noticed that the tooth next to the painful one was also coming with it. Fauchard stopped immediately, and upon further examination discovered that the external part of the alveolus, including the wall between the two teeth, was adhering firmly to both of them: the force he had needed to exert to loosen the carious one had broken this wall away from the rest of the alveolus, bringing the other tooth with it. He immediately pushed both teeth back into their sockets, and filed the alveolus in two before resuming the removal of the carious tooth. By this means, he completed the extraction successfully, and the loosened tooth once again became firm. He noted in his *observation* that if he had simply carried on with the operation he would not only have removed a good tooth with the bad, but would also have left his patient with a large hole in both his gum and his upper jaw.

Fauchard reflected that in the removal of teeth the *dentiste* would often come across new difficulties that he had not foreseen, as he had in this case. If there was a way of avoiding the problems which could ensue, it was 'd'opérer avec prudence & sans précipitation'.[112] It was essential to take care while first starting to apply force to the tooth, noting the resistance to movement and, above all, watching what happened to the neighbouring teeth. If they moved, it might be that the teeth were joined either to each other or to the alveolus very firmly, as in the case recorded in this *observation*. But if the *dentiste* were well instructed, circumspect, shrewd and ingenious, such an episode might be used to establish further *principes* for operating and thus to contribute further to the perfection of his practice: 'Quand on est bien instruit, circonspect, avisé & ingénieux, on est en état non-seulement d'éviter plusieurs accidens, mais encore d'inventer par la pratique, de nouvelles maniéres d'opérer, dont le Public peut retirer de grands avantages.'[113]

There could also, on occasion, be cases in which the *dentiste* would not be able to uncover the problem at all; and in the absence of theoretical foundations on which to base his treatment, would refuse to act empirically. Thus, in 1722, when M. l'Abbé de Rothelin called Fauchard to draw a tooth which was causing him much pain, the *dentiste* initially refused as he could see nothing wrong – and he was not the only one to have done so, noting in his *observation* that 'Plusieurs de mes confréres à qui il s'adressa, refusérent aussi de l'entreprendre.'[114] M. l'Abbé tried everything to ease his pain for ten days or so, but to no avail. He eventually called Fauchard a second time and demanded that he pull his tooth, even adding that if the pain were not eased by so doing the *dentiste* was to draw another. Fauchard acquiesced, drew the tooth, and the pain ceased immediately. But on examination, it appeared completely clean and without caries. Fauchard noted that this tooth had been a late one growing, which had therefore not had sufficient space in the gum, and in his *réflexion* he provides a long, theoretical analysis of how it could have caused the pain. He also admitted that perhaps he should have drawn it sooner – but it would have been apparent to others that such an act would not have been based on sound theoretical knowledge.

> J'avouë que je ne devois point balancer à ôter la dent de M. l'Abbé de Rothelin; mais je crus devoir différer, parce que je craignois qu'il ne fût dit dans le monde que j'eusse tiré une dent saine à une personne de cette considération, sans que l'on sçût les raisons indispensables qui m'y avoient obligé.[115]

It was therefore of central importance to Fauchard and, presumably, those of his *confrères* who had similarly refused to draw the Abbé's tooth, that none could accuse him of performing operations that were not based on sound theoretical knowledge of the teeth.

The dangers of consulting 'les Chirurgiens peu expérimentez'[116]

It should now be apparent that the operations for the teeth performed by the *dentiste*, as evidenced by the examples above, were founded on firm theoretical knowledge of the structure of the teeth and of the ways in which their diseases should be treated. For Fauchard, a lack of this knowledge in those attempting to treat teeth could be dangerous – failure to perform an operation, through either neglect or ignorance, could lead to disastrous consequences, as nearly befell the subjects of two of the *observations* recorded in *Le Chirurgien Dentiste*. In both of these instances, the unfortunate patients came close to losing their lives, and Fauchard laid the blame firmly upon the surgeon who first attended them. The patients' prolonged suffering and near-submission to their diseases was a direct result of ignorance of the particular knowledge of the teeth, the possession of which, for Fauchard, was essential to obtain a cure.

The first of these sufferers was Le Sieur Nicolas de Louviers, a bookbinder of Paris, who in 1719 had two very carious *dents molaires* in his lower left jaw, which were causing a 'fluxion si extraordinaire, & des douleurs si insupportables'[117] that he thought he was going to die. His face became 'monstrueux', and three glands under his chin had swollen to the extent that they each appeared the size of a pigeon's egg. His throat and mouth were swollen to the point where it was almost impossible to open them, or to take food, even the most liquid variety, into his stomach. Seeing himself in this *triste état*, he sent for M. Chauvet, Chirurgien-Juré à Paris, who examined him and decided to bleed him at once, also applying a 'cataplâme émolliant'.[118] These measures had no effect, however, and unfortunately the disease increased to such an extent that the affected parts of the mouth and the throat became even more swollen, so that the patient could neither swallow nor retain his saliva. As a result, fluid flowed from his mouth as abundantly as if he had 'un pthyalisme occasionné par l'effet de quelques remédes mercuriaux'.[119]

On his return, M. Chauvet was surprised to see that his patient was still in such a pitiable state. He decided that he was suffering with a quinsy and, feeling obliged to consult a physician, called M. de Jussieu[120] to visit. The two gentlemen had great trouble examining the mouth, because the patient could not open it far enough to allow them to see the cause of the problem. Nevertheless, de Jussieu judged that his sorry state was not due to a quinsy, but to carious teeth: the gum on one side of M. de Louviers's mouth was swollen, so much so that it was covering the teeth and almost hiding them from view. It was decided that an abscess had developed, and that this would require prompt opening to allow the matter within to drain. The surgeon duly opened the swelling, but only a little pus flowed out, because most of it was enclosed at the bottom of the alveolus and around the angle of the jaw; however, this slight evacuation did allow the parts to be distended a little more, and as a result the patient could now open his mouth a little bit more widely.

De Jussieu now decided it was time to obtain the services of a *dentiste*, and Fauchard was duly called to draw the teeth that were causing the pain. On arrival at the patient's house, he examined the offending teeth as well as he could, identifying the two last *dents molaires* of the lower left jaw as being carious and having therefore caused all the patient's suffering ('comme M. de Jussieu l'avoit très bien observé').[121] He had great difficulty in getting his *pélican* into the patient's mouth, however, due to the severely restricted opening, which caused him to consider carefully which would be the best instrument to use:

> Je choisis une de celles dont le crochet étoit moins long & le plus large pour le pouvoir porter plus aisément sur la surface intérieure des deux dents cariées, afin de les pouvoir tirer d'un seul coup, & d'éviter par ce moyen la récidive de l'effort & de l'ébranlement; ce qui me réussit très-bien.[122]

As soon as the teeth were drawn, there was a considerable flow of escaping pus from their empty sockets – enough to fill three bowls, and all of it 'verdâtre & d'une puanteur insupportable'.[123]

Sieur de Louviers, who had endured 'de très-cruelles douleurs'[124] for eight to ten days, was delivered from it speedily by these two extractions and the huge evacuation of pus which ensued; but François le Blanc, Compagnon Maçon of Ville-Neuve-le-Roi, was not so lucky with his carious teeth. In 1725, he was smitten with a pain so violent and a fluxion so considerable that he could no longer resist it. The last *grosse dent molaire* of his lower right jaw was carious, and he was forced to consult his 'Chirurgien ordinaire'[125] who duly bled him and applied *cataplâmes* to the swelling. However, these remedies proved useless. The fluxion persisted, and an abscess formed at the side of the tooth. The pain and fluxion appeared to diminish, but the matter which had not been released returned to the blood and caused a violent fever and delirium, placing the patient 'en danger de perdre la vie'.[126] The surgeon again bled him two or three times and purged him. Alternating between high fever and a discharge in the mouth, which brought some relief but produced only thin matter which was, nevertheless, of a 'fœtidité insupportable',[127] the patient, whose cheek was now extremely swollen, was again dressed with *cataplâmes* and embrocations in an attempt to reduce the swelling. The surgeon's treatment continued in this way for a whole month with no success.

Eventually, the Maître-chirurgien M. Montaut was called. He examined the patient's cheek, which he found hard and as large as a one-pound loaf. The lower jaw had lost its action, the lower teeth were separated from the upper by no more than the width of a little finger and the patient could barely move his lips to spit or to take *bouillon*. M. Montaut concluded that the thickest matter was retained in the jaw, and only the thin fluid was discharging; but the *chirurgien ordinaire* disagreed and refused to operate, certain that there was no matter to drain as he could feel no fluctuation. Montaut, however, reasoned that there was no other means of treatment than to open the tumour from within the mouth, and that this was absolutely essential as the bone of the jaw was at risk of becoming carious also. The *chirurgien ordinaire* persisted in his opinion, and so it was Montaut who took a lancet and plunged it into the sac of the abscess. He made a large opening, but only a little thin fluid issued from it, so he replaced the lancet with a *bistouri* and enlarged the hole still further. By pressing his hand hard on the swollen cheek, he managed to express a large amount of very thick matter, which was full of clots 'gros comme des noisettes'.[128] Having emptied the sac, he dressed the patient's cheek and, having probed the extent of the sac with a *stilet* as far as the angle of the jaw, decided he would need to make another opening the following morning.

The next day's operation turned out to be extensive. On making his new incision with a razor and exploring it with his probe and *bistouri*, Montaut discovered that the jaw-bone was already carious. In order to reach the caries, which extended 'jusqu'au condille & jusqu'à la cavité glénoïde de l'os temporal',[129] he was forced to make a further incision in the shape of an inverted 'T', in the course of which he could not avoid cutting a large branch of the external carotid artery. This he mastered with a ligature and the tourniquet, and then dressed the carious bone with a great variety of spirits and infusions. Fifteen days later, the surgeon removed four large pieces of exfoliated jaw-bone, which consisted of 'une portion de l'apophyse coronoide, le condille entier de la machoire, une moyenne portion de son angle, & une autre portion plus considérable du même angle'.[130] When the last of these pieces was removed, the carious tooth which had caused all the trouble came with it.

With the carious bone thus removed, Montaut now had a good view of the bone forming the base of his patient's skull, which for a long time had given pain as if it were home to 'quatre ou cinq batteurs de ciment'.[131] There was much damage:

> la cavité glénoïde étoit découverte & de même l'apophise zigomatique & le stiloïde, que tous ces os étoient dépouillez jusqu'au trou auditif externe; ce que ce Chirurgien découvrit au moyen de son stilet, avec lequel il rencontra l'os temporal carié à un tel point, que son stilet le traversa jusqu'à la dure mére: il le passa par-dessous l'arcade zigomatique, & il pénétra jusqu'à la fente orbitaire externe ...[132]

Refusing to give up on this desperate state of affairs, Montaut dressed the wound again, fearing, however, that an exfoliation of the temporal and sphenoid bones forming the base of the skull would ensue. But the patient's luck had turned: this did not happen, and by repeated and careful dressing the beatings ceased and the pain receded.

After two months of treatment and many operations, the patient was left with an incurable fistula from the duct of the parotid (salivary) gland which had necessarily been cut. The lower eyelid on the same side remained everted and rendered paralysed by the destruction of a branch of the fifth nerve which supplied the face, and a cataract had started to form due to obstruction of the 'corps graisseux & au vaisseaux sanguins, qui se distribuent au globe de l'œil'.[133] Apart from this, the patient could now enjoy 'une parfait santé'.[134] Although his operation had been performed by M. Montaut, M. le Blanc (both the patient and his now separate jaw-bone) would be examined closely by Messieurs Winslow, de Manteville, Verdier, de Saint Yves and Fauchard shortly afterwards.[135] Fauchard describes de Saint Yves as a 'Chirurgien Oculiste';[136] thus, we can see that as the patient's problems had involved the teeth, Fauchard, a *chirurgien dentiste* was present – and as they also had involved the eyes (or, more specifically, the orbit), so was de Saint Yves, a *chirurgien oculiste*.

It was not only the *chirurgien ordinaire* who could neglect to treat a tooth appropriately, however; on occasion even a *dentiste* could cause his patient to suffer unduly because of a lack of experience. Fauchard recounts the story of M. Octavien, Peintre de l'Académie Royale de Peinture à Paris, who in 1721 was enjoying a 'fricassée de pieds de Mouton'[137] when he accidentally bit down hard on a small bone lodged between two teeth. This action fractured his lower right first *grosse molaire*, and led to a very uncomfortable chain of events for the unfortunate painter. The cavity of the tooth was thus opened and as a result the tooth, although not decayed, 'lui occasionna des douleurs insupportables'.[138] Desperate to be delivered from this pain, M. Octavien sought out one of Fauchard's *confrères* to request the tooth be drawn; but his request was refused, as the *dentiste* consulted believed it would be 'dommage d'ôter une dent qui n'étoit cariée'.[139] A remedy was given instead, but the fluxion and inflammation increased considerably. Fauchard was called, and went to see the sufferer whom he found 'dans un fort triste état'.[140] Now with a greatly disfigured face and feeding from a baby's bottle, M. Octavien had also succumbed to a fever. Fauchard immediately bled him and applied *cataplâmes* made of milk, dough, egg yolk, saffron and oil of lilies, which was changed morning and evening. After several days, the patient was again bled, and his dressings continued. Some days later, Fauchard met M. Juton, Maître Chirurgien, who knew M. Octavien, and the two called round together to examine his mouth. Finding no improvement, they changed the *cataplâmes* for some made with 'herbes emoliantes'[141] which, after several applications, had the desired effect: the swelling burst and duly receded. Nevertheless, the opening of the swelling was dilated with an instrument and a basin-full of matter released. This was repeated several times over the next few days, during which the patient was 'cruellement tourmenté' – a torment which would continue for nearly two months: 'Il resta dans ce pitoyable état pendant près de deux mois, sans sortir de sa maison, & sans pouvoir vaquer à ses affaires.'[142] When things had calmed down, Fauchard drew the broken tooth which had caused all the trouble, thus releasing the painter from his suffering: 'par-là je terminai heureusement la cure d'une maladie, qui l'avoit tourmenté pendant longtemps'.[143] In his opinion, had the tooth been drawn earlier the patient would not have come as close as he did to succumbing to the torments he had suffered, inflicted by 'la négligence d'un Dentiste peu expérimenté'[144] who had not recognized the need to act.

The practice of the *dentiste*: 'particularization' within the practice of the surgeon

In addition to enabling us to view the way *dentistes* like Pierre Fauchard built their practice on theoretical knowledge, and in turn used that practice to extend that knowledge, the *observations* in Le Chirurgien Dentiste help to reveal a great deal about the position the *dentiste* would hold in the surgical world of eighteenth-century France, and how he came to achieve that position. We shall see that the *dentiste* could indeed now be seen by his contemporaries as a 'particular' surgeon, one who had particular knowledge of a particular part of the practice of surgery. The surgical world was growing rapidly: we have already noted Dionis's comment in the preface to his Cours d'opérations, published twenty years before Fauchard's book, that the *science* of surgery was now of 'une étendue infinie'.[145] He had pointed to a number of gentlemen whose sole employment lay in treating the teeth alone, thereby requiring the possession of one particular part of that infinite surgical *science* only. He had implied that it was because these gentlemen were restricting themselves in this way that they could perform its operations more successfully than the 'general' surgeon,[146] and many of Fauchard's *observations* serve to support such an implication. Fauchard records many instances in which a 'general' surgeon had been consulted concerning either problems of the teeth themselves or problems of other parts which had been caused by the teeth, and their theoretical knowledge had been found wanting. We have already seen the examples of the Marquise de Trans and Mlle Chabot, whose severe headaches were treated by surgeons as rheumatic in origin, and the unfortunate le Blanc, whose problems were made far worse by his *chirurgien ordinaire*'s lack of particular knowledge of the teeth (although le Blanc was saved by the actions of another 'general' surgeon of wider experience). Further examination of Fauchard's *observations* and *refléxions*, focusing on the performance of the practitioners involved, will show how the particular knowledge of the *dentiste* could exceed that of the surgeon in that one area.

According to Fauchard, some surgeons had simply neglected their knowledge of the diseases of the mouth. But such neglect was not only characteristic of the *chirurgien ordinaire*, as it had been in the case of le Blanc. In 1713 a *domestique* of M. le Curé of the Parish of Saint-Germain in Rennes 'fut attaqué du scorbut à la bouche'.[147] He had put himself in the hands of the most able master surgeon of the town, who had failed to elicit a cure despite giving treatment for a considerable period of time. On turning to Fauchard for help, the patient quickly had several carious teeth removed from his mouth along with some splinters of decayed bone. Any areas of ulcerated and dead gum, which 'lui rendoient l'haleine d'une odeur insupportable',[148] were also removed, his teeth cleaned and mouthwashes prescribed. After bleeding and purging for three weeks, the *domestique* was perfectly cured. However, Fauchard felt that the 'Maître Chirurgien des plus habiles'[149] to whom the patient had originally turned for treatment had failed to gain knowledge of the diseases of the mouth. This patient had required nothing more than the dilation of the small sinuses, the removal of the stony growths, the assisted exfoliation of the carious bone, cleaning, reduction of the ulcers and the removal of the diseased teeth. This list of operations was, despite its length, 'ce que les Chirurgiens pratiquent journellement avec succès en pareille occasion'.[150] This surgeon should have acted accordingly: 'Par conséquent on ne peut imputer l'inutilité de son premier traitement qu'à beaucoup de négligence.'[151]

The importance of consulting a surgeon who had not neglected to acquire this knowledge was emphasized still further by the sorry chain of events which befell M. Henri Amariton, the son of M. Amariton Ecuyer, Seigneur de Beaurecœuil of the parish of Nonette.[152] On deciding to have an uncomfortable and painful *dent canine* removed, he had had recourse to an *opérateur* (Fauchard's word) named la Roche, in his home town. This charlatan, as Fauchard also calls him, sat his patient on the ground, positioned his extracting key on the tip of the crown of the tooth and struck it with a large stone until the tooth had disappeared from view. 'Cet empirique'[153] then assured his patient that the tooth had been swallowed, which seemed likely as it could not be found. A few days later, however, M. Amariton began to suffer with considerable pain in his face, and duly consulted his physician, M. Duver. Duver noticed a small but firm tumour appearing on the cheek, by the nose; inside the mouth, there were three small fistulous holes from which was discharging a fetid humour. Soon, discharging fistulae appeared on the cheek also, and the patient was taken to Clermont to consult with the surgeons of the town. Feeling the case to be too difficult, details were sent to two Paris surgeons, Arnault[154] and Petit who, having examined the account thoroughly, decided the problem was too serious to treat informally by postal recommendation.[155] The patient therefore travelled to Paris, and once in the hands of Arnault and Petit was quickly cured. Petit made an incision next to the nose, and having thus exposed the tooth which had previously been supposed swallowed, removed it with a pair of pincers. Fauchard, in his *réflexion* on this case, regretted the long-drawn-out nature of the cure. Had the surgeons of Clermont been better instructed by *observations* such as his own, and had they possessed a proper theoretical knowledge of the teeth, that is, an understanding of the structure of the parts and an ability to reason seriously on the technique to be followed in the operation, it would have been easy for them to have effected a quick and satisfactory cure for their unfortunate patient.

By the 1720s, the extent of the theoretical knowledge possessed by surgeons of even the highest calibre would not necessarily include an understanding of the *science* for the teeth. This was demonstrated in November 1724, when Fauchard was required to attend to M. Tartanson, 'Chirurgien-Juré à Paris & ancien Prévôt de sa Compagnie', who had been attacked by a 'cruelle douleur aux dents incisives & canines de la machoire inférieure'.[156] The senior surgeon could not see how teeth could cause such severe pain when they were not carious, simply a little worn at the tips – the *dentiste*, however, held the advantage over his colleague by virtue of his focus on the *science* for the teeth. He examined Tartanson's teeth with his probe, and assured him that the cause of his pain was just one canine on the right side of his mouth. He could see that this tooth was more worn down than the others, and his knowledge of its anatomy allowed him to reason that the nerve inside had therefore become damaged by the air which could now impinge upon it more easily. Fauchard knew what had happened as a result of this damage, and what should be done to cure it and to save the tooth: 'Je lui dis, que j'étois persuadé qu'il y avoit une matiére purulente épanchée dans cette cavité, & qu'il faloit perforer cette dent pour l'évacuer; que par ce moyen la douleur cesseroit bientôt, qu'on lui conserveroit sa dent.'[157] Having convinced M. Tartanson of the need for an operation, Fauchard went to work. He took a *burin*,[158] which he used as a perforator, and placed its point on the tip of the worn canine near the cavity. By repeatedly turning it from right to left and from left to right, he made the cavity larger until it was big enough to take the point of an *équarrissoir*, which he used in the same manner to make the hole larger still. Once the cavity of the tooth was opened, out flowed a considerable amount of blood and pus, which Fauchard took great delight in demonstrating to his prestigious patient: 'ce que je fis voir au malade par le moyen d'un miroir, en présence du sieur Larreyre son Garçon Chirurgien'.[159]

Tartanson, despite being a surgeon who was 'tres-habile dans son art',[160] was astonished at the success of this operation. Fauchard had to admit, however, that his was not a common problem; and on those occasions when others *had* been called upon to treat similar cases, none had thought to employ such means to treat them. The principal means which should be used was the trepan, as Fauchard had used on Tartanson, coupled with the knowledge of when to use it. Whilst this operation may have been an unusual one in general, for Fauchard it was not out of the ordinary. He had performed it many times for other patients, notably one M. le Nain, for whom he had trepanned many teeth before filling them with lead some months later.[161]

M. le Nain was a 'Lieutenant de Roi de la Province de Dunkerque & Colonel d'Infanterie',[162] whose experiences at the hands of Fauchard will help to reveal the great advantage which could accrue by consulting a *dentiste* over problems with the teeth. In 1723, he had suffered with 'une fluxion & une douleur si considérable, que la joüe du même côté en devint extrémement tuméfiée',[163] caused by the second *petite molaire* on the lower right, which was a little worn down. He went to find Fauchard, who, on examining his mouth, found the gum tender and very inflamed. Knowing that an abscess was forming, the *dentiste* advised bleeding and a series of mixtures and *cataplâmes* to be held in the mouth. Later, Fauchard and M. Sauré, Maître Chirurgien, returned to see the patient, whose abscess was now open and releasing much matter. The next day he was bled again, and treatment continued for many days, relieving the fluxion and pain successfully. A fistula remained on the gum, from which issued 'une matiére purulente'.[164]

Three weeks after being delivered from his pain, M. le Nain returned to see Fauchard to inquire if anything could be done to cure this fistula. The *dentiste* replied that he only had to have the tooth that had caused the trouble removed, and the fistula would disappear; if, however, he wished to keep it, many incisions would need to be made around the fistula, which would need frequent dressing – but by this means, it would be cured completely. The patient much preferred to follow this latter course of action, not wishing to lose his tooth, and Fauchard duly commenced his complicated and delicate treatment.

After having probed the fistula, the *dentiste* made an incision right to the extent of its depth, ensuring that the lips of the wound could not reunite too soon. He cut the angles of the wound with scissors, and dressed it with a mixture which was held in place with 'un petit tampon de charpie',[165] carefully introduced into the opening of the fistula. After five or six days, Fauchard noticed a small piece of alveolus just beneath the fistula which was ready to exfoliate. He made a small incision, continued his dressings, and after another three or four days three small pieces of alveolus exfoliated from the gum. The dressings were continued, and soon the patient was 'parfaitement guéri'[166] – and his tooth was saved.

The need for such treatments only came about, according to Fauchard, as a result of neglect in remedying caries of the teeth by appropriate means, thereby rendering future cure very difficult. But his operation, elegant in both conception and performance, shows clearly that successful treatment was nevertheless possible. He noted that those who suffer in this way are often not fortunate enough to encounter 'des Praticiens assez expérimentez':[167]

> D'où il faut conclurre qu'il y a des moyens pour guérir certaines maladies, qui ne sont connus que de peu de personnes; quoique la connoissance de ces mêmes maladies, & de ces mêmes moyens ne soit pas difficile à ceux qui se sont sérieusement attachez à acquérir la capacité, l'expérience & l'adresse nécessaire. Sans le secours de tels Dentistes, les personnes atteintes de ces maladies se trouvent exposées à courir de très-grands risques; parce qu'étant négligées, le progrès de leur mal a souvent des suites si fâcheuses, qu'elles sont exposées à essuyer des opérations longues & douloureuses; ensorte que des sujets foibles & cacochimes sont quelquefois en danger de perdre la vie.[168]

Thus Fauchard concluded that the methods for curing such *maladies* were known only to a few, despite the ease with which they could be acquired by those who wished seriously to acquire the ability, experience and necessary skill. Without the help of the particular surgeon, the *dentiste*, persons attacked by such maladies ran great risks: neglect of their disease would expose them to long and painful operations, in the course of which the weak and unhealthy were in danger of losing life.

The operation on the Comte de Corneillan: a consultation of equals

The *dentiste*'s possession of theoretical knowledge of the teeth and their operations could, as we have seen, now far surpass that of the 'general' surgeon. For *dentistes* such as Fauchard, this particular knowledge enabled them to construct a practice using a highly respectable clientele which, in turn, both granted and maintained a position of respect within the surgical hierarchy of eighteenth-century France – sometimes at the very highest level. Other medical men, called upon to treat high-ranking members of the court for diseases which involved the mouth, would now be encouraged to include the *dentiste* not only in the treatment itself but also in the decisions to be made about that treatment. The *dentiste* could thus be considered to be a specialist, in the modern sense of the word: not as a practitioner who was *restricted* to performing a few operations only, but as one who, possessing knowledge of the practice of surgery, had chosen to *extend* that knowledge in one particular direction and could therefore, when appropriate, be included in a technical consultation of equals. The elements of this kind of relationship, and the way in which it could work to the benefit of both patient and practitioner, are illustrated clearly by the part played by Fauchard in the cure of the Comte de Corneillan in 1727.[169]

Fauchard was not the principal practitioner involved in the treatment of M. le Comte, but his specialist role in this cure was absolutely central to its success. The count had suffered for a long time with two swellings in the mouth: these were 'une tumeur carcinomateuse aux gencives intérieures des deux petites dents molaires du côté gauche de la machoire inférieure, & une autre tumeur sur les gencives extérieures de ces mêmes dents'. The first tumour 'étoit du volume d'un œuf de Pigeon',[170] and both of them were hindering M. le Comte's eating while making his mouth very unpleasant due to the large amounts of tartar surrounding the neighbouring teeth. Having come to Paris in search of treatment, he travelled to Versailles to seek attention from no less an authority than François Gigot de la Peyronie, the king's *premier* surgeon *en survivance*. Having seen the patient, la Peyronie subsequently called a joint consultation with the highly respected physician M. Mailhes and, *because the disease involved the mouth*, the *chirurgien dentiste* Fauchard. On examining the sufferer's mouth, the practitioners agreed that the tartar covering the teeth should be removed, along with the gum which the tartar had caused to swell (in accordance with the principle which, as we have seen, was applied in and reinforced by Fauchard's treatment of M. Bretonnier two years earlier); the blood with which the rest of the gums were engorged should also be expressed thoroughly. Following this, they concluded that the second *petite dent molaire* on the left side of the lower jaw should be drawn, even though it was clean and free from caries, because this was the only way they would get a better view of the points at which the tumours were attached, and thus be enabled to remove them more easily. They also concluded that the root of the second *petite dent molaire* of the upper jaw on that side should be removed in addition, as it was very carious and had produced a fungal growth of the gum which was effectively stopping the patient from eating on that side.

It was Fauchard, the particular surgeon for the teeth, who performed these operations on M. le Comte's teeth and gums. When he had done so, the trio retired until the evening to allow the patient time to rest. At five o'clock, it was the 'general' surgeon la Peyronie's turn to take up his instruments, and with the aid of a small curved *bistouri*, he removed the tumours in the manner which should, perhaps, be expected of the king's *premier* surgeon: 'avec toute l'adresse qu'on pouvoit attendre'.[171] Over a period of several days, the wound was dressed and washed, and within a short time the patient was 'parfaitement guéri'.[172]

Fauchard's narrative description of the way in which his services were employed in the treatment of this important member of the nobility provides a clear illustration of the respected position which the *chirurgien dentiste* could occupy within the surgical hierarchy. Whilst this operation was not the first to be performed on the mouth of an important person by one whose activities focused on the teeth,[173] it serves to provide a clear picture of how the *dentiste*-as-specialist could now bring his *science* to complement that of others. Here was a very important patient, who had sought treatment from a very important surgeon in the person of la Peyronie. At this time (1727), la Peyronie had succeeded Dionis in demonstrating at the Jardin Royal,[174] and he was successor designate (*en survivance*) to the king's surgeon, his former teacher, Georges Mareschal. He had assumed most of Mareschal's duties, and served as a sort of co-*premier* surgeon until Mareschal's death in 1736.[175] La Peyronie was in great favour with Louis XV, having enjoyed a close relationship with him since childhood: Toby Gelfand has pointed out that 'From 1719, when the king was only nine years old, until la Peyronie's death in 1747, the absolute lawgiver of France entrusted his health absolutely to his premier surgeon.'[176] Gelfand also notes la Peyronie's dominance over the king's physician, quoting the Duc de Luynes who noted in his memoirs that the surgeon 'guides and absolutely controls M. Chicoyneau, the premier physician'.[177] Thus we have an image of la Peyronie, the most important 'medical' man in France (and therefore, by implication, Europe), *not* performing the removal of overgrowths of gum, deposits of tartar or diseased teeth from his distinguished patient – procedures which, as we have seen, had traditionally been considered as the province of the surgeon. Two men consult *with* the surgeon who is to operate on the tumours: one is a highly respected physician, who is a Médecin du Roi, a Docteur en Médecine de l'Université de Montpellier and a royally appointed professor at Cahors[178] and, *because the problems are of the mouth*, the other is a specialist surgeon who has particular knowledge and experience of that part of the body and its operations: a *chirurgien dentiste*. According to Fauchard's account, these three make the decisions *between* them. 'Lorsque je fus arrivé, & que nous eûmes examiné la bouche du malade, nous fûmes tous d'avis de commencer'[179] – 'after I had arrived, and *we* had examined the mouth of the patient, *we were all* of the opinion'. 'Ensuite nous conclûmes ... Nous conclûmes de même'[180] – '*we* concluded'. But, while the planning of M. le Comte's treatment was a joint activity between physician, surgeon and *dentiste*, the physical removal of the teeth and gum was performed by the *dentiste* alone: 'Lorsque j'eus fait ces opérations'.[181] However, all three would preside over the recovery. 'Pendant quelques jours nous ne mîmes sur la gencive que de petits plumaceaux trempez dans un digestif'[182] – 'For some days *we* put on the gum'. Thus the Comte de Corneillan was cured by three men who possessed particular abilities in their own particular fields and who formed, therefore, on a technical basis, a consultation of equals. For Fauchard, the consultations he had played a part in and the operations he had performed on such a prestigious patient were neither the work of the simple tooth-drawer, nor of the 'general' master surgeon, however senior in standing; they were part of the complex and carefully executed business of a specialist surgeon, their performance based on reasoning and decisions whose foundations lay in a *science* of the mouth and teeth.

The *chirurgien dentiste* as specialist surgeon, practising an indispensable part of surgery

Pierre Fauchard should be seen, therefore, as a representative of a new class of surgeons who had turned to the treatment of teeth to make their living, creating and applying a *science* for the mouth and teeth in the process – and taking a new title both to indicate and to celebrate this particular interest in the teeth. According to Fauchard, writing around fifteen years after Dionis had identified a group choosing to treat the teeth only, the title of *chirurgien dentiste* was an appropriate one for this kind of practitioner, signifying one whose interest lay in all aspects of treating the teeth rather than in their simple removal alone. Indeed, a *dentiste* would do all he could to avoid such an operation, not because of the violence and pain which would be inflicted upon the patient, or the problems which could follow, but because of the great importance attached to the use of the tooth.

> Ce n'est qu'avec regret que je me détermine à ôter des dents, non
> pas par rapport à la violence de l'opération, qui n'est jamais si
> considérable, que les douleurs qu'elles causent, ni par rapport aux

suites fâcheuses qui peuvent en arriver; mais j'hésite, j'élude & je différe à les ôter par le grand cas que j'en fais, & à cause de l'importance de leur usage.[183]

In Fauchard's opinion, if all who treated teeth shared this view, their activities would be held in much higher regard. Thus, whilst there were those who undoubtedly deserved the title of *arracheur de dents*, there were also those who deserved the title of 'Conservateur de dents',[184] because that was precisely what they did – and not only did they strive to conserve teeth by applying the 'régles de l'art'[185] to their fullest extent; they also applied their innovative genius: 'mais encore qu'ils employent leur génie, en imitant la nature, à réparer les défauts qui restent à une bouche, lorsque l'ouvrage de cette même nature vient à manquer'.[186] In his opinion such practitioners deserved the descriptive title of *chirurgien dentiste*, as they practised this one particular part of surgery to its fullest possible extent: 'On ne scauroit refuser à des derniers le titre de Chirurgiens Dentistes; puisqu'ils pratiquent exactement dans toute son étenduë une partie de la Chirurgie'.[187] This opinion was reinforced by his *confrère* M. Laudumiey, *dentiste* to the king of Spain, who celebrated Fauchard's use of a title which had been built on a broad body of knowledge gathered by such genius, great attention and assiduous work: 'Le titre de *Chirurgien Dentiste* ... est soutenu par tout ce qu'un génie heureux, une grande attention & un travail assidu pouvoient rassembler de connoissances.'[188]

The particular practice of the *dentiste* was, for Fauchard, just as useful and important for the preservation of mankind as any other part of surgery. Thus, as the *science* of the surgeon was absolutely necessary for the survival of man, so was the *science* of the *chirurgien dentiste* – which could *only* be the province of that particular part of surgery: 'le Dentiste & sa profession, qui ... auroit toujours été considérée autant que plusieurs autres parties de la Chirurgie, qui ne sont ni plus utiles, ni plus importantes à la conservation de l'homme'.[189] But it was not just Fauchard and his *confrères* who placed the practice of the *dentiste* in context as a part of surgery. Surgeons, too, saw Fauchard's writings in *Le Chirurgien Dentiste* as representative of a complete and perfected body of theoretical knowledge of the diseases of the teeth and their operations, which formed an essential part of their own wide-ranging practice. We have seen in this chapter that in the early decades of the eighteenth century the *dentiste* would work alongside some of the most respected medical men in France, sometimes literally. Men such as the physicians Winslow and de Jussieu[190] and not least the *premier* surgeon la Peyronie enlisted the particular knowledge of the *dentiste*, and Fauchard's *observations* also reveal that some patients who were recognized as suffering with specific problems of the teeth would, on occasion, be sent direct to a *dentiste* by such prominent physicians as Helvetius and Hecquet.[191] But perhaps the clearest view of the way in which men of such high standing would acknowledge the role of the *dentiste* is provided by the *approbations* printed at the end of *Le Chirurgien Dentiste*.

These *approbations* allow us to see the light in which other types of practitioner presented the practice of the *dentiste* when asked to do so. The gaining of an *approbation* was required by law, and acted as a form of registration without which publication would be illegal. The *Encyclopédie* of Diderot and d'Alembert describes the *approbation* as

> un act par lequel un censeur nommé pour l'examen d'un livre, déclare l'avoir lû & l'avoir rien trouvé qui puisse ou doive en empêcher l'impression. C'est sur cet acte signé du censeur, qu'est accordée la permission d'imprimer; & il doit être placé à la tête ou à la fin du livre pour lequel il est donné.[192]

M. le chancelier would nominate an official body of *censeurs*[193] whose members, numbering around one hundred at the time of the publication of Fauchard's book, would be expected to possess a particular understanding of what they would be asked to read.[194] *Le Chirurgien Dentiste*, however, carries thirteen separate *approbations*, indicating between them that six physicians, thirteen surgeons and one *chirurgien dentiste*, all bearing the highest credentials, had each read Fauchard's book. Only the first of these, written by the highly respected physician Winslow, makes mention of having been made at the chancellor's request and of having found nothing that should prevent publication.[195] It seems unlikely that the authors of all the other *approbations* should have been members of the body of official *censeurs*; however, whether they were written at the chancellor's request, or at the request of Fauchard, they nevertheless provide us with an insight into how these other, various Parisian practitioners now viewed the practice of the *chirurgien dentiste*.

The physicians who had studied Fauchard's writing placed much emphasis on what they saw as its construction on sound theoretical knowledge. Former dean of the Paris Faculté Hecquet, for example, states in his *approbation* that the practice described by Fauchard was built not on imagination or a collection of empirical remedies, but on sound theoretical foundations: 'Ce Livre n'est point un ouvrage d'imagination, ni un ramas de moyens, d'opérations, ou de remédes à essayer pour la guérison des maladies des dents: C'est une méthode tirée de l'étude, & sortie de l'expérience'.[196] Another senior physician, M. Silva, noted that *Le Chirurgien Dentiste* was built on facts: it was 'fondé sur un grand nombre de faits bien observez, dont il a tiré des conséquences très justes & très-utiles'.[197] Similarly, the physician Finot, who had read *Le Chirurgien Dentiste* with pleasure, had found it to be full of highly detailed facts on which knowledge of the diseases and their treatments could be built.

> Il [*Le Chirurgien Dentiste*] contient en effet beaucoup de faits exactemement [*sic*] détaillez, des Réflexions judicieuses sur les maladies des dents & sur les moyens de les guérir. Ces Réflexions fondées sur un travail assidu & tirées d'une expérience confirmée, à laquelle on ne peut rien ajouter, lui ont donné une connoissance parfaite de ces maladies différentes ...[198]

For Finot, therefore, the *chirurgien dentiste* would use his mind, making judgements, 'des Réflexions judicieuses', about the diseases of the teeth and the ways in which they should be treated. For Winslow, Fauchard's writing was built on a fund of knowledge regarding that particular part of surgery which concerned the teeth. He had, 'déja plusieurs années, remarqué dans son Auteur un grand fond de connoissances, d'habileté & d'observations, par rapport à cette partie de la Chirurgie'.[199] Those who had seen Fauchard working would also claim from the evidence of their own eyes that his practice was built on an exact theory, such as the surgeons Sauré and Gramond, who noted of his book that 'On y trouve une exacte théorie & une pratique confirmée par un grand nombre de cures & d'observations, qui sont les fruits d'une longue expérience accompagnée d'heureux succes, dont nous avons été les témoins oculaires en plusieurs occasions.'[200]

Surgeons, however, saw the work of the *dentiste* as forming an important part of the practice of surgery which had hitherto been consigned to obscurity, and dealt with only superficially in surgical texts. Duplessis stated that the diseases of the teeth had long awaited the foundation of a body of *préceptes* and *regles* for their treatment: 'Les maladies des dents, quoique fréquentes & en si grand nombre, faisoient attendre depuis longtems que quelqu'un par ses propres Observations pût donner des préceptes & des regles pour remédier à ces maladies.'[201] Fauchard's book provided such a body of knowledge, which had hitherto been lacking in surgery. For Duplessis, it was 'un Ouvrage aussi utile, aussi nécessaire, & qui manquoit à la Chirurgie'.[202] The surgeon Tartanson who, as we have seen, had enjoyed the benefits afforded by Fauchard's knowledge personally when he had been suffering from a toothache that he himself could not explain, stated that surgery had previously been lacking in a part no less necessary than any other; but that Fauchard's writing had rendered the art complete.

> Il manquoit à la Chirurgie une partie qui cependant ne lui étoit pas moins nécessaire que toutes les autres, qui ont été perfectionnées avec tant de soin. M. Fauchard vient de la donner cette partie, en mettant au jour son Traité sur les dents, que j'ai trouvé contenir les explications les plus claires, les opérations les plus sûres, les remédes

les meilleurs & les Réflexions les plus judicieuses. Par cet excellent
Ouvrage cet Auteur rend notre Art complet ...[203]

The senior surgeons of Paris also recognized in *Le Chirurgien Dentiste*
an essential contribution to the practice of surgery. They had 'reconnu
que cet Ouvrage étoit très-essentiel à la Chirurgie': in his writing,
Fauchard had shown how 'une longue pratique & un grand discernement
lui ont fait recueiller de connoissances sur cette partie de notre Art', and
they could not fail to praise 'l'honneur qu'il fait à sa profession'.[204]

For the surgeon de Vaux however, the knowledge contained within
Fauchard's book would be of principal benefit to the *particular* surgeon
– he who had chosen to practise this part of surgery only. In his
approbation, de Vaux paints a broad picture of surgery: whilst he was
sure *Le Chirurgien Dentiste* would be of use to surgeons 'de toute
espéce', and to those patients who would have need of 'cette Chirurgie',
the century should nevertheless be congratulated for producing *both*
excellent courses in surgery and anatomy (for which the public should
be grateful to 'Chirurgiens célébres') *and* particular surgeons, those
who would devote themselves to one part of surgery only: 'il se trouve
encore des particuliers qui s'étant dévoüez à une seule partie de la
Chirurgie'. It was writing such as Fauchard's which was 'le moyen de
porter un Art si utile à sa plus haute perfection', and to de Vaux its
principal value would lie in instructing the particular surgeon – it would
be 'très-instructif pour ceux qui se proposent de faire leur capital de
cette Chirurgie particuliére'.[205]

Perhaps the greatest implications for the rise of the *dentiste* as particular surgeon, however, may be found in the remarks of two surgeons
of high status who were also teachers by royal appointment. As we have
seen in our analysis of the rise of surgery in Paris, from 1724 the École
de Chirurgie at Saint-Côme would form a surgical focal point with
Mareschal and la Peyronie's securing of royal letters patent, which
would establish and endow five public courses in surgery at the amphitheatre.[206] The five *démonstrateurs royals* who would present these
courses were named by the *premier* surgeons the following year: amongst
their number were César Verdier, 'Chirurgien Juré de Paris, &
Démonstrateur Royal en Anatomie', and Sauveur-François Morand,
'Associé de l'Académie Royale des Sciences, Chirurgien Juré de Paris &
Démonstrateur Royal des opérations'[207] at Saint-Côme. Both men would
publish their approval and endorsement of Fauchard's book three years
later. Toby Gelfand has identified Morand as one of the most popular
teachers of anatomy and surgery in Paris during the 1730s,[208] and it is
of particular significance that Morand, especially, found that *Le
Chirurgien Dentiste* 'paru contenir d'excellentes choses; mais nous ne
prétendons connoître ni juger de la pratique qui s'y trouve'.[209] Morand

was *not familiar* with the practice found in Fauchard's writing: this claimed unfamiliarity with the particular field of operations performed by the *chirurgien dentiste* would imply that this senior demonstrator of operations did *not* consider them to be a part of 'general' surgery. This omission, coming forty-five years after Dionis had devoted a large part of his seventh demonstration to the teeth and their operations, lends powerful support to the argument that the operations for the teeth had ceased to be part of 'general' surgery, and were now the sole province of a particular type of surgeon.

The specialist surgeon as mountebank: the case of 'Le Grand Thomas'

The practice of the *dentiste*, as exemplified by the activities of Fauchard, was not the only way in which the specialist surgeon could exercise his knowledge and experience of the treatment of teeth. The surgeon Jean Thomas had worked in 'les Hôpitaux du Roy', and was 'experimentée sous les yeux de Messieurs Fermelhuys et Lemery, Docteurs-Régents en Medecine de la Faculté de Paris'.[210] Thomas had been received as a *maitre chirurgien* at Saint-Côme: he, too, had chosen to specialize in the treatment of teeth – but he did not do it in the same manner as Pierre Fauchard.

Jean Thomas, or 'Grand Thomas' as he was known, performed in the fairground atmosphere of the Pont-Neuf in the 1720s in a most spectacular manner, which has encouraged recent writers to describe him deprecatingly as a quack or charlatan;[211] yet as we shall see his activities appear to present us with something of an anomaly. Flamboyant and showman-like, his appearance was indeed so dramatic that it could even perhaps be considered to have *caricatured* that of the charlatan or mountebank. This appearance is evident in Sébastien Mercier's colourful description of Thomas in the *Tableau de Paris*, which describes his booming voice and the imposing figure he presented as he stood on his steel chariot, with the badge of the mountebank tooth-drawer, an enormous sabre, hanging from his belt.[212] According to Mercier, toothache seemed to expire at his feet, drawing admiration from the crowd and jealousy from the physicians:

> Il étoit reconnoissable de loin par sa taille gigantesque & l'ampleur de ses habits; monté sur un char d'acier, sa tête élevée & coëffée d'un panache éclatant, figuroit avec la tête royale d'Henri IV;[213] sa voix mâle se faisoit entendre aux deux extrêmités du pont, aux deux bords de la Seine. La confiance publique l'environnoit, & la rage de dents sembloit venir expirer à ses pieds. La foule empressée de ses admirateurs, comme un torrent qui toujours s'écoule & reste toujours égal, ne pouvoit se lasser de le contempler; des mains sans

> cesse élevées imploroient ses remedes, & l'on voyoit fuir le long des
> trottoirs, les médecins consternés & jaloux de ses succès. Enfin,
> pour achever le dernier trait de l'éloge de ce grand homme, il est
> mort sans avoir reconnu la faculté.[214]

Grand Thomas was well known to the people of Paris, and his show-manship was extremely popular. On the birth of the Dauphin in 1729, the city was overflowing with parades, processions and special services of celebration. The Opéra Comique presented a free show at its stage in the *foire* Saint-Laurent, entitled 'L'inpromptu de Pont Neuf',[215] in which Grand Thomas and his assistants played a part. He announced that he would offer his services for free: 'pendant quinze jours consecutifs, j'arracherai *gratis* les dents, les laverai, les nettoyerai et les rendrai blanches comme du Lait'.[216] At the end of this period, he promised a free all-day banquet, which would close with a firework display. The authorities eventually refused to allow the banquet, but instead Grand Thomas travelled in a flamboyant procession to Versailles to pay his respects in person to the royal family (Figure 5.3). The spectacle provided by this procession was recorded by the printer Coignard, who noted in particular the fine head-dress worn by this 'Illustre Opérateur sur les machoires humaines'.[217] Grand Thomas wore a

> Caparasson brodé de Dents humaines avec des Daviers passez en sautoir aux quatre coins de la Housse; l'amplitude de son chef sera couverte et ombragée de fameux Bonnet dont tout le monde est prevenu et qui d'argent d'Orphevrerie pese 6 marcs 7 onces, de la hauteur de 16 pouces sur 7 de diametre, sur le haut duquel est un Cocq les ailes épanouies, le bec ouvert et imitant si bien le naturel qu'il n'y manque que la voix et l'accent, avec une aigrette des plus fournies pour égaler le volume de sa Perruque, et sur son estomac une Égide representant le Soleil dans tout son éclat. Ce Heros Dentiste sera precedé d'un Drapeau émaillé de goutes de sang avec des dents en étoiles; ensuite viendra un Tambourg de Basque avec une Trompette marine ...[218]

How should we read this complicated picture of a master surgeon dressed as a mountebank, which seems so at odds with itself? If we view the activities of Grand Thomas in an open light, looking *through* his extravagant stage appearance, we shall see an image that reveals a link between the *science* of the surgeon and the lucrative theatrical performance of the successful mountebank. He was *not* itinerant: in addition to pulling the crowds, and their teeth, at his stall on the Pont-Neuf, he would also attend patients at his *hôtel* in the Rue Tournon.[219] Grand Thomas, unlike many performers of similar appearance, possessed the knowledge and the experience required to perform the operations for the teeth. The anonymous composer of the *Apothéose du Docteur Gros Thomas*, published in the *Chansonnier Française*

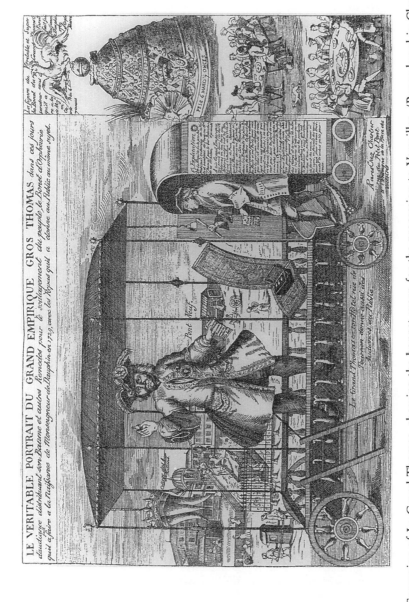

5.3 Engraving of Le Grand Thomas, showing the bonnet worn for the procession to Versailles. (Reproduced in Chevalier, 'Un charlatan du XVIIIᵉ siècle', 1880.)

three years after his death in 1757, appears to have made use of this ability:

> Sa main surpassoit son conseil,
> J'en atteste l'expérience,
> Et le titre de Sans-Pareil
> Lui fut acquis par sa science.
> Dentistes, qui suivez ses pas,
> Bientôt vous n'en douterez pas.
> Lisez sa mémorable histoire:
> Elle annonce pour évident
> Qu'il arrachoit une mâchoire
> Plus vite que vous une dent.[220]

Treating teeth was a part of the practice of the surgeon – and Thomas was received as a master surgeon at Saint-Côme. As we have seen, a number of surgeons were choosing to specialize in the treatment of the teeth, creating and developing as they did so a body of knowledge built around the structure, diseases and operations of those parts. Grand Thomas also chose to specialize in that part of surgery which involved treating the teeth; however, unlike his direct contemporary Pierre Fauchard, rather than contribute to any body of theoretical knowledge he chose instead to make his mark in a different way, in the provision of a kind of robust and enthusiastic treatment which the *dentiste* did not offer.[221] Jean Thomas would use his pitch on the Pont-Neuf to make money, for which a parody of the style and appearance of the mountebank could be turned to his great advantage. He would eventually retire in 1754 to his house in the quai d'Orléans, where he would die three years later leaving 55 000 *livres* in cash.[222] Le Grand Thomas, the surgeon, could indeed remove teeth quickly and effectively – and in the process he out-mountebanked the mountebanks.

Notes

1. I shall use the term 'particular' surgeon to indicate a surgeon who *chooses* to practise one particular part of surgery only. This is intended to form a distinction from the *expert*, who was only officially *entitled* to practise a part (or parts) of surgery.
2. This title would now be used extensively on the title pages of books written about the teeth. The first to do so was Pierre Fauchard (*chirurgien dentiste*), in his book of 1728. He would be followed by Geraudly (*chirurgien dentiste*, 1737); Bunon (*chirurgien dentiste*, 1741 and 1746); Mouton (*chirurgien dentiste*, 1746); Lécluse (*chirurgien dentiste*, 1754); Jourdain (*chirurgien*, then *dentiste*, 1757); Bourdet (*dentiste*, 1757, 1764 and 1771); Beaupréau (*chirurgien dentiste*, 1764) and so on.
3. Pierre Fauchard, *Le Chirurgien Dentiste, ou Traité des Dents, ou l'on*

enseigne les moyens de les entretenir propres & saines, de les embellir,
d'en réparer la perte & de remédier à leurs maladies, à celles des Gencives
& aux accidens qui peuvent survenir aux autres parties voisines des
Dents. Mariette, Paris, 1728. For most of what follows, unless indicated
otherwise I shall refer to the second edition of 1746. Where appropriate
however, I shall refer to the first edition.

4. According to Prinz, for example, it was an 'epoch-making publication
    on the science and the art of dentistry' (H. Prinz, 'Pierre Fauchard and
    His Works', *Dental Cosmos,* LXV, 1923, p. 830). Guerini describes
    Fauchard as 'the founder of modern scientific dentistry' (V. Guerini, *A*
    History of Dentistry from the Most Ancient Times until the End of the
    Eighteenth Century, Lea and Febiger, Philadelphia, 1909, p. 259. See
    also Malvin Ring, *Dentistry: An illustrated History*, Abrams, New York,
    1985, p. 8: Lindsay, *The Surgeon Dentist* (English translation), 1946,
    translator's introduction and many others. In her introduction, Lindsay
    makes the odd remark that 'Very little is known of his [Fauchard's] life
    except what may be gleaned from this book.'
5. Many writers on the history of dentistry have analysed particular as-
    pects of Fauchard's life in detail. Amongst the most prominent
    publications which do so are Campbell, *Dentistry Then and Now* (pri-
    vate publication, Glasgow, 1963), Lindsay, *A Short History of Dentistry*
    (Bale, Sons and Danielsson, London, 1933) and Ring, *Dentistry: An*
    illustrated history. In 1923 an issue of *The Dental Cosmos* (LXV (8),
    1923) was produced to celebrate Fauchard, which contains articles by
    Prinz ('Pierre Fauchard and his works', 827–30), Viau ('The Life of
    Pierre Fauchard (1678–1761)', 797–808) and Walsh ('Fauchard, the
    Father of Modern Dentistry', 809–23), all of which contain much per-
    sonal detail. Perhaps the most impressive collection of biographical
    material concerning Fauchard, and even his relatives, may be found in
    André Besombes's and Georges Dagen's book *Pierre Fauchard, Père de*
    l'Art Dentaire Moderne (1678–1761) et ses contemporains (Société du
    publications médicales et dentaires, Paris, 1961).
6. Fauchard, *Le Chirurgien Dentiste*, vol. I, p. xiv.
7. 'Comme je n'ai composé ce Livre qu'après avoir recueilli beaucoup de
    connoissances puisées dans la bonne Chirurgie, & confirmées par différens
    succès'. Fauchard, *Le Chirurgien Dentiste*, vol. I, p. xxiii.
8. Fauchard, *Le Chirurgien Dentiste*, first edition (1728), vol. I, preface
    (not paginated).
9. Fauchard, *Le Chirurgien Dentiste*, vol. II, p. 354.
10. Barbier, *Chronique de le Régence et du regne de Louis XV (1718–1763),*
    ou Journal de Barbier, Charpentier, Paris, 1857. In the entry for October
    1740 Barbier relates the unfortunate tale of a *chirurgien dentiste* by the
    name of Gaulard, who 'était garçon ou associé de Fauchard, qui est le
    premier homme de Paris pour dents, demeurant rue de la Comédie, dans
    la même maison où il a été assassiné une femme par le sieur Mauriat'.
    Gaulard, whom Barbier estimated to earn 3–4000 *livres* in a year, called
    at a young lady's house to escort her to dinner. Whilst dining, he
    remembered that he must spend an hour 'chez une femme de qualité
    pour les dents', whereupon he made his excuses, returned to his com-
    panion's house and stole her valuables before returning to finish his
    dinner. Barbier relates that on Gaulard's subsequent arrest even Fauchard,

who had 'beaucoup d'amis dans les gens de considération', could not influence the court and the unfortunate *chirurgien dentiste* was duly hanged for his crime. Fauchard's influence with his friends, always assuming he chose to attempt to use it, clearly had its limitations.

11. See, for example, Fauchard, *Le Chirurgien Dentiste*, vol. I, pp. 285, 291 and 332; see also a discussion on tooth-powders (vol. I, p. 79) and comments on various designs of artificial teeth (vol. II, p. 219), amongst many other instances.

12. See the map of Paris, 'après le plan de La Caille, dressé en 1714', reproduced in Franklin, *La vie privée d'autrefois ... Variétés chirurgicales* (vol. 14), p. 211.

13. G. Viau, 'The Life of Pierre Fauchard', *The Dental Cosmos*, LXV (8), 1923, 797–808, 805.

14. This notice of interment is reproduced in Besombes and Dagen, *Pierre Fauchard*, p. 6.

15. 'Docteur en Médecine de la Faculté de Paris, de l'Académie Royale des Sciences, & Professeur en Botanique au Jardin Royal des Plantes.' Fauchard, *Le Chirurgien Dentiste*, vol. I, note to p. 441. Fauchard worked with de Jussieu on more than one occasion; see, for an example, *Le Chirurgien Dentiste*, vol. I, p. 453.

16. 'Docteur-Régent en la Faculté de Médecine de Paris, de l'Académie Royale des Sciences, Professeur en Anatomie & en Chirurgie au Jardin Royal, &c.' Fauchard, vol. II, 1st approbation. Fauchard would work alongside Winslow in 1725, on a case which would also require the services of M. Saint-Yves. This, as we shall see, is of further significance: Fauchard refers to Saint-Yves as 'Chirurgien Oculiste à Paris'. Fauchard, *Le Chirurgien Dentiste*, vol. I, p. 451.

17. Ibid., p. 310.

18. I shall use the French form, *fait* or *faits*, to indicate that I am referring to phenomena that Fauchard described as facts.

19. This classification of the diseases of the teeth is taken from Fauchard, *Le Chirurgien Dentiste*, vol. I, p. 106 ff.

20. Ibid., p. 117.

21. Ibid., p. 118.

22. Ibid., p. 185.

23. And would, in the process, present a better target than the tooth-drawer for the mountebank drug-seller's parodic performance.

24. Fauchard, *Le Chirurgien Dentiste*, vol. I, pp. xii–xiii.

25. Ibid., chapter XII.

26. Ibid., p. 183.

27. Ibid., p. 184.

28. Ibid.

29. Ibid.

30. Ibid.

31. Ibid.

32. Ibid.

33. Ibid., p. 154.

34. Ibid., p. 136.

35. Ibid., p. 135.

36. Ibid., p. 136.

37. Ibid.

38. Ibid., p. 137.
39. Ibid.
40. 'Ces explications qui paroissent très-vraisemblables'. Ibid., p. 138.
41. Ibid.
42. *Ébranler*: 'to shake, rattle or weaken' (*Grand Dictionnaire*, Larousse, Paris, 1993). All translations given in the following section will be my own: where necessary, I have included the term used by Fauchard in the original French. Page references are to Fauchard, *Le Chirurgien Dentiste*, 1746, second edn.
43. Ibid., vol. I, p. 143.
44. M. de la Hire, 'Mathématicien & membre de l'Académie Royale des Sciences... [writing in the] Mémoires de l'Academie de 1699'. Ibid., pp. 24–5.
45. M. de Manteville, Chirurgien-Juré à Paris. Ibid., p. 152.
46. Ibid., p. 144.
47. Ibid., pp. 144–5.
48. Ibid., p. 119.
49. The following is taken from ibid., pp. 119 ff.
50. Ibid., p. 121. 'Virus', in early eighteenth-century England, was applied to 'a morbid principle or poisonous substance produced in the body as the result of some disease' (*OED* entry).
51. Fauchard, *Le Chirurgien Dentiste*, vol. I, p. 154.
52. Ibid.
53. Ibid., p. 155. I take Fauchard to use *sensibilité* here to mean the ability to perceive sensation: 'Disposition des sens à recevoir les impressions des objets ... La *sensibilité* du parties nerveuses.' Entry for *sensibilité*, Furetière, *Dictionnaire Universel, contenant géneralement tous les mots françois, tant vieux que modernes, et les termes des sciences et des arts*, The Hague, 1727.
54. Fauchard, *Le Chirurgien Dentiste*, vol. I, p. 155.
55. Literally, 'gnawing humour'. Ibid.
56. Ibid.
57. Ibid., p. 157; see also Chapter One, pp. 25–6.
58. Ibid., p. 158.
59. Ibid.
60. Dionis, *Traité* [*sic*] *d'opérations*, vol. I, p. 509, cited in ibid., p. 161.
61. Ibid., p. 162.
62. Ibid., 161.
63. Ibid., pp. 162–3.
64. Ibid., pp. 163–4.
65. Ibid., p. 169.
66. Literally, a 'squarer' for cutting. Ibid., p. 170.
67. 'Alors on se servira d'un foret convenable, monté sur son chevalet, qu'on teindra de la main gauche; & avec son archet tenu de la main droite'. Ibid., p. 171.
68. Fauchard, *Le Chirurgien Dentiste*, vol. II, p. 54.
69. Ibid., pp. 54–6.
70. Ibid., p. 57.
71. Ibid., p. 282.
72. Ibid., p. 283.
73. The following is taken from ibid., pp. 415 ff.

74. Ibid., p. 415.
75. Ibid., p. 417.
76. Ibid., p. 418.
77. Poultices.
78. Fauchard, *Le Chirurgien Dentiste*, vol. I, p. 419.
79. Ibid., p. 420.
80. See p. 104.
81. Fauchard, *Le Chirurgien Dentiste*, vol. I, p. 376.
82. Ibid., p. 378.
83. Ibid.
84. Ibid., p. 379.
85. Ibid.
86. Ibid., p. 385.
87. Ibid., p. 386.
88. 'Capitaine dans le second Bataillon de Bourbonnois, & à présent Lieu-tenant de Roi à Bayonne'. Ibid., p. 383.
89. Ibid., p. 119: also see this chapter, p. 106.
90. Henri Baudean, Marquis de Parabére, who was 'Brigadier des Armées du Roi, Chef d'une Brigade du Regiment Royal des Carabiniers'. F. A. A. de la Chesnaye-Dubois, *Dictionnaire de la Noblesse de France*, 1770–78 (12 vols).
91. Fauchard, *Le Chirurgien Dentiste*, vol. I, p. 467.
92. Ibid.
93. 'Après avoir mûrement réfléchi sur la singularité de cette maladie, je jugeai, que quoique cette carie fût peu apparente, elle pouvoit par quelques petits conduits s'être communiquée dans la cavité du corps de la dent, par où l'air s'étant introduit, avoit pénétré les parties membraneuses & nerveuses renfermées dans cette cavité, qu'il avoit irritées & enflammées en altérant les liqueurs qui y circulent; de maniére qu'il s'y étoit formé un abcès.' Ibid., pp. 468–9.
94. 'Comme je l'avois prévû'. Ibid., p. 469.
95. Ibid.
96. 'Outside the arch', that is, irregularly. Ibid., p. 362.
97. Ibid., p. 363.
98. Ibid.
99. Ibid., p. 364.
100. Ibid., pp. 364–5.
101. Ibid., p. 403.
102. Ibid., p. 404.
103. Ibid., p. 400.
104. See ibid., pp. 397 ff.
105. Ibid., p. 406.
106. Ibid.
107. Ibid., pp. 320–21.
108. Ibid., p. 323.
109. Ibid.
110. Ibid., p. 324.
111. Ibid., p. 347.
112. Ibid., p. 348.
113. Ibid., pp. 348–9.
114. Ibid., p. 299.

THE MAKING OF THE *DENTISTE* TECHNICALLY   151

Ibid., pp. 301–2.
116. Ibid., p. 450.
117. Ibid., p. 440.
118. A softening poultice. Ibid.
119. Ibid., p. 441.
120. 'Docteur en Médecine de la Faculté de Paris, de l'Académie Royale des Sciences, & Professeur en Botanique au Jardin Royal des Plantes'. Ibid.
121. Ibid., p. 442.
122. Ibid., pp. 442–3.
123. Ibid., p. 443.
124. Ibid.
125. Ibid., p. 444.
126. Ibid.
127. Ibid.
128. Ibid., p. 446.
129. Ibid., p. 447. The condyle is the part of the lower jaw which moves on the base of the skull, forming the jaw joint; the glenoid fossa is the surface which it contacts, immediately in front of the ear.
130. A large section of the vertical part of the jaw-bone, the entire moving part of the jaw joint, a piece from the middle of the angle of the jaw, below the ear and another considerable part of the same angle. Such injuries would represent the loss of most of the jaw-bone on that side. Fauchard, *Le Chirurgien Dentiste*, vol. I, p. 448.
131. Ibid.
132. The base of the patient's skull was exposed, along with the zygoma and the styloid process, all the way up to the external auditory meatus. Probing further revealed the temporal bone (forming the base of the side of the skull) to be so carious as to allow the probe to travel through it, thereby pressing on the membrane covering the brain. The probe had passed beneath the zygomatic arch, which forms the cheek-bone, and penetrated the external orbital fissure, just below the back of the eye. Ibid., pp. 448–9.
133. Ibid., p. 450.
134. Ibid.
135. These were very important men: in particular Winslow who, as we have seen, was 'Docteur-Régent en la Faculté de Médecine de Paris, de l'Académie Royale des Sciences, Professeur en Anatomie & en Chirurgie au Jardin Royal', and Verdier was 'Chirurgien-Juré de Paris, & Démonstrateur Royal en Anatomie' (these descriptions are given in the approbations at the end of *Le Chirurgien Dentiste*, vol. II).
136. Fauchard, *Le Chirurgien Dentiste*, vol. I, note to p. 451.
137. Ibid., p. 290.
138. Ibid., p. 291.
139. Ibid.
140. Ibid.
141. Ibid., p. 293.
142. Ibid.
143. Ibid., p. 294.
144. Ibid., p. 295.
145. Dionis, *Cours d'opérations*, p. 608.
146. 'Il faut convenir que ces Messieurs qui n'ont pour objet de leur travail

que ces seuls parties peuvent exceller dans cet art plûtôt que le Chirurgien'. Ibid., pp. 416–17.

147. Fauchard, *Le Chirurgien Dentiste*, vol. I, p. 424.
148. Ibid.
149. Ibid..
150. Ibid., p. 426.
151. Ibid.
152. Ibid., p. 392.
153. Ibid., p. 393.
154. 'Chirurgien-Juré à Paris, & ancien Prévôt de sa Compagnie'. Ibid., note to p. 393.
155. It was by no means unknown for consultations to be made by letter in early eighteenth-century France. For a full discussion of this phenomenon, see Laurence Brockliss, 'Consultation by Letter in Early Eighteenth-Century Paris: The Medical Practice of Etienne-François Geoffroy', in Ann La Berge and Mordechai Feingold (eds), *French medical culture in the nineteenth century*, Rodopi, Amsterdam, 1994, pp. 79–117.
156. Fauchard, *Le Chirurgien Dentiste*, vol. I, p. 470.
157. Ibid., p. 471.
158. A graver.
159. Fauchard, *Le Chirurgien Dentiste*, vol. I, p. 472. Larreyre would later become surgeon to the Duc de Condé.
160. Ibid.
161. Ibid.
162. Ibid., p. 456.
163. Ibid.
164. Ibid., p. 457.
165. Ibid., p. 458.
166. Ibid., p. 459.
167. Ibid., p. 460.
168. Ibid., pp. 460–61.
169. This patient was a high-ranking nobleman of a 'Maison aussi illustre qu'ancienne': François-Victor de Corneillan, Vicomte de Corneillan, Siegneur de Saint-Germain, Orlhonac, la Bastide and Capdenac. He had been a *page du roi*, and a *mousquetaire de la première Compagnie*. He had also been appointed to the office of 'Gentilhomme à la Venerie du Roi'. Chesnaye-Dubois, *Dictionnaire de la Noblesse de France*.
170. Fauchard, *Le Chirurgien Dentiste*, vol. I, p. 309.
171. Ibid., p. 311.
172. Ibid.
173. As we shall see in Chapter Six, when we examine the activities of the king's *dentiste*.
174. Yves Laissus, 'Le Jardin du Roi', in René Taton (ed.), *Enseignement et diffusion des sciences en France au XVIIIᵉ siècle*, Hermann, Paris, 1964, pp. 287–341, 329.
175. Toby Gelfand, *Professionalizing modern medicine: Paris surgeons and medical science and institutions in the 18th century*, Greenwood, Westport, 1980, p. 60.
176. Ibid., p. 61.
177. Charles-Philippe d'Albert de Luynes, *Mémoires sur la cour de Louis XV*,

Paris, 1860–65, 6, p. 60 (1 September 1744), cited in Gelfand, *Professionalizing modern medicine*, p. 61.

178. Fauchard, *Le Chirurgien Dentiste*, vol. I, note to p. 310.
179. Ibid., p. 310.
180. Ibid.
181. Ibid., p. 311.
182. Ibid.
183. Fauchard, *Le Chirurgien Dentiste*, vol. II, p. 200.
184. Ibid.
185. Ibid.
186. Ibid., pp. 200–201.
187. Ibid., p. 201.
188. 'Monsieur Laudumiey, Chirurgien Dentiste de Sa Majesté Catholique Philippe V. Roi d'Espagne'. Ibid., *approbations* (not paginated).
189. Ibid., p. 201.
190. At the time Fauchard published his book, Winslow was 'Docteur-Régent en la Faculté de Médecine de Paris, de l'Académie Royale des Sciences, Professeur en Anatomie & en Chirurgie au Jardin Royal': de Jussieu was 'Docteur-Régent en la Faculté de Médecine de Paris, Professeur en Botanique au Jardin du Roi, de l'Académie Royale des Sciences, des Sociétez Royales de Londres & de Berlin' (ibid., *approbations*). De Jussieu's full title at the Jardin Royal was 'démonstrateur de l'interieur des plantes sous le titre de professeur en botanique', and from 1722 he was joined at the Jardin by his younger brother Bernard who was appointed 'sous démonstrateur de l'extérieur des plantes'. Laissus, 'Le Jardin du Roi', pp. 325 and 332.
191. See chapter XXXVI of vol. I, in which Fauchard records the cases of two patients, both sent to him by Helvetius: the second of these was the well-known Imprimeur & Marchand Libraire of Paris, M. le Mercier. It was in 1710 that Hecquet sent a lady who was suffering with a great pain in her lower incisors to see Fauchard. Fauchard, *Le Chirurgien Dentiste*, vol. I, p. 302.
192. *Encyclopédie, ou Dictionnaire Raisonné des sciences, des arts et des métiers, par une societé de gens de lettres*, compiled by Diderot et d'Alembert, Paris, 1757, entry under *approbation*.
193. *Encyclopédie*, entry under *censeur*. In this case, the *chancelier* was the 'Chevalier le Sieur Daguesseau, Chancelier de France'. Fauchard, *Le Chirurgien Dentiste, privilege du roy.*
194. Robert Darnton and Daniel Roche, in their study of the press in France before 1800, have noted that 'the effectiveness of the state's system of control was established by 1699, when the abbé Bignon became director of the book trade. Under the supervision of the chancellor or the keeper of the seals, the Office of the Book Trade entrusted to its censors the examination of all works destined for legal publication; to be legal, all books had to be registered. After examination, they received either "privileges" (the exclusive rights of publication and sale) or "tacit permissions" (authorization given to works the state could not sanction openly yet did not want to condemn).' Darnton and Roche (eds), *Revolution in print: the press in France, 1775–1800*, University of California Press, Berkeley, 1989, pp. 6–7.
195. Winslow, in his glowing *approbation*, remarks that he has read *Le*

Chirurgien Dentiste 'par ordre de Monseigneur le Chancelier' and that he has found it 'ne rien contenir qui en doive empêcher l'impression'. Fauchard, *Le Chirurgien Dentiste*, vol. II, *approbations*.

196. *Approbation* of M. Hecquet, 'Docteur-Régent en la Faculté de Médecine de Paris, & ancien Doyen de ladite Faculté': ibid. Laurence Brockliss has shown that until the mid-1720s at least, Hecquet believed a true system to be based on facts, built in their turn on *réflexions, observations* and on *conséquences tirées de la nature*. For him, it was these *observations* which would provide the basis for the principles of knowledge. For an analysis of Hecquet's life, see Laurence Brockliss, 'The medico-religious universe of an early eighteenth-century Parisian doctor: the case of Philippe Hecquet', in Roger French and Andrew Wear (eds), *The medical revolution of the seventeenth century*, CUP, Cambridge, 1989, pp. 191–221.

197. *Approbation* of M. Silva, 'Docteur-Régent en la Faculté de Médecine dans l'Université de Paris, Médecin de son Altesse Sérénissime Monseigneur le Duc, & Médecin-Consultant du Roi': Fauchard, *Le Chirurgien Dentiste*, vol. II.

198. *Approbation* of M. Finot, 'Docteur-Régent en la Faculté de Médecine de Paris, & Médecin de leurs Altesses Sérénissimes Monseigneur le Prince de Conti & Mesdames les Princesses de Conti': ibid.

199. *Approbation* of M. Winslow, 'Docteur-Régent en la Faculté de Médecine de Paris, de l'Académie Royale des Sciences, Professeur en Anatomie & en Chirurgie au Jardin Royal': ibid.

200. *Approbation* of MM. Sauré and Gramond, 'Chirurgiens Jurez à Paris': ibid.

201. *Approbation* of M. Duplessis, 'Chirurgien Juré à Paris': ibid.

202. *Approbation* of M. Duplessis, 'Chirurgien Juré à Paris': ibid.

203. *Approbation* of M. Tartanson, 'Chirurgien-Juré de Paris, & ancien Prevôt de sa Compagnie': ibid.

204. *Approbation* of MM. Bourgeois, Mouton, Chauvet, Routhonnet, Mothereau and Bertrand: 'Lieutenant du premier Chirurgien du Roi, Prévôts & Gardes & Receveur en charge'. Ibid.

205. *Approbation* of M. de Vaux, 'Chirurgien-Juré à Paris, & ancien Prévôt de sa Compagnie': ibid.

206. See Chapter Four, p. 66.

207. Verdier's and Morand's titles are taken from the *approbations* in Fauchard, *Le Chirurgien Dentiste*, vol. II.

208. Toby Gelfand, 'The "Paris Manner" of dissection: student anatomical dissection in early eighteenth-century Paris', *Bulletin of the History of Medicine*, **XLVI** (2), 1972, 99–130, 119.

209. *Approbation* of M. Verdier, 'Chirurgien Juré de Paris, & Démonstrateur Royal en Anatomie', and M. Morand, 'Associé de l'Académie Royale des Sciences, Chirurgien Juré de Paris & Démonstrateur Royal des opérations': Fauchard, *Le Chirurgien Dentiste*, vol. II.

210. Avis Salutaire au Public, Par Brevet et Permission de M. Dodart, Premier Medecin du Roy, reproduced in A. Chevalier, 'Un charlatan du XVIIIᵉ siècle: Le Grand Thomas', in *Mémoires de la Société de l'Histoire de Paris et de L'Ile-de-France*, VII, 1880, Champion, Paris, 1881, pp. 61–78, 64–5.

211. See, for example, Ring, *Dentistry,* p. 157. Ring states that 'It is difficult

to imagine that there were many quacks in Europe with such panache as Thomas, but certain it is that many thousands of equally unqualified specialists had no difficulty in attracting customers.'

212. For the implications of the sword, see Chapter One: Grand Thomas, however, removed teeth with the forceps. See *L'ordre et la marche de l'entrée du Grand Thomas*, in Chevalier, 'Un charlatan du XVIIIe siècle', p. 70.

213. Grand Thomas set up his stall directly facing the equestrian statue of Henri IV which was in the middle of the bridge – hence the resemblance could easily be spotted.

214. Sébastien Mercier, *Tableau de Paris*, Amsterdam, 1782, vol. I, p. 161.

215. Chevalier, 'Un charlatan du XVIIIe siècle', p. 64.

216. *Harangue du Grand Thomas, Opérateur pour les Dents*, Coignard, Paris, 1729. Reproduced in Chevalier, 'Un charlatan du XVIIIe siècle', p. 66.

217. *L'ordre et la marche de l'entrée du Grand Thomas en habit de Cérémonie*, L. Coignard, Paris, 1729. Reproduced in Chevalier, 'Un charlatan du XVIIIe siècle', pp. 69–70.

218. Ibid., p. 70.

219. See the inscription below the cart in Figure 5.3.

220. *Apothéose du Docteur Gros Thomas* (*Air*: Un jour le malheureux Lysandre), verse 9, in Chevalier, 'Un charlatan du XVIIIe siècle', p. 76.

221. Grand Thomas could certainly be aggressive in his methods. He would operate with his patients kneeling before him, and it was said that on at least three occasions he would lift them clear of the ground with his forceps as he removed their teeth. J. B. Gouriet, *Personnages célèbres dans les rues de Paris*, Lerouge, Paris, 1811; quoted in Chevalier, 'Un charlatan du XVIIIe siècle', p. 62.

222. Franklin, *Variétés chirurgicales*, p. 163.

CHAPTER SIX

The Making of the *Dentiste* Socially: Appearance, Ennoblement and the Court

In the previous chapter, Fauchard's writings in *Le Chirurgien Dentiste* were used to view the activities of the new group of specialist surgeons who appeared around the start of the eighteenth century in Paris, taking the descriptive and celebratory title of *chirurgien dentiste*. This reading of Fauchard illustrated the way in which the practice of the *dentiste* was built using both hand and mind – that is, not only on the acquisition of practical skill and manual experience, but also on the creation and extension of a body of theoretical knowledge, coupled to experience gained in how and when to apply that knowledge. We have seen how the development of this *science* was considered by some surgeons to have rendered the whole art of surgery complete: an art so wide-ranging that the *chirurgien dentiste*, practising a part of it only, could be considered as a particular surgeon in his own right and could therefore gain acceptance by those occupying the very highest levels of the French surgical hierarchy.

This intimate analysis of Fauchard's work has been highly technical in nature, an approach which, at first sight, would perhaps appear unavoidable given the nature of the material contained within his writing; but looking at it from this perspective alone will leave us with a picture which is at best incomplete, and at worst dangerously unbalanced. While it will, to some extent, help to reveal the standing of the *dentiste* amongst other contemporary practitioners, we can go further in our aim to reveal how he would be viewed by those he treated. In order to do so, we shall need to ask how the *science* of the *dentiste* was applied to the mouths of eighteenth-century France, and what those mouths asked of it: in other words, we should place this *science* within its social context. As noted in the Introduction, it is not the intention of this book to tell either a purely technical or a purely social story of the history of dentistry. Rather, by taking advantage of the narrow focus provided by the practice of the *dentiste*, it will prove possible to examine both technical *and* social stories and explore their relationship more fully. In this way, the broader picture may become clearer; and by taking a balanced view of both technical and social histories in this way, we shall see that just as *science* (theoretical knowledge as the basis for technical innovation) did not drive fashion (as social strength), so fashion did not drive *science*. Each would act in support of the other – and neither would be able to act alone. In order to achieve this aim and to establish this balance, in this chapter I therefore intend to expose the social element of the equation to our view more clearly: first by analysing the social importance of the appearance of the teeth, and later by examining the implications of the king's ennoblement of the royal *dentiste* at the end of our period, around the middle of the eighteenth century.

So far, in our examination of the practice of the *dentiste* as viewed through Fauchard's *observations* in *Le Chirurgien Dentiste*, we have seen that it was, to a great extent, constructed on the pain caused by such phenomena as carious teeth and swollen faces, accompanied by fluxions, putrefaction and bleeding gums. But such suffering did not form the only foundations upon which the *dentiste* could build. If we examine some of the consultations and operations described, looking beyond the fine technical detail, we shall uncover a completely different type of relationship altogether – we shall see that the *dentiste* could also be consulted by people who were *not* in pain. The *science* for the teeth could meet the demand for a different kind of treatment, founded on different principles and with a different aim: a treatment for the *appearance* of the teeth, driven by the social strength of fashion and fuelled by the powerful desire for social emulation. The appearance of the mouth and teeth was of great importance to the fashionable members of Parisian society, and the *dentiste* possessed both the knowledge and the experience essential for the effective improvement of that appearance.

In this chapter, I shall suggest that the *dentiste* could achieve such an improvement in four principal ways: by the cleaning of teeth; the straightening or regulation of unsightly existing ones which had grown out of place; the provision of replacement teeth for those that were missing; or the repair of diseased or damaged teeth, thereby allowing for their retention instead of extraction. These types of operations, both built on and contributing to the development of the *science* for the teeth, were of central importance to the establishment of the *dentiste*'s specialist practice within surgery. As we have seen in Chapter Three, in the one-hundred-year period before the publication of Fauchard's book, surgeons who had written on the operations to be performed on the teeth *by the surgeon,* such as Fabricius, Scultetus and Dionis, had described such procedures as extraction, filling and filing: Dionis had discussed the cleaning of teeth and the provision of replacements in some detail, but other surgical writings had made little more than passing reference to the replacement of missing or damaged teeth. Teeth that had grown out of their natural position had been the subject of

Fabricius's 'the removal of protruding teeth',[1] whilst Scultetus had made no mention at all of irregularities; Dionis had written only of 'the opening or widening [of] the Teeth when they are set too close together'.[2] Fauchard, on the other hand, would fill thirty pages with detailed accounts of the operations which should be employed to straighten irregular teeth, and would use twelve *observations* to describe both the improvement in appearance he had brought about by their use and the way in which this type of operation had been perfected. The consultations thus described were not, as we shall see, due to emergencies, but were called by the patients at a time of their own choosing. Neither were they called only by anxious parents, concerned over their children's appearance – adults, too, wished to alter the personal presentation afforded by the face. We need to ask how this demand was created; but in order to do so, we first need to examine the importance of appearance, and the role played by the teeth in that appearance, in France in the late seventeenth and early eighteenth centuries.

In Chapter Four I touched on the social rise of the surgeon, and noted the part played by technique and theory in this rise in such instances as the curing of the king's fistula; but at the beginning of the eighteenth century the treatment of teeth had as yet enjoyed no such social boost to prestige. In the second part of this chapter, I shall examine the importance that was attached to the procedures of court etiquette and behaviour in maintaining and indicating social standing within the court. An intimate part of this etiquette was the 'contrived opulence and hierarchical significance'[3] of court dress under Louis XIV, which by the final decades of the seventeenth century would present what Christopher Breward has called 'the dual images of increased artifice and visual grandeur'.[4] It was just at this time, as Louis XIV's reign was giving way to the regency and the reign of Louis XV, with the increasing dissemination of this 'artifice and visual grandeur' which would accompany it, that the services offered by the *chirurgien dentiste* would begin to flourish. Our search for the force behind this rise in standing will therefore gain by focusing on the importance of appearance at court, for the non-aristocratic noble and for the upper echelons of the *bourgeoisie*.

Artifice and ornament as necessities for *les gens de considération*

Only a few nobles at the court of Louis XIV, such as the princes of the blood, the dukes of Orléans, Condé and Conti and the legitimized children, could sustain a level of consumption which came near to approaching that of the king. For most of the Parisian nobility, expenditure was high but relatively limited.[5] The historian Daniel Roche has said that

> The dress of the nobility thus takes its place within a luxury economy in which it had considerable impact, on manufacture on the one hand, on commercialization on the other, through the imitation it inspired and through the changes dictated by fashion, of which it was the principal client. This was the beginning of a major trend which ... affected every social milieu, and in which economic determinants and aspirations, the purchasing power of individuals and the ploys of presenting an appearance all played a part ... The conspicuous consumption which permitted social differentiation in the external aspects of life was an instrument of group self-affirmation in the constant competition for rank and prestige. Expenditure on clothes corresponded less to actual economic possibilities than to the desire to be different. But rather than the financiers spurring on the great lords, it was more that, for the bourgeois gentleman, the quest for distinction began by acquiring a noble appearance.[6]

Roche's argument focuses on dress and costume in particular, but it may also be applied to the wearing of wigs and hair powders, to face-painting and to the appearance of the mouth and teeth, each of which played an important role in the never-ending quest to present a prestigious image. However, it is important that the concept of a 'prestigious image' should by no means be confused with the *natural* (in the modern sense): it was the decoration and embellishment of the face and body which would serve as the personal display-case for an individual's rank and status. In the early decades of the eighteenth century this particular 'instrument of self-affirmation in the constant competition for rank and prestige',[7] which had gained significant momentum during the reign of Louis XIV, would further increase in refinement and social importance.

With the political regime of Louis XIV built so strongly on personal allegiances to the body and person of the king, the appearance of the body itself was of central importance, particularly for those struggling to climb the hierarchical ladder – and the focal point of that appearance was the face. The *perruque*, first introduced to the court by Louis XIII to hide his premature baldness at the age of twenty-three and which would endure in popularity throughout the *ancien régime*, provided an ornamental 'frame' for presenting the face to the world and thereby accentuated this focus. Worn by both men and women, wigs were heavily powdered and scented and would be worn in increasingly extravagant styles. However, such use of artifice did not stop at the 'frame' of the face. The ladies of the court in particular would make extensive use of face-painting to ornament their appearance. This practice was deplored by Jean de la Bruyère, writing of the manners of the age in 1688:

> The Women of this Country hasten the decay of their Beauty, by their Artifices to preserve it: they paint their Cheeks, Eye-brows and Shoulders, which they lay open, with their Breasts, Arms and Ears, as if they were afraid to hide those places which they think will please, and never think they shew enough of 'em.[8]

La Bruyère extended his argument against face-painting by claiming that *no* men approved of the practice or found it alluring:

> If 'tis the Ambition of Women only to appear Handsome in their own Eyes, they are in the right without doubt, to take what course they please to Beautify themselves, and in the choice of their Dress and Ornaments, to follow their own caprice and fancy. But if 'tis the Men whom they wou'd charm, if 'tis for them they Wash and Paint; I have told their votes in that case, and I do assure them from all the Men, or from the greatest part, that, the White and Red they use, make 'em look hideous and frightful; ... If Women were form'd by Nature what they make themselves by Art; if they were to lose in a Minute all the freshness of their Complexion, and were to have their Faces as thick with Red and Paint, as they lay 'em on, they wou'd look on themselves as the most Wretched Creatures in the World.[9]

The whiteness of the painted face was brought into sharper relief by the application of scented black patches. In his *Précieuses,* first published in 1683, Molière wrote of ladies who, 'to assure their beauty'd be un-matched, appeared with faces thoroughly patched'.[10] In addition to their decorative function, the wearing of face patches developed into an elaborate means of expression, whose messages were clear: *la passionnée* was indicated by a patch worn in the corner of the eye, *la coquette* one near the lip (signifying flirtation) and *la majestueuse* was worn, majesti-cally, in the middle of the forehead.[11]

By the beginning of the eighteenth century the voluptuous look of the mid-seventeenth had given way to one of painted porcelain, which would endure until the revolution.[12] Men, women and children wore perfumed and powdered wigs, and the court at Versailles would become known as 'la cour parfumée' with Louis XV's court etiquette demand-ing a different scent to be worn on each day.[13] To a 'lady of fashion', make-up was essential, and as the century progressed more and more was applied. Court ladies whitened faces, pencilled eyebrows, blued veins and 'rouged to the limit'.[14] This art form was not lost on its audience – the Turkish ambassador at Versailles, when asked for his opinion of the French ladies, is reputed to have declined to comment on the grounds that he was no judge of painting.[15] Such fashionable use of the brush was not the prerogative of the ladies alone, with men's painting considered extremely stylish, and particularly suitable in the evening.[16] Patches, referred to as *mouches de Massilon* following a strong anti-patch sermon by Massilon, the bishop of Clermont, were generally considered to make a woman look younger[17] and had taken up more complex forms such as stars, lozenges, squares and even the outline of a coach and horses. At the court of Louis XV, Madame Pompadour would place her spots on 'the most alluring parts of her body'[18] for the king to search for. Whether removed if found, or simply prone to falling off, most well-prepared ladies would keep several spots in an ornamented box with a mirror to allow for speedy replacement.

The mirror itself was becoming an important instrument in the armamentarium of the fashionable. At the beginning of the eighteenth century, its popularity was increasing as a feature of the well-to-do French household. To own a mirror was now a sign of belonging to the town, of being one of the *gens de considération*: Saint-Gobain's new manufacturing process had moved it from its affluent 'luxury' status to that of a 'decency', making it available to a large urban market.[19] As Daniel Roche has said, 'The Parisian mirror symbolized the pursuit of superfluity, of a doubling of appearances for people and things. It provided an opportunity to contemplate, and if necessary correct, the outward appearance of the fashionable ... [it was the] instrument of integration into the socialized world of superior practices.'[20]

The impact which the popularity of copious facial ornamentation on the part of the ladies of the French court could wield may be gauged from a letter sent from Paris by Lady Mary Wortley Montague in 1718:

> *A propos* of countenances, I must tell you something of the French ladies; I have seen all the beauties, and such – (I can't help making use of the coarse word) nauseous creatures! so fantastically absurd in their dress! so monstrously unnatural in their paints! Their hair cut short, and curled round their faces, and so loaded with powder, that it makes it look like white wool! and on their cheeks to their chins, unmercifully laid on a shining red japan, that glistens in a most flaming manner, so that they seem to have no resemblance to human faces. I am apt to believe that they took the first hint of their dress, from a fair sheep newly raddled. 'Tis with pleasure I recollect my dear pretty country women; and if I was writing to any body else, I should say, that these grotesque dawbers give me still a higher esteem of the natural charms of dear Lady R——'s auborne hair, and the lively colours of her unsullied complexion.[21]

A few high-ranking women would attempt to flaunt the requirements of fashion at the French court, however. Marie-Thérèse of Spain, first wife of the Dauphin, objected to the practice of face-painting and refused to do so herself; but upon her arrival in France in 1745, the king made it clear that she would be expected to follow the French fashion, which demanded a chalk-white face, black patches, and flaming red cheeks.[22]

The importance of *l'ornement* of the mouth and teeth

We now have a picture of an established court society in which physical *ornement* and artifice played an important role in the struggle for social emulation, via a personal display which could indicate individual standing and status within court hierarchy. We have seen what degree of importance could be attached to the various elements of this appearance; however, identification of the part played by the mouth and teeth in physical *ornement* or artifice is problematic. While many pictures and written descriptions have survived which depict the designs and opulence of costumes and dress, the length and extravagance of wigs and *perruques* and, to a lesser degree, the effects created and achieved by face-painting, almost all of the little evidence which relates to the appearance of the teeth and gums is to be found not in the writings of contemporary commentators but in the writings of those who could change that appearance – notably in books such as Fauchard's *Le Chirurgien Dentiste* and the many others written by those who would follow him. However, evidence may be found on occasion which indicates that great importance could be attached by some to the way in which teeth could contribute towards the appearance and artificial ornament of the face. When Jean de la Bruyère, writing just four years before the date of the first of Fauchard's published *observations*, had wished to assure the ladies that their painting and ornamentation did not attract the gentlemen, he had included in his tirade those who chose to wear false teeth, thereby implying that they were worn for the same purpose:

> that they hate as much to see Women with Paint on their Faces, as with false Teeth in their Mouths, or Balls to plump out their Cheeks, that they solemnly protest against all Art; which indeed does make 'em ugly, and is the last and infallible means that Heav'n takes to reclaim Men from their Love.[23]

La Bruyère noted that men could also consider the shining display of a smiling set of white teeth to be an important element in the ornament of the face, and therefore central to the picture presented in public display.

> *Iphis* at Church sees a new fashion'd Shoe, he looks upon his own, and blushes, and can no longer believe himself drest; he comes to Prayers only to shew himself, but now he hides himself, and you may see him held by the foot in his Chamber all the rest of the day. He has a soft hand, with which he gives you a gentle pat; he is sure

to laugh often, to shew his white Teeth; he sets his mouth in order, and is in a perpetual smile: he looks upon his Legs, he views himself in the Glass, and no body can have so good an opinion of another, as he has of himself.[24]

These various comments and remarks, regarding dress, wigs, painting, facial appearance in general and the appearance of the teeth in particular, were all made *at the same time* that surgeons such as Fauchard were creating the practice of the *dentiste*. Close examination of some of the innovative operations involved in this creation will provide us with a clear impression of the way in which the *science* of the *parfait dentiste* could be employed to the advantage of la Bruyère's *Iphis*, and others like him.

The *chirurgien dentiste* and the appearance of the mouth

We have seen in the previous chapter how the newly established practice of the *dentiste*, as demonstrated in Fauchard's *Le Chirurgien Dentiste*, was imitating that of the 'general' surgeon in the establishment of a *science* upon which that practice could be both based and extended. In this way, Fauchard's writing followed that of surgeons such as Dionis, in the construction of categories of disease and the particular operations for their treatment; but unlike that of the surgeon, the writing in *Le Chirurgien Dentiste* also contains a strong social element in the importance attached to the form of the picture which the teeth will present to others. It is clear that in some instances the *appearance* of the *dentiste*'s work matters greatly, and this is illustrated in the book's full title: *Le Chirurgien Dentiste, ou traité des dents, ou l'on enseigne les moyens de les entretenir propres & saines, de les embellir, d'en reparer la perte & de remédier à leurs maladies* ... .[25] Fauchard's treatise on the teeth, therefore, described the means by which they may be maintained properly and healthily, *embellished* or adorned (the German edition of 1733 translates *embellir* as 'sie schöner zu machen.'[26] – to make more beautiful), their loss made good and their diseases remedied. The appearance of the teeth thus formed a central part of their treatment, and emphasis was placed not only on the maintenance of this appearance but also on the means which might be employed to *improve* it.

For Fauchard, the appearance of the mouth, and the equally important 'appearance' of the voice, was held to be of great value. Before considering any operations to cure disease or repair damage to the teeth, the third chapter of *Le Chirurgien Dentiste* places strong emphasis on 'l'utilité des dents'.[27] While briefly noting their functional importance, Fauchard states that the teeth are *absolutely necessary* for the beauty of the voice and of the face: 'Si les dents sont très-importantes pour la conservation de la santé, elles sont aussi absolument nécessaires pour l'agrément de la voix, la prononciation du discours, l'articulation des mots & l'ornement du visage.'[28] For him, it is the regular arrangement of the teeth which allows the voice to 'charme l'oreille',[29] and it is by 'l'effet de cette harmonie que le discours est plus intelligible & plus gracieux qu'il ne le seroit, si les dents étoient mal arrangées, ou qu'elles laissassent des places vuides'.[30] Care of the teeth should, therefore, be of principal concern to those who spoke in public or who enjoyed making music. In a letter of 1714 Louis XIV's fourth and last wife, Madame de Maintenon, had lamented the signs of her ageing, complaining that she could no longer be understood as her pronunciation had gone with her teeth: 'Je ne vois presque plus, j'entends encore plus mal, on ne m'entend plus, parce que la prononciation s'en est allée avec les dents.'[31] When Fauchard discussed techniques for transplanting teeth from one mouth to another, he noted that such an operation was usually requested for the resulting improvement in clarity of speech as well as for a better appearance, and hence the most commonly replaced teeth were 'les incives, les canines & les petites molaires; parce que ce sont celles qui servent le plus à la prononciation & à l'ornement de la bouche'.[32]

The appearance of the lips and cheeks was also governed by the teeth within, and the loss of a tooth, particularly for members of the 'beau séxe',[33] could be a disaster:

> Elles ne sçauroient ouvrir la bouche, dire une parole, ou faire le moindre soûris, sans montrer des défauts qui leur reprochent la négligence qu'elles ont euës à remédier aux affections contre nature, qui sont arrivées à ces parties.[34]

The gums, too, had an important part to play in the presentation of the face. While their primary role was, of necessity, a supporting one, their shape and colour could nevertheless contribute to a gracious appearance:

> Elles contribuent aussi à l'ornement de la bouche, quand elles sont bien configurées & découpées en forme de demi croissant. Lorsqu'elles se manifestent à l'occasion du ris, elles étalent un rouge vermeil, qui reléve l'éclat de la blancheur des dents, & qui est réciproquement relevé par cette même blancheur: Cette opposition de couleur, avec l'ordre & la régularité des dents, & du bord des gencives, offre à la vûë un objet des plus gracieux.[35]

For Fauchard, the *dentiste* clearly had an important role to play in the public presentation of a gracious appearance, in the maintenance and repair of the all-important *ornement de la bouche*.

Operations performed by the *chirurgien dentiste* to improve *l'ornement de la bouche*

What could the practice of the *dentiste* bring to the repair and improvement of this *ornement*? I have already identified four principal types of operation which could improve or restore the look of a patient's mouth: the cleaning of unsightly scale and staining; the straightening of irregular teeth; the provision of replacement teeth for those that were missing or broken; and the repair, and therefore the retention, of damaged or diseased natural teeth. In the performance of this last group of operations, examined in some detail in the previous chapter, it is apparent that the importance of preserving the teeth for appearance's sake was, on occasion, the patient's prime concern. For example, the daughter of M. Tribuot, whose suffering with an extremely painful carious tooth we have already followed, had nevertheless been keen *not* to have it extracted because of 'la difformité qu'auroit causé la perte de cette dent'.[36] We have also seen that Mlle de la Roche had kept her painful *petite dent molaire*, wary of 'la difformité que son extraction auroit faite à sa bouche'.[37] Both women had pleaded with the *dentiste* to retain their teeth *for this reason*; and his theoretical knowledge and experience had allowed them to do so.

The cleaning of teeth, both by the provision of powders designed to polish them and particularly by the act of scraping them with a metal instrument, was an established part of the surgeon's repertoire. However, in the 1670s Pierre Dionis had remarked that such cleaning should no longer be considered the province of the 'general' surgeon:

> 'Tis so common to clean the Teeth, that it seems not to deserve the particular Application of a Chirurgeon: 'Tis true indeed, every Body usually after eating picks their Teeth with the Tooth-picks, or the Quills, common cleanliness obliging them not to fail, because there remains betwixt the Teeth some particles of the Meats, which, putrifying there, occasion a stinking Breath. We should also wash our Mouth every Morning, and with one of the small Spunges rub the Teeth, to clear off the Foulness which gathers on them, and preserve them in their natural Whiteness: But how careful soever we are, near the Gums there yet grow thin Crusts which render the Teeth yellow, and within-side there grow certain Shells so hard, that they require strong Instruments to disengage them from the Teeth: Wherefore those who are curious of their Mouth, from time to time have Recourse to those whose daily Practice 'tis to clean Teeth.[38]

Nevertheless, Dionis provided a full description of the instruments which should be used, along with a series of practical rules indicating how they should be employed and how both patient and operator should be positioned for the successful performance of this operation. Twenty years later, Fauchard's writing places the cleaning of teeth firmly within the province of the specialist surgeon for the teeth. He notes that while many judge this operation to be dangerous, accompanied by the risk of damaged enamel and broken teeth, there will be nothing to fear if its performance is placed 'entre les mains d'un habile Dentiste'.[39] To avoid problems, it should be performed frequently: he suggests that those who care for the health of their teeth should 'faire visiter une ou deux fois tous les ans par un Dentiste expérimenté'.[40] His book contains a long and finely detailed chapter describing the instruments which should be used for this cleaning, together with an equally detailed description of the manner in which the operation should be performed.

It is clear from Fauchard's writing that for most people the primary aim of this activity was not the preservation of the health of the teeth, but of their whiteness. He dismisses many of the powders and acids sold for this purpose as causing more harm than good, and demonstrates this with his *science*: after such cleaning, 'si l'on examine avec une loupe, (*a*) & même sans loupe, les dents ainsi blanchies plusieurs fois, on appercevra sans peine le ravage que les liqueurs qu'ils employent, y ont fait dans toute leur surface'.[41] Clearly the use of the correct recipe could, however, be beneficial as he then devotes twenty-four pages to detailed descriptions of his own mixtures. The cleaning of teeth, and the preservation (or acquisition) of their whiteness, formed the focus of the writing of the *chirurgien dentiste* Geraudly, whose very brief *L'Art de conserver les dents* would be published nine years after Fauchard's book, in 1737.[42] Six years later another *chirurgien dentiste*, Robert Bunon, would follow Fauchard in stating that such cleaning should be done regularly by a *dentiste*, despite the warnings given otherwise by some: 'il faut avoir recours au Dentiste. C'est pour cela qu'il est à propos de faire visiter sa bouche une ou deux fois par an, & il ne faut point écouter ceux qui prétendent que quand on fait nettoyer ses Dents par l'*Opérateur*, elles se salissent plûtôt.'[43] Bunon indeed stated that the advice contained within his book would follow 'l'exemple de deux célébres Dentistes': this was accompanied by a footnote which identified those *célébres dentistes* as 'MM. Fauchard & Geraudly'.[44]

'Les dents difformes & mal arrangées'[45] made regular by the *dentiste*

Possibly the most dramatic way in which the *dentiste* could improve the appearance of a face was by straightening teeth which had become misaligned, or had grown in an irregular manner. Fauchard had demonstrated his ability to do this successfully as early in his career as 1696, in his treatment of M. de Crespy de la Mabilière;[46] however, the dates of the *observations* in *Le Chirurgien Dentiste* show that it was not until around 1720 that he began to perform this kind of operation more commonly. While this was mostly on young patients, typically aged twelve to fourteen and at the instigation of their mothers, some adults, too, sought treatment. In some of the *observations*, those wishing to have their teeth straightened are in their twenties, and in his description of the way in which the operation should be performed Fauchard claims to have performed it 'même à des personnes àgées de trente à quarante ans'.[47] Thus, it appears that by the second decade of the eighteenth century the *chirurgien dentiste* would possess both the theoretical knowledge and the experience required to perform this type of operation. But here, once again, we should exercise caution. As noted previously, we should not assume that Fauchard acted alone simply because he is the most visible to us through his writing. As we shall see, he noted that there were indeed others who could perform this type of operation; however, according to him, no one had applied ingenuity and experience to it in the same way that he had. From his knowledge of the anatomy of the mouth and the operations performed upon it, he had devised a quick and effective way of straightening teeth using a development of the *pélican*, an instrument more commonly associated with extraction. This operation appears to have been innovatory: 'Il n'est pas encore venu à ma connoissance qu'aucun Dentiste avant moi se soit servi du pélican pour redresser les dents.'[48] An examination of its performance, as recounted in some of Fauchard's *observations*, will reveal how important the appearance of the teeth could be – it will also reveal how ingenuity and theoretical knowledge could be applied to this 'social' marketplace.

The usual way in which the early eighteenth-century Parisian *dentiste* straightened misaligned teeth was by binding them with thread or thin strips of silver, the pressure of which would move the teeth over a period of months. But for some of Fauchard's patients this was too long to wait. The wife of the Correcteur des Comptes wanted her twelve-year-old daughter's *moyenne dent incisive* of the upper left jaw straightened, and Fauchard noted that it was 'fort dérangée & inclinée vers le palais: Madame sa mére me demanda s'il étoit possible de donner à cette dent son arrangement naturel, & d'ôter par ce moyen la difformité qu'elle causoit à la bouche de la jeune Demoiselle'.[49] On being told that the operation would certainly be a success if the young lady presented herself to the *dentiste* each day for eight to ten days, to have threads attached and tightened, the mother declined, as this would interfere with her daughter's studies. This prompted Fauchard to say that if she wished, he could place this tooth in its natural position within a few minutes. The surprised mother agreed to his suggestion, not realizing that he would do it there and then. Turning immediately to his task, the *dentiste* filed the tooth to allow it to pass between its neighbours, and pulled it into its natural position with his *pélican*. The patient's mother was astonished at the result, as were 'sa sœur & plusieurs autres personnes qui se trouvérent présentes'.[50] They had all seen the method of 'redresser & arranger des dents' used by the late *dentiste* M. Carmeline and many others, but never before had they seen teeth moved by *this* method; neither had they witnessed the achievement of a successful result in such a short time.[51]

Not all *dentistes* possessed the necessary experience or knowledge to perform this kind of operation successfully. In 1719, M. l'Abbé Morin de Chartres en Beausse, aged twenty-two, had consulted several of Fauchard's *confrères* to see if they could straighten his 'dents canines & les incisives trè-dérangées & très-difformes'.[52] They had all advised against treatment, which to them seemed too difficult, and, seeking further advice, he had called upon Fauchard. His visit coincided with that of one of the *dentiste*'s *confrères*, and the two together examined M. l'Abbé's irregular teeth. As the visiting *dentiste* was Fauchard's senior, and Fauchard believed him to be more experienced than himself, he asked him for advice as to the method he should follow to treat cases such as this; but no satisfactory reply was forthcoming. This lack of response prompted Fauchard to claim that in three or four days his patient's teeth would be 'parfaitement bien arrangées'.[53] His colleague did not think that this was possible, but curiosity made him return – and he was duly astonished at the successful result.

The use of the *pélican* to straighten teeth, in the hands of an experienced and knowledgeable *dentiste*, could produce spectacular results. In 1712 the wife of M. Maziére, premier Commis to the Directeur des Aydes & Gabelles at Angers,[54] sent Fauchard to see her eleven-year-old daughter, who was a 'Religieuse dans le Couvent des Filles-Dieu' in the rue S. Denis.[55] This young lady had two teeth at the front of her upper right jaw 'fort mal arrangées & inclinées en dedans du côté du palais'.[56] Without causing her much pain, the *dentiste* rearranged these teeth with his *pélican* and placed them in their natural positions. He fixed them with thread to maintain their position and to prevent them from springing back with the force of the gum. He succeeded so well that it appeared as if the teeth had never been out of place, and when he removed the thread eight days later they were firmly fixed in their new position.

For Fauchard, this last *observation* clearly demonstrated how the skill of 'un habile dentiste'[57] could transform the appearance of an ugly mouth. According to him, surgery had no operation as successful as that performed by a 'Dentiste [qui] est adroit, ingénieux & expérimenté',[58] be it cleaning and whitening the teeth or improving their shape. After such an operation, the teeth 'ne sont pas reconnoissables, & paroissent beaucoup plus uniformes & plus réguliéres, qu'elles n'étoient auparavant'.[59] A skilful *dentiste* could transform a mouth which was defective, ugly and objectionable to the sight:

> Les dents sont-elles mal placées, rendent-elles par-là une bouche défectueuse, vilaine & insupportable aux yeux, on n'a qu'à souhaiter de se défaire de cette difformité, recourir à un habile Dentiste, se confier à lui & le laisser faire; l'arrangement des dents changera de telle maniere, qu'on aura le plaisir de surprendre ceux qui ne seront pas accoutumez à voir ces petits prodiges de l'art. C'est ce qui arriva à cette compagnie que Mademoiselle Maziére fut rejoindre deux heures après que j'eus redressé ses dents.[60]

The implications for the desirability of the services of the *dentiste*, performing spectacular transformations of ugly mouths as in this case, would not be lost on the *gens de considération* of Paris. As we have seen in the previous chapter, Fauchard was building his practice on an eminent clientele and, by performing operations such as these, he could improve the appearance of the daughter of the Auditeur des Comptes,[61] the grandson of the Prévôt des Marchands de Paris,[62] the son of an Ecuyer de la petite Ecurie du Roi[63] and the son of M. le President Amelot de Gournay,[64] amongst others.

The construction of artificial teeth to produce *la bouche ornée*

The fourth of the ways in which the appearance of the teeth could be improved was by the replacement of missing teeth. Again, Dionis's writings reveal that for him such an operation was considered to be the province of the surgeon – and that in its performance, appearance was the primary concern of the patient.

> The seventh and last Operation performed on the Teeth, is the inserting of Artificial ones in the Place of those which are lost. Two Reasons are alledged to authorize this Practice; the first is drawn from the Ornament which they afford, it being a disagreeable Sight to see a Mouth ill furnish'd, in which there wants one or several Teeth; and the second is grounded on the Necessity of articulating the Voice, it not being possible for those who want Teeth to pronounce so well certain Words, as when they have them all. To obviate these two Inconveniences are reccommended [*sic*] Ivory Teeth, very near the Size of those in whose Place they are to be substituted ...[65]

Dionis gives a description of the way in which such teeth should be constructed, with each one pierced, bored and fastened to its natural neighbours with gold thread. Their success seems to have been some-what limited, however, as

> We know some old Women who wear a whole Row of false Teeth, and dare not open their Mouths for fear of discovering the Substitution. But the mischief is, that Ivory in a small time grows yellow in the Mouth; wherefore *Fabritius* advises the making them of Oxes shin-bones, and *Guillemeau* of a certain Paste ...[66]

With the arrival of the specialist surgeon for the teeth, more attention could be paid to the way in which unsightly gaps in the teeth could be filled successfully. This is evident in the second volume of Fauchard's book, which contains many chapters on the construction and attachment of *dentiers artificiels* and obturators, using either human or artificial teeth. In every instance, great emphasis is placed on the appearance of the result. For Fauchard, it is important that a replacement tooth should be of the same length, thickness and width as the one it is to replace: 'Lorsqu'on veut mettre une dent ... artificielle, il faut qu'elle ait à peu près la longueur, l'épaisseur & la largeur de la dent naturelle, qui en occupoit la place'.[67] Many different materials may be used:

> Pour faire des dents artificielles, on employe ordinairement des dents humaines, des dents d'hipopotame, ou cheval marin, des dents de bœuf, même l'os de ses jambes, les défenses de vache marine, & le cœur de l'yvoire le plus fin & le plus beau.
> Les dents humaines & celles de cheval marin sont à préférer à toute autre matiére; parce qu'elles ont leur émail, & qu'elles résistent davantage à l'action des corps qui les touchent, & que par conséquent elles durent plus longtems, & conservent une couleur beaucoup plus belle, que tout autre matiére, dont on pourroit se servir en pareil cas.[68]

Thus, the choice of a material is governed principally by the appearance it will produce. Human teeth, and those of the *cheval marin*, are to be preferred because they have a covering of hard enamel which will preserve their colour better, but the teeth of oxen could also be used in those cases where a human tooth cannot be found which is of sufficient size or whiteness.[69] Whiteness is of particular importance, and Fauchard devotes an entire chapter to the way in which the leg-bones of oxen should be bleached for use as artificial teeth.[70]

Having established that the material to be used will provide the desired appearance, there is a complicated body of practical rules which govern the way in which artificial teeth should be constructed by the *dentiste*. Single, or small numbers of adjacent teeth, should be joined to their neighbours by thread or wire, or fixed by means of a gold post cemented into a retained root; but more substantial replacements would require a more complex method of construction altogether. Replacement sets of teeth could be provided for both upper and lower jaws, even if there were *no* natural ones remaining. If, however, problems were encountered with the wearing of both together, then, for Fauchard, it was the lower set which should be considered to be the most important due to its direct effect on the wearer's appearance. The lack of lower teeth would allow the cheeks and lips to sink into the mouth, thus clearly indicating to all the patient's lack of teeth:

> Les jouës & les lévres sont, par le défaut des dents inférieures, comme perduës & enfoncées dans la bouche: Il arrive de-là qu'on se contente souvent de réparer les besoins pressans de cette machoire, sans avoir égard à ceux qui se rencontrent à la machoire supérieure.[71]

As a result, therefore, the needs of the lower jaw took precedence over those of the upper, driven by the importance attached to the patient's appearance. For those who still possessed those all-important lowers however, the *dentiste* could design and construct a set of artificial upper teeth which would be kept in place by the natural lowers, and held against the upper jaw by springs. Fauchard's design for this *pièce de dents artificielles* would be of such an appearance that it would 'tromper les yeux par son aspect'[72] (see Figure 6.1).

Thus, for many patients, the appearance of their artificial teeth was of paramount importance. The *dentiste*, using his knowledge and experience, could go to great lengths to meet their desires. Fauchard, for example, had devoted much time to the enamelling of artificial teeth with the intention of achieving a 'decoration plus regulière & plus agréable'.[73] The purpose of this enamelling was to try to match the whiteness of the artificial or replacement teeth to that of those left in the mouth, perhaps even to *enrich* the ornament of nature – 'J'ai tâché d'imiter la nature, & même de l'enrichir par ces dentiers artificiels dans les circonstances qui concernent l'ornement de la bouche.'[74] Noting that artificial eyes had been made of enamel but that teeth as yet had not, Fauchard emphasized that beyond every advantage which artificial teeth had over enamel eyes, they served in the same way *as ornaments*, repairing those deformities which were shocking to the sight.

> On a imité les yeux naturels par des yeux composez d'émail; mais on a négligé la même application de l'émail à l'égard des piéces de dents artificielles, qu'on substituë aux dents naturelles; cependant outre tous les avantages que les dentiers artificiels ont au-dessus des yeux d'émail, ils servent comme eux à l'ornement, & reparent de même les défauts des parties dont les difformitez choquent au premier aspect.[75]

By the late 1730s, the *science* of the *dentiste* could be brought to bear on the problems of appearance suffered by those in the highest echelons of Parisian society. In 1737, a 'Dame de la première condition'[76] who

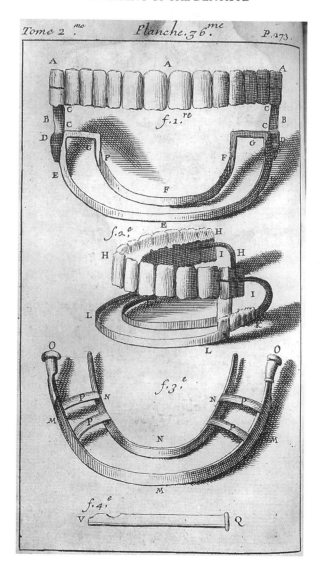

6.1 'Planche XXXVI. qui contient plusieurs dentiers ou pièces artificielles. La Figure I. représente une pièce, ou machine pour la machoire supérieure, dont le ratelier est joint à deux demis cercles par deux ressorts, vûë antérieurement.'

The *dentier artificiel* depicted in this plate illustrates clearly how much attention was paid to the appearance of the artificial teeth. It also illustrates how much complicated metalwork would be accepted by the wearer in the interests of that appearance. It is perhaps of interest that Fauchard suggested that this device need only be removed from the mouth in order to replace the springs when they became worn. (Fauchard, *Le Chirurgien Dentiste*, 1746.)

was aged about sixty and who had lost all the teeth in her upper jaw, despite retaining a full lower set, had addressed 'M. Caperon Dentiste du Roi, & très habile'[77] in the hope that he could 'garnir sa bouche d'un dentier supérieur'.[78] The royal *dentiste* had informed her that as she had no natural upper teeth remaining to which an artificial set could be attached, such a task would be like trying to 'bâtir en l'air'.[79] He suggested she try Fauchard who, having examined her mouth, spent many days meditating on her problem. Only appearance, and the 'appearance' of the voice mattered to his patient: 'Cette Dame ne voulant qu'avoir le devant de la bouche orné & une prononciation plus parfaite.'[80] The *dentiste* therefore made her *dentier* very small and light, and retained by springs and a lower arch frame which enclosed her natural teeth.[81] In the interests of cleanliness, two of these elegant devices were constructed which could be worn on alternate days. In the account of a similar, yet undoubtedly more demanding case, Fauchard describes the design of a complete upper denture which was held in place solely by the support of the cheeks and lower teeth, which as a result had to be very light indeed and was intended to improve the appearance and the voice only: 'il faut qu'il soit léger, & il ne sert guéres que pour l'ornement & la prononciation'.[82] Such a denture could only have been constructed with the intention of contributing to the artifice of the face.

Fauchard relates the tale of a set of artificial teeth which further helps to illustrate the lengths to which some would go in the interests of presenting an attractive mouth. He describes a typical structure, consisting of a row of artificial teeth for the upper jaw which were retained only by a thread piercing the gum. In their resemblance to 'pendans d'oreilles',[83] he describes them as 'floating teeth', moving with the tongue and the passage of air through the mouth: 'des dents flottantes, qui obéissoient non-seulement aux impulsions de la langue, mais encore à celles de l'air qui entre dans la bouche & qui en sort'.[84] He had heard of a lady so equipped, who had enjoyed nothing but discomfort as a result of such continuous movement of her teeth until 'un heureuse toux'[85] had shot this sorry structure into the fire, from which it was retrieved half-consumed. Not knowing if it had been repaired or not, Fauchard remarked that she must have been extremely keen to have a decorated mouth. He could not understand how any *dentiste* who valued his reputation could have exposed her to such treatment, above all in Paris where, he wrote, so many able members of all sorts of professions may be found contributing by their work to *l'ornement* of that great city.[86]

Looking forward to the latter decades of the eighteenth century reveals that the importance of the appearance of the teeth was, by then, a long-established part of being a well-to-do Parisian. Sebastien Mercier wrote in his *Tableau de Paris* of 1782 that the most beautiful mouth was not beautiful if it lacked teeth: 'La plus belle bouche n'est plus belle si les dents lui manquent. Otez une dent à la belle Hélene, la guerre de Troyes n'a plus lieu, & la divine Illiade rentre dans le néante.'[87] Mercier suggested that good teeth were an indicator of good health, whose lack could cause women to hide their disfigured smile.

> Les dents fraîches annoncent la santé, & c'est un charme préférable à tout autre. Les dents & les levres! Les voluptueux seront de mon avis.
>   La femme à qui les dents manquent fait mille grimaces pour voiler de défaut; elle n'ose rire que sous sa main ou sous l'eventail.[88]

The *science* of the *dentiste* could therefore, perhaps, bring the smile out from behind the fan.

From 'necessary' to 'indispensable': the ennoblement of the king's *dentiste*

From the evidence provided in the preceding chapters, we have seen how the mouths of the aristocracy and the *gens de considération* of Paris provided the *dentiste* with an important and highly visible foundation on which to build the *science* of his own particular part of surgery (see Figure 6.2). We have also seen how social pressure helped to reinforce that *science* in creating and encouraging a demand for it. Along the way, we have seen that the nature of what was on offer, and the status and standing of those who both offered and consumed it, declared the practice of the *dentiste*, and the *dentiste* himself, to be highly respectable. The second part of this chapter will focus on an event which takes this social story on to a higher plane: the ennoblement of the king's *dentiste* in the years around the middle of the eighteenth century.[89] This act would represent the stamping of the royal seal of approval on the practice of the specialist surgeon for the teeth, indicating an acknowledgement of respectability at the highest level of *ancien régime* society.

By the close of the eighteenth century, the royal mouth of Louis XIV had drawn plenty of attention from various practitioners. The *premier physician* d'Aquin, who provided the king with cures for the toothache,[90] had noted in 1685 that there was, in Louis's upper jaw,

> un trou qui, toutes les fois qu'il buvoit ou se gargarisoit, portoit l'eau de la bouche dans le nez, d'où elle couloit abondamment comme d'une fontaine. Ce trou sétoit fait par l'éclatement de la mâchoire arrachée avec les dents, qui sétoit enfin cariée et causoit quelquefois quelqu'écoulement de sanie de mauvaise odeur.[91]

6.2 A *dentiste* attends to the mouth of a gentleman.[92] (Eighteenth-century painting by Nicolas Lefebvre.)

The surgeon Dubois, who had mostly been responsible for what had by now become the toothless state of the king's upper jaw, the near-toothlessness of the lower and possibly the hole itself, had nevertheless treated it successfully with applications of the actual cautery.[93] By 1712, a specialist surgeon was attending to royal teeth: Charles-Arnault Forgeron was paid 2295 *livres* as 'chirurgien-opérateur pour les dents' to the king, and a further 1500 for treating the mouths of the Dauphin and the Dauphine.[94] The *État de la France pour 1712* described Forgeron's duties as the cleaning and cutting of the king's teeth, and supplying him with the roots and opiates with which he washed his mouth.[95] However, as we have seen from Fauchard's record of his provision of artificial teeth for a 'Dame de la premiére condition' in 1737,[96] by this date Jean-François Capperon held a post which Fauchard, writing in 1746, described as that of 'Dentiste du roi'.[97]

Service within the royal household was highly prestigious. As we have seen in our examination of the hierarchical structure of surgery, by the early eighteenth century it was the senior court surgeon, as exemplified by Mareschal and, in particular, la Peyronie, who would stand at the very top of the surgical ladder. In his analysis of the position of the king's *premier* physician at the end of the *ancien régime*, Colin Jones has noted that although *of* the court, the physician was *not* a courtier; he was not aristocratic. However, although the

> *premier médecin*, and others who were entitled to call themselves *médecin du roi*, cut little ice at court, being part of the court meant a lot in the smaller and more parochial world of medical institutions. Indeed, the royal medical household which the king's *premier* médecin headed constituted one of the most important and prestigious parts of the medical establishment of *ancien régime* France ...[98]

Thus, for a medical man, being part of the court carried status *outside* it, but not necessarily *within* it. Nevertheless, there was still a 'courtly' hierarchical ladder to climb as well as a 'professional' one. Higher standing at court could do nothing to harm status either inside or outside it; and, although the servant may not be aristocratic by birth, if his service were outstanding in the eyes of the king he could *become* noble.

How did the royal *dentiste* gain such a high honour at court? In order to answer this question, we shall first need to place this act of ennoblement in the context of the court and the social hierarchy within, and examine it with regard to other, similar acts. But the route to an understanding of the structure of the noble hierarchy of the *ancien régime* can appear to modern eyes to be highly complex and poorly defined.[99] In searching for an easier pathway, I shall take as my principal guide Gilles André de la Roque, whose *Traité de la Noblesse, et de toutes ses differentes espéces* was published in a new edition in 1735, ten years before the granting of *lettres d'anoblissement* to Jean-François Capperon, *dentiste du roi*. La Roque gives a brief account of seven principal types of ennoblement in France: '*Noblesse Féodale*' and '*Noblesse de Chevalerie*' (long-established military honours), noblesse '*de privilége ou de Mairie*' (honours for service in government office), *noblesse de* '*l'Avoüée*' (for the illegitimate offspring of established nobility), ennoblement for holders of the office of Sécretaire du Roi, *noblesse* '*Accidentelle*' or '*Graduelle*' ('indirect' nobility, acquired in office) and noblility originating in '*Lettres particuliéres, ou des Edits & Déclarations des Rois, ou des Chartes générales*'.[100] However, la Roque provides a clearer view of this complex situation in concluding that there are, in effect, only two types of nobility – that conferred by birth or noble extraction, and that acquired by royal decree in recognition of virtue and merit in those who perform a notable service.[101] Jean-Pierre Goubert has described these two groups as 'ancient' and 'modern',[102] and it is within this second group that we shall find the ennoblement of the king's *dentiste*.

The route to *lettres d'anoblissement*

The most common route by far to ennoblement for *roturiers* (common-
ers) recruited from the ranks of financiers, the liberal professions, the
law courts, administrators and the military, was by appointment to
office, but a few could find their way via *lettres d'anoblissement,* the
last route described by la Roque. He states that this type of nobility was
held in the lowest esteem due to the presumed common standing of the
recipient – but that in reality it was the *most* glorious, serving as
evidence of a particular virtue. 'Cette sorte de Noblesse est la moins
éstimée, parce qu'elle présupose roture: mais elle est la plus glorieuse,
parce que le Titre est un témoignage d'une vertu particuliére'.[103] The
usual route, ennoblement by office, was a collective and automatic
process which was largely beyond the control of the king and usually
expensive for the recipient. Letters of ennoblement, however, with their
origins in 'la grace spéciale du Roi',[104] allowed him to reward fidelity
and devotion, thereby ennobling whom he liked.[105] In this way, the
barrier could be crossed in one step, allowing what Guy Chaussinand-
Nogaret has described as 'explosive arrivals'. Recipients could 'arrive'
for many reasons, ranging from sudden enrichment or contacts in high
places to exceptional merit or a lucky marriage, but above all such
movement remained exceptional and stood out against the more usual
protracted climb which could often take two generations.[106]

The *lettre d'anoblissement,* which had been in use from the thirteenth
century up to the time of the Revolution, was not necessarily a cheap
undertaking for the recipient. The granting of letters was usually accompanied by a charge or *finance* payable to the royal exchequer to
cover registration dues and by way of compensation for the new noble's
likely exemption from taxation.[107] In order to gain this exemption, and
for the holder and all his legitimate offspring to enjoy all the benefits
and immunities of nobility to the full, *lettres d'anoblissement* were
required to be authenticated and registered by the Chambre des Comptes
and the Cour des Aides in Paris. These benefits were stated precisely in
the customary wording of the letters patent:

> By Our special grace, plenary power and royal authority, given
> under Our own hand, We have ennobled and do hereby ennoble
> *sieur* X, and have conferred and do confer the title of noble and
> squire, being pleased and desirous that he be held and reputed
> noble ... together with his children, posterity and descendants,
> male and female, born now or in future, in rightful wedlock; that
> as such they may in all documents and in all places assume the
> rank of squire, that they may have access to all the degrees of
> chivalry and other dignities, titles and qualities set apart for Our
> nobility, be inscribed upon the roll of noblemen, and enjoy all

rights, privileges, prerogatives, preeminences, franchises, liberties, exemptions and immunities which the other nobles of Our realm enjoy and are accustomed to enjoy ...[108]

But what sort of person was receiving these honours, and enjoying their benefits? Uncovering the identities of the recipients of *lettres de noblesse* and the mechanisms by which they acquired their rewards does not seem to be as straightforward as for other nobles, such as the members of the 'ancient' or hereditary nobility, due principally to the lack of useful records and the confusing nature of those that do exist. Ruth Kleinman, writing of the reign of Louis XIII, has noted that 'the study of French royal households suffers from a particular handicap: the absence of continuous and consistent documentation such as exists, for example, for English royal households. Questions are therefore apt to be tantalizing and answers somewhat tentative. ... Trying to determine who was or was not noble in the king's household is therefore an unprofitable exercise.'[109] Such a view may be extended to the eighteenth century. Guy Chaussinand-Nogaret, who also notes the absence of a general register of the *noblesse*, looks beyond the royal household in stating that 'In France it was never entirely clear who was and who was not in the nobility.'[110] The registers and dictionaries that do exist, such as de la Chesnaye-Dubois's *Dictionnaire de la Noblesse de France* or Père Anselme's *Histoire généalogique et chronologique de la maison royale de France*,[111] focus only on families carrying a long tradition of inherited 'ancient' nobility. Such records make little or no mention of those lower down the noble hierarchy who may have been granted honours for reasons of merit, the performance of a personal service for the king or other similar and relatively unusual reasons. As a result, those accorded honours in this way can appear to be difficult to identify; but, as we shall see, sources other than traditional ones can be very helpful.

The second apparent difficulty lies with the contemporary *recognition* of nobility and its various degrees. Merely describing someone as 'noble' meant little: as may perhaps be expected in a society in which the acquisition of nobility went hand-in-hand with social success, many different types and shades of *noblesse* abounded, with varying degrees of acceptance by the nobility itself. Ruth Kleinman, whilst once more lamenting the lack of a comprehensive register, draws attention to this lack of reliability in stating that 'There has never been a complete roster of nobility for seventeenth-century France, let alone one upon which all contemporary nobles would have agreed.'[112] But perhaps such contemporary disagreement should come as no surprise. Members of the higher echelons of the ancient *noblesse d'epée* in particular, their nobility rooted in generations, would be unlikely to consider the 'explosive arrival' of any *roturier,* for whatever reason, as an indication of real nobility. It is likely, however, that those whose personal or family status would be directly affected by any such argument or discussion would be extremely aware of their own position within this complex hierarchy.

Third, the identification of 'modern' nobles, particularly those ennobled by letters, can appear to be further obscured by uncertainties over noble status arising from the constant need of the French eighteenth-century noble to present and verify proofs to the court.[113] As we have seen, in order for the prospective noble to enjoy the privileges accorded by *anoblissement par lettres* to the full, the recipient's letters were required to be registered at parliament in the Chambre des Comptes and in the Cour des Aides.[114] At registration, these courts exercised caution in the acceptance of such letters, requiring verification before the new noble could enjoy the benefits which would accompany his title.[115] Ennoblement of any kind could only be accorded to a man of substance, and although the king could exercise a powerful element of personal choice, the candidate's letters of proof, often in the form of a *curé*'s affidavit, would be required to demonstrate the high standard of his 'life' and his 'morals'.[116] Such letters were required to be submitted within a year, after which *lettres de surannation*[117] (or *relief de surannation*) may have been presented. But uncertainty did not end with verification, for even if such proofs were accepted, and nobility accorded, honours carried no guarantee of permanence. The *Encyclopédie* of Diderot and d'Alembert illustrates the long tradition of inconsistency in the according and recognition of honours: in 1588 Letters of Restoration had re-established a group of nobles whose titles had been revoked earlier, and in an edict of January 1598 Henri IV had revoked all ennoblements made for money. These were later restored in a further edict of March 1606. Louis XIII, by an edict of November 1640, had revoked all those made in the previous thirty years, and *lettres de noblesse* accorded since 1630 were also revoked in August 1664. Two years later in 1666, a grand royal *enquête* into noble titles was held, requiring further proofs of nobility.[118] In 1696 Louis XIV created five hundred nobles, followed by two hundred in an edict of May 1702 and a further one hundred in December 1711; however, in August 1715, he did away with all *anoblissements par lettres* and privileges of nobility granted since 1 January 1689 to *offices* (that is, those in military, judicial or financial posts).[119] Although the reasons for such repeated revocations and reinstatements are not clear, it would appear that nobility for the ennobled *roturier* was not necessarily for life.

What was required in the first half of the eighteenth century to trigger the 'explosive arrival' of a new noble? For a small number of those who became 'modern' nobles, particularly those who were so rewarded for the provision of a highly personal service to the king, these exceptional social movements could be made along a relatively smooth path. In these cases, ennoblement was granted in recognition of doing something completely different from what had gone before. This kind of ennoblement for merit – that nobility which la Roque had described as '*la plus glorieuse*' – would acknowledge the respectability of that activity by the highest authority: it would represent a kind of royal seal of approval. These activities may seem, at first sight, to have been those that were traditionally manual or mechanical in nature, the performance of which would have instantly invited derogation in a noble and precluded *anoblissement* in a *roturier*. But these new nobles brought something completely new to the material on which they worked. They brought the application of the *mind*; and in doing so, they created a new type of activity altogether. Although still of necessity using their hands, the outstanding way in which the mind was applied would distract the observer from noticing those hands.

I shall suggest that for a small number of exceptional cases, the conferring of *lettres d'anoblissement* would require the fulfilment of four particular and well-defined criteria. Three of these, which we shall see later to have been stated clearly in documents relating to the granting of *lettres d'anoblissement*, were the possession of (i) *l'expérience*, (ii) *la sagesse* and (iii) *la conduite*. The first required the candidate to have great experience and ability in the performance of his particular service, whilst the second demanded the application of mind rather than might – that is, the possession of theoretical knowledge and the ability to apply that knowledge. The third requirement, *la conduite*, related to the way in which the service was performed. To become noble, the candidate would first have to behave as a noble: whatever the activity, it should be performed in a genteel, respectable manner. But a fourth quality clearly set such ennoblements apart from other, more commonplace rewards. Some *lettres d'anoblissement*, granted by the grace of the king, would require the performance of (iv) a personal service which 'touched' the king himself, the *corps du roi*, closely. We shall see that the fulfilment of all four of these criteria could produce a particular and unusual type of ennoblement which was attainable only by a small and select group of the king's servants, but which could have a profound effect on their domains of service.

Royal recognition of the specialist surgeon: the ennoblement of Julien Clément, *chirurgien accoucheur*

In Chapter Four, we have already caught a glimpse of the reward which could accrue to the surgeon for the performance of a particular personal service for the king in the granting of *lettres d'anoblissement* to Charles-François Félix in 1690. To earn this reward, Félix had performed a highly personal service for the king in the form of a successful operation, for which he had devised a new type of *bistouri*, on an extremely uncomfortable anal fistula.[120] The *premier* surgeon had duly received a very generous financial reward in addition to his honour; but despite becoming noble, he was to continue to use his hands in the application of his theoretical knowledge of surgery. His nobility was granted under the express understanding that he would continue to serve the king's person whilst running no risk of *dérogeance* for doing so: 'à la charge de vivre noblement, sans néanmoins que l'exercice de notre premier chirurgien que nous voulons être continué par ledit sieur Félix, lui puisse être imputé à dérogeance'.[121] We have also caught sight of the way in which this episode could influence the court, albeit for a brief period. For a time, many aspiring courtiers would come to Versailles to (as Dionis had put it) 'turn up their Posteriors to a Chirurgeon, for him to make Incision'.[122] The turning up of the posterior was, for these hopefuls, a *social* gesture, not a medical one. Dionis wrote that he had 'seen above thirty who desir'd to have the Operation perform'd, and whose Folly was so great, that they seem'd angry when they were assured that they did not at all want it'.[123] The king's submission to the surgeon's knife had acted as a sure signal that to undergo such an operation, necessary or not, could take the supposed sufferer towards the next rung up the courtly ladder.

But it is in the less well-known story of the ennoblement of a specialist surgeon twenty-one years later, the surgeon-turned-*accoucheur* Julien Clément, that the particular mechanism by which *lettres d'anoblissement* could be gained for the personal touch becomes most readily visible. Clément was a royal surgeon who was required to bring his skills to the birth of royalty itself – and, having fulfilled the four criteria which I have suggested above, would be granted letters of ennoblement in 1711. Clément could claim great experience and ability in his practice, bringing his wisdom and knowledge of theory very close to the king's personal interest. Some *accoucheurs* had been building their reputations at court,[124] but most royal deliveries had actually been performed by midwives or *sage-femmes*. Louis XIV's mother, Anne of Austria, and his wife Marie-Thérèse had both used the services of midwives; but the king's mistress, Mlle de la Vallière, and his daughter-in-law the Dauphine would have their children delivered by Clément.[125]

Clément's first royal delivery was that of the Dauphine's first-born in 1682, the Duc de Bourgogne, who thus provided the first exciting spectacle for the newly installed court at Versailles. As was usual for a royal birth, huge crowds filled the palace. Clément directed the birth from the start – he had not been called in his capacity as a surgeon to take over because of problems[126] – but the arrival of the Duc de Bourgogne was difficult and protracted, so much so that all present expected the mother to die (including the Dauphine herself). By the end of the second day of agony for the Dauphine (passed in an August heat-wave), all present appeared exhausted, with the exception of the *accoucheur*. Throughout the ensuing delivery, Clément exercised great noble behaviour: he remained calm and in control, occasionally bleeding his patient and promising the king that everything would be all right. He was as good as his word, and not only the baby but the mother, too, survived the experience.

The safe delivery of the Duc de Bourgogne was the first of many performed at court by the able Clément, setting him on the path to his ennoblement. He directed the births of the Dauphine's other two children, Phillipe (the future king of Spain) and the Duc de Berri at Versailles. In the letters of ennoblement granted to Clément, Louis, after remarking that the majority of such rewards were made for military service,[127] declared that he would also honour those serving in office close to the royal person, who exercised their experience and wisdom in the correct manner: 'ceux qui ont eu l'honneur de nous rendre leurs services dans des charges qui les ont approchez de plus près de notre personne, ou qui dans des professions ou emplois qui demandent de l'expérience, de la sagesse et de la conduite'. The king knew that Clément indeed possessed long experience, particularly in delivering babies 'of the blood'. The *accoucheur* 's'être appliqué pendant plusieurs années aux accouchemens', and he had 'reçu de même les enfans dont il a plû à Dieu de bénir le mariage de ces princes et princesses de notre sang royal depuis plus de trente-cinq ans'. The letters clearly acknowledge Clément's great wisdom, due for recognition: 'Nous avons cru que sa grande capacité, ses soins et sa sagesse méritoient une marque d'honneur'. But of principal importance, in delivering children of 'notre sang royal', the *accoucheur* had performed a personal service for the king, which approached 'de plus près de notre personne'. Therefore, the criteria suggested above were met – and, as a result, Julien Clément could add a golden *fleur de lis* to his coat of arms[128] and enjoy the advantages it would bring.

Royal recognition of the specialist surgeon: the ennoblement of Jean-François Capperon,[129] *chirurgien dentiste*

Examination of the reasons for the honouring of the king's *dentiste* Jean-François Capperon, and particularly of his successor Etienne Bourdet, will, as in the case of the *accoucheur*, reveal once again the fulfilment of the particular criteria which I have suggested were essential for the granting of this type of ennoblement. The earliest evidence of nobility conferred upon a *dentiste* may be found in the *lettres de surannation* obtained by Jean-François Capperon in 1759, in support of the ennoblement by letters granted to him by the king in 1745.[130] Unfortunately, these particular *lettres d'anoblissement* have not survived, and evidence relating to Capperon's activities appears at present to be almost non-existent. We have, however, seen that Pierre Fauchard was familiar with his work, remarking that even though Capperon could not 'bâtir en l'air' when asked to build a set of artificial teeth in 1737 by a lady of the highest standing,[131] he was, nevertheless, as 'Dentiste du Roi ... très-habile'.[132] The chronicler Barbier recorded what must have been a difficult moment for the *dentiste* in 1742, when he managed to break two of Louis XV's teeth while attending to his mouth: the king, however, exhibited admirable patience, apparently suffering greatly yet managing to retain regal control of his tongue:

> Malgré l'habileté du Sieur Capron et l'opinion que tout le monde a de sa réputation, il cassa avant-hier deux dents au Roi, en les lui accommodant, et l'on a admiré la patience de Sa Majesté, qui a souffert extraordinairement sans se plaindre et sans dire des choses trop désagréables à ce dentiste. Ce n'est pas la première fois qu'on se plaint de lui dans le monde sur de semblables sujets.[133]

Despite this unfortunate incident, in December 1745 the king granted Capperon his *lettres d'anoblissement* and, some years later, the king's counsellor would perform the customary *enquête de noblesse* by acquiring letters of support.[134] These letters indicate that Capperon did indeed possess long experience in the practice of the *dentiste*: according to Michel Le Duc, who was a 'capitaine général, colonel des trois compagnies des gardes de la ville ... dès sa plus tendre jeunesse [Capperon] s'est appliqué à sa profession de chirurgien-dentiste'.[135] Antoine Bandezy de la Val, 'compositeur des ballets dy Roy',[136] noted Capperon's *sagesse*: he had known 'depuis longtemps ledit Sieur Capperon, qu'il s'est adonné avec tant d'application à l'art de sa profession'.[137] In an example of the *curé's* affidavit (as suggested by Goubert[138]) M. Rémy Chapeau, 'Prêtre bachelier de Sorbonne' and 'curé de l'Eglise de Saint-Germain l'Auxerrois',[139] stated that the accordance of letters of ennoblement to Capperon was a mark of distinction appropriate to one of such merit, and due reward for his services rendered to the king. He knew

> ledit Sr. Capperon pour être de bonne vie et mœurs, de la religion catholique, apostolique et romaine, très affectionné au service du Roy, que les lettres de noblesse que Sa Majesté a bien voulu lui accorder, sont une marque de la distinction qu'Elle fait de son mérite et une récompense des services qu'il lui a rendu et au public ...[140]

Thus Capperon had letters of proof which could show that he had experience in the practice of the *dentiste*, and that he had exercised *conduite* in his performance of a personal service for the king; but it would be difficult to draw any firm conclusions regarding the effect of this ennoblement, if it *was* indeed finally conferred, on the practice of the *dentiste*.

The 'royal person' and the *science* of the *dentiste*: the ennoblement of Etienne Bourdet

Our view of the 'arrival' at court of the king's *dentiste* is made much clearer by the image of the royal *dentiste* Etienne Bourdet, who was granted *lettres d'anoblissement* in 1767.[141] Ten years prior to this act Bourdet, who had been 'reçu au Collége de Chirurgie',[142] had published his *Recherches et observations sur toutes les parties de l'art du dentiste*: a book which the French writer François Vidal has described as 'certainement le plus important ouvrage d'odontologie publié après le «Chirurgien-dentiste» de Fauchard'.[143] Having already become well acquainted with Fauchard's writings in our exhaustive investigation into the construction and extension of the *science* of the *dentiste*, we shall now look to Bourdet's *Recherches et observations* of 1757 to help us to understand the reasons for his ennoblement.

Bourdet had been born in Agen, southern France, in 1722. In Paris, he had married the daughter of one of his *confrères*, and succeeded Capperon's short-lived successor, Mouton, as *dentiste* to the king *en survivance* in 1760.[144] In the introduction to his *Recherches et observations*, Bourdet reveals that he, like Fauchard, had been destined for surgery from childhood, and had been drawn to that part which related to the teeth:

> Formé d'ailleurs dès mon enfance, dans la pratique des opérations, j'ai eu pour celles de Dentiste toutes les ressources qu'une main exercée trouve dans l'habitude du travail. C'est avec des dispositions, c'est après avoir passé une grande partie de ma jeunesse à suivre d'habiles Maîtres en Chirurgie & les Hôpitaux, que ... je me suis fixé à la partie des Dents.[145]

He had gained much advantage from the study of surgery, from whose *science* (in his opinion) the art of the *dentiste* should never be separated, as it provided the *principes* essential to that art.

> Mais dans l'application continuelle que j'ai donnée a toutes les parties de notre Art, je ne dois point dissimuler les secours & les avantages que j'ai tirés particulierement de l'étude de la Chirurgie. Cette science si étendue dont l'Art du Dentiste est une partie qui n'en devroit jamais être separée, m'a rempli de principes qui s'étendent & qui s'appliquent à tous les objets de cet Art.[146]

Bourdet had been greatly influenced in his work by the writings of Fauchard. For him, it was Fauchard who had prepared the ground for a *science* for the teeth, ground which he himself had then trodden. Thus it was 'M. Fauchard qui l'a si bien défriché [qui] a été mon guide'.[147] He had stated in the introduction to his book that his work followed that of Fauchard, who had produced the most complete work on the teeth: 'J'avouerai que c'est embrasser à peu près toute la matiere de l'ouvrage de Monsieur Fauchard, le plus complet qui'il y ait sur les Dents.'[148] In his discussion of 'Des différentes Opérations qui se pratiquent sur les Dents',[149] he identified Fauchard as having 'déja donné le détail des opérations que j'entreprends de représenter'.[150]

Recherches et observations does indeed appear to follow Fauchard's work, in placing the practice of the *dentiste* firmly on foundations constructed on theoretical knowledge, using operations which would both demand the application of that knowledge and contribute to its extension. Bourdet described it as a 'Livre de Théorie & de Pratique',[151] which was written not only for 'general' surgeons, but also those who had chosen to specialize in the operations for the teeth: 'des Maîtres en Chirurgie qui ont donné quelque attention à l'objet des Dents, mais encore des Dentistes mêmes qui voudront examiner sans passion'.[152] For him, *principes* were essential building blocks. The *dentiste* should be 'sufissament pourvûs de principes, pour exercer plus sûrement un Art tout Chirurgical, & qui demande plus que de la main'.[153] *Recherches et observations* contains a full description of the anatomy and *physiologie* of the teeth, the different diseases which may attack them, along with their causes, both internal and external, and the remedies which should be used to prevent them, both general and particular. There follows a chapter on the diseases and other causes which will affect the whiteness of the teeth and another on the diseases of the gums. The operations for the teeth are discussed in great detail, along with the whole *manuel* of the *Dentiste* concerning artificial teeth. Appearance, again, plays a central part: artificial teeth were, for Bourdet, an important means by which the loss of the most beautiful teeth could be remedied. 'Il est bien vrai qu'on remédie à ces inconvéniens extérieurs, par le moyen des

Dents artificielles. Lorsque ces Dents sont bien faites, & d'une proportion exacte, elles remplacent les plus belles Dents naturelles'.[154] Bourdet
placed much emphasis on 'l'ornement naturel que les Dents forme de la
bouche',[155] an emphasis which is readily apparent in some of the *observations* recorded in his book. For example, after he had performed an
operation to straighten irregular teeth in 1751, 'Cette Demoiselle [his
patient] a présentement les plus belles Dents du monde'.[156] In the interests of obtaining such a result, Bourdet had invented a new type of
pélican (see Figure 6.3) which, whilst fulfilling the normal requirements
of such an instrument, was designed to be particularly useful in the
realignment of irregular teeth (an operation for which, significantly,
Fauchard had been the first to use such an instrument).

On taking up his royal post on Mouton's death in 1762,[157] Bourdet
also held the positions of *dentiste* to the *famille royale*, and to the École
Royale Militaire.[158] He would die in 1789, an extremely wealthy man,
having sold his royal office *en survivance* to the *dentiste* and fellow
Chirurgien-Juré Jean-Joseph Dubois-Foucou in 1783 for 120 000 *livres*.[159]

Bourdet fulfilled with ease the four criteria suggested previously for
the successful candidate for *anoblissement par lettres*. At midday on
Saturday, 6 August 1768, an *enquête de noblesse* was made in the Cour
des Aydes by Claude François de la Ville du Portault, Conseiller du Roi,
'à la requeste du sieur Etienne Bourdet, chirurgien-dentiste du Roy',[160]
in order to verify the *lettres d'anoblissement* accorded to him in the
previous year at Versailles. One of Bourdet's *confrères*, Jean-François
Fontaine, 'maitre chirurgien-dentiste, demeurant à Paris',[161] noted in his
supporting letter of proof the merit of Bourdet's writing on their particular part of surgery; but that his personal merit and *qualités sociables*
also rendered him worthy of ennoblement. For Fontaine, it was

> tout le méritte d'un ouvrage considérable que le dit sieur Bourdet a
> donné au public sur cette partie intéressante de la Chirurgie, que
> d'ailleurs son méritte personnel et ses qualités sociables l'ont rendu
> digne de la distinction que le Roy lui a accordé.[162]

M. François Théodore Regnard, avocat au Parlement, knew Bourdet
well and attested to his experience and character. He avowed

> qu'il connoit parfaitement le dit sieur Etienne Bourdet dentiste de
> Roy, de la Reine et de toute la famille royale, qu'il sait que son
> application à son art lui a fait entreprendre un ouvrage considérable
> pour le perfectionner, que son caractère bienfaisant luy fait donner
> au public tous les moments que luy laissent ses occupations près de
> la famille Royale ...[163]

Jean Anger de Montignac, ancien officier d'Infanterie, stated that the
king's *dentiste* was highly industrious and well known; he knew that he
was

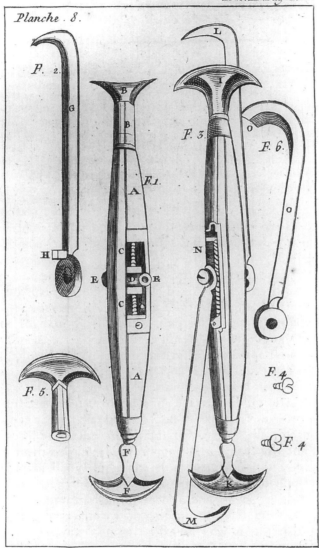

6.3   Bourdet's *pélican*. This instrument had been submitted to an examination by the Académie Royale de Chirurgie: 'Monsieur Dupouy qui avoit été nommé pour examiner un Pélican particulier, de l'invention de Monsieur Bourdet, Dentiste à Paris, on ayant fait son rapport: l'Académie a jugé que cet Instrument est applicable à des usages dont le Pélican ordinaire est privé, qu'il a le mérite essentiel de servir à l'arrangement des Dents, & qu'il est digne d'être approuvé. A Paris ce 19 Mai 1753, Signé, MORAND, Sécrétaire perpétuel'. (Bourdet, *Recherches et observations*, 1757.)

fort appliqué à sa profession, très connu et employé dans cette partie, qu'il ne doutte pas que la distinction que sa Majesté a fait de luy en luy accordant des lettres de noblesse ne soit fondé que de très justes motifs ...[164]

According to Jean-Louis-Nicolas Jarry, chirurgien-major des Gardes Suisses, Bourdet's merit made him a worthy successor to Capperon who had served the royal family and the public well. Bourdet was

distingué dans cette partie de la chirurgie par un ouvrage considérable ayant pour but la perfection de cet art, que son mérite connu l'a fait classer pour succéder au sieur Caperon, qu'il scait qu'il employe à la satisfaction du public les moments que luy laissent ses occupations près de la famille royale, que par ses sentiments soutenus lui ont mérité la distinction que le Roy lui accorde par les lettres de noblesse dont il s'agit ...[165]

From the evidence provided by these letters, it would appear therefore that Bourdet's experience in his profession, and his suitability for ennoblement (in other words, his possession of the necessary *conduite*), were well recognized.

Bourdet's *sagesse*, his application of the mind to the operations for the teeth, had been demonstrated clearly in the *ouvrage considérable* referred to in the letters of proof above: his *Recherches et observations sur toutes les parties de l'art du dentiste* would run to several editions throughout the eighteenth century, not all of them French.[166] The king himself noted that in writing this book, Bourdet had contributed to the progress of his art: 'le S. Estienne Bourdet notre chirurgien dentiste après avoir beaucoup contribué au progrès de l'art qu'il exerce par la publication d'un ouvrage considérable sur cet art fruit de son aplication et de ses Travaux'.[167] Bourdet had taken what he saw as the foundations for the *science* for the teeth which had been laid by Fauchard and, by their further application, built on them to extend that *science* – and, as *dentiste* to the king, queen and royal family, he was both applying and building it on the most prestigious mouths possible. In doing so, he had also performed an important personal service for the king, *literally* touching the royal person and his family. It may be that this is why Bourdet was not expected to make the payments that were usually required of those accorded honours, his ennoblement being granted 'aucune finance ni indemnités';[168] however, as we have seen in the case of the *accoucheur* Clément, personal service was a central factor in promoting the king's desire to grant noble status. As with Clément's *lettres*, those accorded to Bourdet state clearly that honour was due to those servants who had not only proved their ability, but whose affection and zeal for the royal person were particularly well known:

Attentif à leur exemple à ne pas laisser sans récompense ceux de nos sujets qui ont donné publiquement des preuves de leur capacité et surtout ceux dont l'attachement et le zele pour notre personne sont particulierement connu ... Sous reconnoitre les bon services qu'il a réndus et rend encore, tant à Notre personne qu'à celle de la Reine, Notre fidelle épouse et Compagne et à notre famille Royale; Tous ces motifs Nous ont porté à lui accorder comme Nous avions fair ci-devant au S. Capperon son prédécesseur, un titre d'honneur ...[169]

Thus the honour was given in recognition of the good service already rendered, and still being rendered, as much to the king's person as to that of the queen and the royal family – the same reasons as those for honouring Bourdet's predecessor, Sieur Capperon. The reward for such service was dazzling:

[nous] donner à ces sujets des marques plus éclatantes et plus précieuses de notre satisfaction qu'en leur accordant un titre qui les éleve autant au dessus des autres que leur mérite personel et leur affection à notre service les ont distingués ...[170]

Such 'precious marks' of the king's satisfaction would raise recipients as far above others as their personal *mérite* and their devotion to the service of the king demanded.

In granting these *lettres d'anoblissement*, the king had conferred on the activities of his *dentiste*, quite literally, a royal seal of approval; and, as we shall see in more detail later, this approval was intended to act as a signal to others. In declaring that such honours might be accorded in this way for 'touching' the king and his family, Louis stated that such an honourable title as that bestowed upon Capperon and Bourdet was intended to encourage others to show themselves equally worthy in the practice of those arts which are useful and necessary for the public: their ennoblement was 'un titre d'honneur capable d'encourager ceux qui s'en rendrons aussi dignes dans l'exercice des arts utiles et nécessaires au Public'.[171] In this way, the king himself was indicating that the treatment of teeth is useful, necessary and therefore desirable and, by this means, that it is *respectable* – despite the apparent manual nature of the operations performed, it is of principal importance that these operations have been constructed and applied by the mind. Social acceptance demanded theoretical knowledge, and conversely theoretical knowledge could not succeed without social acceptance. The *dentiste* had been signalled as noble, his activities stamped with the impress of Louis's 'grand sceau de cire verte'.[172]

The importance of the 'personal touch': the power of the body of the king

In the preceding paragraphs, I have suggested that the ennoblements of Clément, Capperon and Bourdet demonstrate the importance of what I have called the 'personal touch' in the acquisition of honours from the king. To place these acts of ennoblement within the context of the court, this 'personal touch' requires a brief analysis. Why was this type of service considered to be so important, and by what social mechanism could it confer status? Answers to these questions will reveal that the king's body, what that body did and what it had done to it, carried great significance at court. We must, therefore, look briefly at the *gloire de l'univers*,[173] the king himself.

In his analysis of court society, Norbert Elias has described Louis XIV as 'the first perfect representative' of the 'court aristocratic type [of king]',[174] noting that it was his grandfather Henri IV who had embodied the transition towards this 'type' from the *roi chevalier*, riding into battle at the head of his troops. Louis XIV became the *only* centre of court society to a greater extent than any of his predecessors, and it was this 'royal power in an entirely secure condition'[175] which Louis XV inherited. Louis XIV, in establishing an unprecedented distance between himself and his nobility, had brought the 'deification' of the king's person to its highest art. Under his successor, the court's centre of gravity would shift from the great royal palaces towards the *hôtels,* the residences of non-princely court aristocrats,[176] but this would not mean that it would lose its significance as the centre of influence. With respect to the central position of the king, the importance of his person and its influence on society, little would change. Traditional historians find less to interest them in Louis XV than in his predecessor;[177] but it is the creation of the tradition surrounding the power of the king's person and the importance of his body itself which is central to the *dentiste*'s path to nobility in the middle of the eighteenth century.

The establishment of Louis XIV as 'great' has been built on strong foundations, with Voltaire (writing after the king's death) describing 'four ages in the history of the world ... of which the fourth is called "The age of Lewis XIV" ... it is, perhaps, of the four, that which approaches the nearest to perfection'.[178] Voltaire noted that

> it may with truth be said, that, from the last years of cardinal Richlieu to the death of Lewis XIV. there happened a general revolution, not only in our government, but in our arts, minds, and manners; which ought to be an eternal epocha of the true glory of our country. And this happy influence was not confined to France,

but extended into England, where it excited the emulation which that sensible and thinking nation then wanted.[179]

According to Voltaire, this 'general revolution' was directly attributable to the king's person in his appearance and his bearing. He

> surpassed all his courtiers by the superior dignity of his person, and the majestic beauty of his countenance. The tone of his voice, which was insinuating and noble, gained the hearts of those which his presence intimidated. His manner of walking was suitable only to his own rank and person, and in any other would have been ridiculous. The confusion into which he threw those who spoke to him, flattered him with a pleasing conviction of his own superiority ...[180]

The display of power was physical: it was 'superior dignity' and 'majestic beauty' which placed the king on his pinnacle, his brilliance unsurpassed, and 'All this gave the court of Lewis XIV. an air of grandeur, which eclipsed every other court in Europe. He was desirous that this lustre should reflect from his own person, down to his brother and the prince, and to all about him ...[181] Louis XIV was light itself – the *roi soleil* stood at the centre of his court, with rays of brilliance radiating outwards. Sun King became Sun God: in discussing the part played by Louis XIV in the development of French absolutism,[182] David Parker has described the king's appropriation of the god Apollo as symbolizing the desire to bring human society into harmony with an idealized universal order. As 'Chief of the Muses, God of Music, Ruler of the Planets, The Sun, God himself – Apollo was the quintessence of the harmony of the cosmos.'[183] Although noting that such deification was, to some extent, an ideological illusion created to encourage the stability of the regime,[184] Parker points out that

> it was not imposed in any crude fashion on an unwilling or hostile public. On the contrary, the educated public were themselves steeped in the classical idiom in which the propaganda was couched: many of its members benefitted from royal patronage, and they certainly accepted, as did the populace at large, the religious foundations of royal authority.[185]

In the resulting 'cult of royal authority ... [which had] no equal anywhere else in Western Europe',[186] to touch the king's person was to touch God himself.

This 'deification' of the king was reinforced by an intricate, complicated and highly reverential ceremonial etiquette which reached its fullest expression in the court of Louis XIV. This etiquette served to distance the king from the court, but it was also an important display of power, as the king's memoirs show:

> Those people are gravely mistaken who imagine that all this is mere ceremony. The people over whom we rule, unable to see to the bottom of things, usually judge by what they see from outside, and most often it is by precedence and rank that they measure their respect and obedience. As it is important to the public to be governed only by a single one, it also matters to it that the person performing this function should be so elevated above the others, that no-one can be confused or compared with him; and one cannot, without doing harm to the whole body of the state, deprive its head of the least mark of superiority distinguishing it from the limbs.[187]

However, this great ritual was perhaps of even greater importance to Louis XV. To his predecessor, who had codified it, it was a tool, a means of controlling the nobility and maintaining the social order of the court. But for Louis XV, who had lived with it from birth, it determined the way his environment functioned, and he was very sensitive to any break in the accepted code, which continued to flourish.[188] The rituals of the king's rising and his retiring, the *levées* and *couchées*, continued much as they had under Louis XIV with the exact order of precedence in the elaborate ritual of the *entrées* of great interest to the whole court. Thus, the Duc de Luynes noted in 1737[189] that the *entrées* in the evening were the same as in the morning, with the *familières*, the *grandes* and the *premières entrées* staying until the king was actually in bed. When the main crowd had gone, the Premier Valet de Chambre, on the king's order, gave a candlestick to one courtier who had been allowed to stay. This honour, of holding the light close to the king to assist him with his undressing and *toilette*, brought the candle-bearer even closer to the royal person. It was a highly valued mark of great favour.

Royal meals were also highly ritualized. The king might eat more formally (the *grand couvert*) or less formally (the *petit couvert*), but on even the least formal occasion (*très petit couvert*, composed of a minimum of three courses and many dishes) these meals were 'performances before an audience',[190] at which it was an honour to be allowed to watch the king eat and a greater honour to be spoken to by the king during the meal. The supreme honour would be an invitation to serve the king his food, or to eat with him;[191] the greatest privilege would again be to come closest to the king's person.

The power of the king's body itself, dazzlingly displayed in these personal rituals, shone even more brightly with the powers contained within it for curing disease. Whilst touching the king was an honour of the highest order, being touched *by* him could be a powerful symbol of his sacred character. Kings of France, marked with 'the impress of the divine finger',[192] had the miraculous power of curing scrofula simply by touch. Immediately before performing this act of healing, the king would receive the sacrament. That his power to cure came directly from God is apparent in the words which would accompany each touch: 'Le roi te touche, Dieu te guérit'.[193] The royal touch was offered regularly to large numbers on days of royal and religious festival – Easter, Pentecost, Christmas Day, New Year's Day, Candlemas, Trinity Sunday and others – the ceremony having been announced several days in advance by public notice.[194] The crowds awaiting the 'touch' could be vast: in October of 1722, the day after his consecration, more than two thousand scrofula sufferers appeared before Louis XV at Rheims,[195] and Louis XVI would touch two thousand four hundred when he became king in 1775.[196]

The outward display of social position: the need to 'consume' an extravagance royally signalled as prestigious

Court society was, therefore, focused obsessively on actions that were highly charged with symbolic meaning, 'performed in public', as Burke has said, 'by an actor whose person was sacred'.[197] All-important etiquette served as a visual indicator of rank within the hierarchy of this court by demonstrating clearly to each an assurance of his own carefully graded social position, always taken with respect to the king's deified position at the very top. One who had the right to attend the *première entrée* or to hold the king's shirt would therefore look down on and would not give way to one admitted only to the *troisième*. The prince would not give way to the duke, as the duke in turn would not yield to the marquis, and all members of the *noblesse* would not and *could* not yield to any *roturier*. Any shifts in standing which might occur would be apparent to all; a change in the hierarchy that was not reflected in a change of etiquette, as directed from on high, could not occur.

To the members of this court, the outward display of social position was of the utmost importance. It was the only certain way of proclaiming stature in an absolutist society of estates, in which the various noble ranks had hardly any corresponding governmental functions. With the nobility only marginally engaged in the exercise of power, which was almost exclusively the province of the king, superiority of one courtier over another of lesser rank had to be displayed in a different manner. Thus it was essential to display one's rank at all times and to all people, declaring one's status at court clearly by the presentation of an appropriate social appearance. The only sure way of doing this was by presenting an ostentatious display of luxury and conspicuous consumption.

Luxury was therefore an *essential* mark of rank, and the most desirable luxuries were clearly those used by the highest rank of all – the king himself.

It would be easy for us to think that the ambitious *bourgeois*, observing this courtly life, was desperate to emulate what appears at first sight to have been a life of comfort, surrounded by wealth and the effortless consumption of superfluous luxury. But what may appear to us retrospectively as 'luxury' in the modern sense, as the cream poured on top of everyday life, was anything but superfluous in the polite society of *ancien régime* France – nor, indeed, was it effortlessly acquired. As Norbert Elias has said of this court,

> In a society in which every outward manifestation of a person has special significance, expenditure on prestige and display is for the upper classes a necessity which they cannot avoid. They are an indispensable instrument in maintaining their social position, especially when – as is actually the case in this court society – all members of the society are involved in a ceaseless struggle for status and prestige.[198]

Luxury, for the courtier in mid-eighteenth-century France, was an essential part of life, a necessary instrument in the full-time business of consuming and being *seen* to consume.

We have seen that the ennoblement of the *accoucheur* and the *dentiste* should be viewed as indicators of the acceptance and endorsement of a luxury by the king, the ultimate arbiter of good taste and style: an authority that was socially unchallengeable. By the declaration of royal approval implicit in this act of ennoblement, the king had demonstrated that the use of their services represented an essential indicator of social rank, thereby compelling those with social ambition to *seek* such services. There was no easy alternative passage to that of the court; as Norbert Elias has said of the court of Louis XIV, so could be said of that of his great-grandson:

> Individuals who ... did not belong to court society, or have access to it, had relatively little chance of proving and fulfilling their individual potential by achievements that would be deemed of importance on the traditional scale of historical values.[199]

Under Louis XV, the tightness with which noble polite society was centred on the court itself started to show signs of relaxing slightly, and a greater degree of diffusion of its influence became apparent. Louis XIV had viewed the formation of social circles outside the court with displeasure, preferring his courtiers to take apartments at Versailles and to stay when he held court there.[200] But on his death this tight rein, which had had the effect of concentrating the highest élite of court society within one place, was gradually loosened. Rank, reputation and

noble income was still decided at a court which, with the king firmly
sitting centre-stage, lost none of its central significance and importance.
But, as the ties were relaxed, it began to share its role as a theatre of
social life and strong cultural influence, first with the palaces of the
royal princes and later with the aristocratic circles of the *hôtels*, the
residences of non-princely court aristocrats. These wider circles, in their
turn, could more easily exert their powers of influence over the rich
bourgeoisie of the third estate. So, as the nobility moved a little closer
to those driven by a desperate desire to emulate them, what was in
favour at court could now find itself in favour with polite society more
rapidly and easily than before.

The rise of the specialist surgeon: the *accoucheur*

The ennoblement of Julien Clément in 1711 came at a time of great
discussion and argument in France regarding the role of the surgeon in
childbirth, and it may well have been highly influential in the outcome
of that argument. Jacques Gélis has suggested that *accoucheurs* were
offered a 'tremplin inespéré',[201] an unhoped-for springboard, by Louis
XIV's calling for Clément to assist at the birth of Mlle de La Vallière's
children in the 1660s. However, although they were becoming accepted
at court, there was no shortage of strong opposition to the use of the
male surgeon in place of the *sage-femmes*. For example, the Jansenist
physician Philippe Hecquet (who would become Dean of the Faculté in
1712) had favoured the use of *sages-femmes*, presenting a powerful
argument for their use on both moral and medical grounds.[202] In 1708,
Hecquet had published a book entitled *De l'indécence aux hommes
d'accoucher les femmes, et de l'obligation aux femmes de nourrir leurs
enfans. Pour montrer par des raisons de physique, de morale et de
médecine que les mères n'exposeroient ni leurs vies ni celles de leurs
enfans en se passant ordinairement d'accoucheurs et de nourrices.*[203] In
this book, as the title suggests, Hecquet argued that the employment of
an *accoucheur* (whose services, in his view, were rarely necessary) was
contrary to the maxims of the Christian religion. The profession of
accoucheur had been unknown in antiquity and therefore, for Hecquet,
it was without title or authority.[204] He had blamed the rise of the
accoucheur on the timidity of wives and the gullibility of their hus-
bands, and had claimed that this 'intrusive profession'[205] could, and
should, be easily passed by.

However, any argument against the use of the *accoucheur*, particularly one based so strongly on religious grounds, seems to have been
completely undermined by the king's ennoblement of Clément, three

years after the publication of Hecquet's book. This royal act served as a clear sign that the king, God's representative on earth, saw the *accoucheur* as a member of a noble and worthy profession. As we have seen, although the delivery of a baby was of necessity performed with the hands, Clément had brought experience and ability, wisdom and *conduite*, 'correct' genteel behaviour, to its performance for the king's own family. Thus childbirth, *if it was performed by a specialist surgeon*, an *accoucheur*, did not carry the stigma of a manual occupation, even though the hands were used in its performance. Clément's letters of ennoblement, like those accorded to the surgeon Félix after his operation on the king's fistula, contained a clause which expressly allowed for the *continued* use of those hands: his nobility was given 'sans ... qu'il soit tenu de cesser l'exercice de sa profession, en considération des secours que les princesses de notre sang pourront continuer d'en recevoir'.[206] Thus the service provided by the *accoucheur* was both approved of *and used by* royalty, and it was therefore a service which should be much in demand by those wishing to climb the hierarchical ladder of French society.

With the acquisition of royal approval by the granting of honours, *accoucheurs* did indeed now come to be in increasing demand at the birth of the children of the nobility and the well-to-do *bourgeoisie*. Mireille Laget, who also notes the implications of Clément's engagement by the king, has suggested that 'women – at least in urban areas – may well have followed a trend of fashion. Once the royal example had been set by Louis XIV, who called the obstetrician Julien Clément to Mademoiselle de La Vallière's childbed, the surgeons' guild began to gain recognition among ladies of quality'.[207] Jacques Gélis has also identified those who would now call upon the services of the *accoucheur*, noting that at the start of the eighteenth century it was 'surtout les femmes des classes aisées qui utilisent les talents de l'accoucheur'.[208] That highly respected contemporary of Clément, the surgeon Pierre Dionis, noted in his *Traité général des accouchemens* (first published in 1717, just six years after Clément's ennoblement) that princesses and 'toutes les dames de qualité' now chose to use the services of *accoucheurs*, and that 'les bonnes bourgeoises suivent leurs exemples'.[209] Dionis claimed that even the lower orders who could afford to use them would now do so in preference to the *sage-femmes*: it was said of the 'femmes des artisans et du menu peuple que si elles avoient le moyen de les payer, elles les préféreroient aux sages-femmes'.[210] Prosper Marchand added a note to his *Dictionnaire de Bayle* of 1720 to the effect that fashionable Paris preferred the *accoucheur*: 'La grande mode de Paris est de se servir des accoucheurs et non pas des sages-femmes.'[211] He also noted that the time would perhaps come when this same fashion would rule through most of Europe. The *accoucheur* had made his 'explosive arrival' at court and, as a result, his newly noble profession could only find it easier to reach a ready market amongst those French families who could afford its services.

That the rise of the new male role in childbirth happened at this time, and happened in France, is confirmed by the critical Philip Thicknesse, writing in England in the 1760s.[212] Thicknesse, whose invective was aimed at the British man-midwife William Smellie, noted with acerbity that the

> scarce ever failing female midwife, Goody Nature ... who had practised the art of midwifery in every corner of the globe, for many generations, with amazing success; was, about fifty years ago [that is, around 1715], stifled in France between two featherbeds, by Messrs. Doctor *La Motte* and *Mauriceau*: and no sooner was the good old lady interred, than these, and many other male impostors in that fantastical country, endeavoured to intrude themselves on the public as her legitimate sons; nay, to be able by their art, and with the help of hooks, crotchets, fillets, forceps, and scissars, to surpass the good old lady.
> The vivacity, and the love of novelty, peculiar to that nation; and the great liberties the two sexes are allowed to take with each other in that kingdom, promoted the designs of these men; and prevented a detection of such impostors, till they became so numerous, and had established so much interest, (owing I presume to their sex) that the old lady, their pretended mother, has there, long since been forgot. That such a practice as this *should begin in France*, be encouraged by the ladies, and permitted by the men, does not much surprize me; because modesty in that country, is rather an unfashionable part of high breeding, and high life ...[213]

Thicknesse chose to identify the *accoucheurs* la Motte and Mauriceau (both of whom had published treatises, la Motte in 1722[214] and Mauriceau in 1668[215]) as his chief culprits, rather than Clément; but he places the *act* of stifling in around 1715, just four years after the green light of ennoblement had first been lit.

The rise of the specialist surgeon: the *dentiste*

The services of the specialist surgeon for the teeth, the *dentiste*, also enjoyed an acknowledgement of respectability and a rising popularity amongst the well-to-do in France throughout the eighteenth century. We have already seen, via the writings of Pierre Fauchard, that the *dentiste* appears to have gained the approval of other medical men with relative ease, as is implied by the identities of some of those who worked alongside him in the 1720s and by an analysis of the *approbations* published in his book.[216] We have also seen the ennoblement of two royal *dentistes*, the first in 1745 and the second in 1767,[217] and we have noted from records relating to these ennoblements that they were made in acknowledgement of each *dentiste*'s merit. In the case of the second, Etienne Bourdet (for whom the original *lettres d'anoblissement* have survived, unlike those of his predecessor, Jean-François Capperon), we have even seen that ennoblement was made with the expressed intention of encouraging others to show themselves equally worthy in the performance of useful and necessary services for the public – Bourdet had been granted 'un titre d'honneur capable d'encourager ceux qui s'en rendrons aussi dignes dans l'exercice des arts utiles et nécessaires au Public'.[218]

The strongest and most readily visible body of evidence for the rise of the *dentiste* in France may be found in the list of original treatises on the teeth, published by *chirurgien dentistes* or *dentistes*, throughout the eighteenth century.[219] The majority of new publications by such writers appeared after the middle of the century, and are therefore outside the scope of the present volume; nevertheless, a look at their numbers, and the way in which their authors saw themselves, will provide us with what Adrian Wilson has called 'a simple index of eighteenth-century change'.[220] In order to do this, I shall examine publications on the teeth which were original in three distinct ways. First, they were no longer part of 'general' surgical books; second, they contain much technical detail, of a type which had not appeared previously, relating particularly to the *science* for the *dentiste*; and, finally, they were written not by 'general' surgeons but by a group of surgeons who were treating teeth exclusively, celebrating this exclusivity in the titles they took for themselves. A simple survey of book titles and authors will reveal that the publication of an original treatise on the teeth in France was a very rare event indeed before the publication of Fauchard's *Le Chirurgien Dentiste* in 1728[221] – but by mid-century, the number of writings concerning the teeth alone would threaten to outstrip those on any other part of surgery. This phenomenon was recorded by the *dentiste* Etienne Bourdet in his *Recherches et observations* of 1757, who noted that the *Journal des Sçavans* of the previous year had claimed that 'on se réprésente, en un mot, dans la seule partie des Dents, un plus grand nombre d'Ecrivains qu'il n'y en a dans aucune autre branche de la Chirurgie'.[222] Over the following decades, this large number of *écrivains* would show no sign of diminishing. Between 1746 and 1778 twelve different writers would publish a total of twenty works dealing exclusively with diseases and operations concerning the mouth and teeth (see Table 6.1). A brief analysis of the dates of these publications reveals the emergence of two distinct periods of activity amongst their writers: one

Table 6.1 Publications in French on the teeth, 1700–80

Date of publication	Author	Short title	Place of publication
1728	Pierre Fauchard	*Le Chirurgien Dentiste*	Paris
1737	Claude Geraudly	*L'art de conserver les dents*	Paris
1746	Pierre Fauchard	*Le Chirurgien Dentiste*, 2nd edn	Paris
1746	Robert Bunon	*Experiences et demonstrations*	Paris
1746	Mouton	*Essay d'odontotechnie*	Paris
1750	Henri de Lécluse	*Traité Utile*	Paris
1753	G. P. Le Monnier	*Dissertation sur les maladies des dents*	Paris
1754	Henri de Lécluse	*Nouveaux éléments d'odontologie*	Paris
1755	Henri de Lécluse	*Eclaircissements essentiels*	Paris
1757	Etienne Bourdet	*Recherches et observations*	Paris
1757	A. Bréchillet-Jourdain	*Nouveaux éléments d'odontalgie*	Paris
1764	Beaupréau	*Dissertation sur la propreté et la conservation des dents*	Paris
1766	A. Bréchillet-Jourdain	*Essai sur la formation des dents*	Paris
1766	Le Roy de la Faudignère	*La manière de préserver et guérir les maladies des gencives et des dents*	Paris
1770	Jean-François Botot	*Observations sur la suppuration des gencives*	Paris
1771	Pierre Auzebi	*Traité d'odontalgie*	Lyon
1771	Etienne Bourdet	*Soins faciles pour la propreté de la bouche*	Paris
1772	Le Roy de la Faudignère	*La manière*, 2nd edn	Paris
1773	J. A. Hebert	*Réfutation d'un nouveau traité d'odontalgie*	Geneva
1775	anon.	*Le dentiste observateur*	Paris
1778	A. Bréchillet-Jourdain	*Traité des maladies et opérations réellement chirurgicales de la bouche*	Paris
1778	J. A. Hebert	*Le Citoyen Dentiste*	Lyon

group seems to have appeared shortly after 1745, at around the time of publication of the second edition of *Le Chirurgien Dentiste*, and a second group seems to have been busy from the mid-1760s onwards. Significantly, *not one* of the writers concerned would describe himself as an *expert* – each title page would proudly proclaim the writer to be a *chirurgien dentiste* or *dentiste*.

Louis Sébastien Mercier, writing in his *Tableaux de Paris* of 1782, implied that towards the latter decades of the eighteenth century the *dentiste*'s sign had become a familiar sight in Paris. According to Mercier, if you were seized by a toothache while walking in the street, you had only to look up to see the *dentiste*'s sign welcoming you:

> Si une rage de dents vous saisit dans la rue, vous n'avez qu'à lever les yeux. Une enseigne qui représente une dent molaire, grosse comme une boisseau, vous dit *montez*. Le dentiste vous fait asseoir, releve sa manchette de dentelle, tire votre dent d'une main leste, & vous offre ensuite un gargarisme; vous le payez & vous continuez votre chemin sans douleur. Cela n'est-il pas commode?[223]

But, for Mercier, the *dentiste* was much more than just a remover of teeth. The most skilful would try to keep teeth rather than remove them, rarely reaching for their *daviets* or *pélicans*. Mercier noted that one, by the name of Catalan, had brought together judicious and careful observations, and by the nimbleness of his hands could create a kind of marvel. He could make a complete set of artificial teeth with which the wearer could grind all his food with neither embarrassment nor effort: he understood mastication, and knew how to imitate it to the point of perfection.[224] For Mercier, therefore, such work deserved the credit due to an artist, and it was built on foundations of an extended knowledge of anatomy – which Dionis had described at the start of the century as 'the *basis* and foundation of surgery'.[225] Surgeons were turning to the teeth in the provinces, too: the historian Pierre Laudet, for example, has shown that the surgeon Guillaume Delga of Toulouse would advertise that he had set up as a specialist 'in the practice of those branches of surgery concerning the treatment of the teeth and hernias' in 1784.[226]

Studies of archive material, performed both recently and in the 1920s, help to reinforce this image of a growth in the numbers of *dentistes* during this period. But much further research awaits the historian of dentistry in France in the second half of the eighteenth century. As I have explained in the Introduction, it has not been my intention here to perform a thorough archive-based analysis of the rise in numbers of *dentistes*, but those who have searched for such evidence have found it exceptionally difficult to uncover.[227] As a result, it seems unlikely that we shall ever be able to arrive at anything approaching firm figures for the number of *dentistes*, even taking Paris alone. However, by combining the little archive material which we *do* have with other written evidence, we may be able to venture a reasonable estimate – but at present this should not be taken to be anything other than a 'first-order' guess. Once again, analysis of such material will require an open reading of the titles used and applied, paying particular attention to *who* is describing *whom* as *what*.

We may reasonably assume that in around 1700 there were very few *dentistes* in Paris. There were perhaps one or two practitioners who had taken that title for themselves: we know that Fauchard had started to focus on the teeth in the 1690s (the earliest-dated *observation* in *Le Chirurgien Dentiste* relates to treatment performed in 1696),[228] and he makes frequent reference to the late M. Carmeline, whom he held in high regard, describing him as 'Maître Chirurgien à Paris, & célébre Dentiste'.[229] There is also a reference to the late M. Dubois, 'Chirurgien Dentiste de Louis XIV'.[230] However, Fauchard's book, published in 1728, reveals that by this time the number of *dentistes* had started to increase. Some of these we know by name: Capperon, Laudumiey and Fauchard himself all rejoiced in the title, and there are many references to others practising in the same way, such as the number of unnamed *confrères* and the body of *dentistes* whom Fauchard considered worthy of the title due to their efforts in conserving teeth.[231] By 1727 more than sixty-five patients had approached Fauchard with problems which were of sufficient importance to warrant inclusion in his *observations* (and which were presumably, therefore, not his only consultations in this period), and the practice of the *dentiste* was well enough known for the physician of the Marquise de Trans to suggest she should consult one.[232] I shall suggest, then, that we may assume a rough estimate of perhaps ten to twelve *dentistes* in Paris at the end of the 1720s.

The earliest documents relating to *dentistes* in Paris which appear to have survived date from just after the middle of the eighteenth century, and from these it seems reasonable to assume that the number in the town had risen to around thirty-five by this time. André Besombes and Georges Dagen, working in the 1920s, noted the existence of a register relating to payments made to the École de Chirurgie at Saint-Côme for the year 1757–58, which lists thirty-four practitioners for the teeth.[233] For the official purposes of Saint-Côme, these are referred to as *experts*; but the list includes names such as Bourdet, Fauchard, Hébert, Jourdain, Lécluse and Le Monnier, all of whom had taken (or would take, in the case of Hébert) the title of *chirurgien dentiste* or *dentiste* to describe themselves, as we have seen in the list of publications in Table 6.1. Similarly, the *Tableau de Paris* for 1759 contains the names of thirty-five practitioners, most of whom also featured on the Saint-Côme document.[234] Jeze's *Tableau de Paris* for 1761 lists thirty-three *dentistes*, three of whom are described as Maistres en Chirurgie and the rest, including Bourdet, Fauchard, Laudumiay (*sic*), Le Monier (*sic*) and Mouton (described as Dentiste du Roi) as *experts*;[235] however, Fauchard's certificate of interment, issued upon his burial at the parish church of Saint-Côme in March of that same year, would describe him only as 'Pierre Fauchard, ancien Maître Chirurgien-Dentiste'.[236] By 1776, according to the *Etat de la Médecine*, the number had increased to forty-three, again including *chirurgien dentistes* such as Bottot (*sic*), Bourdet, Bunon, Jourdain, Landumiey (*sic*), Lécluse and Mercier's favourite, Catalan.[237]

More recent research has uncovered archive material relating to those treating teeth in the latter part of the eighteenth century in provincial France, and this, too, points to an increase in the numbers of *dentistes*. Pierre Baron in particular has made a detailed archive study of those treating teeth in Lyon in this period, drawing on his examinations of the *Livre pour les actes de légère experience*[238] and the admissions register for the Lyon guild of surgeons. This study shows that just five practitioners treating teeth were newly recognized by the guild between 1742 and 1763, but that from 1767 to 1788 the number rose to ten – double the number for the same time-span.[239] Extending his research to the *Almanach de Lyon*, Baron notes that the first appearance of a particular surgeon for the teeth was in 1768, listed immediately after the master surgeons and a single surgeon-oculist.[240] The numbers soon increased, however: there were two in 1769 and five in 1774–75, rising to nine in 1788.[241] If we build on these figures, which mostly relate to the acceptance of new practitioners, it seems reasonable to arrive at an estimate of around fifteen to twenty *dentistes* in Lyon by the end of the 1780s; but again, it must be emphasized that at present such a figure should only be taken as a first-order guess.

If we combine the estimates suggested above with the evidence provided by publications, and place them alongside the technical and social stories told in this book, we can see that for Paris, at any rate, the number of *dentistes* increased gradually from the start of the eighteenth century. After around 1745, the date of Capperon's ennoblement, this increase became more pronounced; and, as the *science* of the *dentiste* expanded over the following decades (as implied by the rise in publications) it would continue, accompanied by the welcoming approval of the surgical establishment and the ennoblement of Bourdet in 1767. This ennoblement, while not, perhaps, having the same sudden impact as that of the *accoucheur* Clément fifty-five years earlier, would nevertheless serve as a celebration of the establishment of those taking the title of *chirurgien dentiste*. Taken together, then, *all* these events would

serve to fuel the fashion for the *dentiste*. It would seem fair to conclude
that by 1760 in France, the *dentiste* had arrived.

Notes

1. Fabricius ab Aquapendente, *Opera Chirurgica,* Venice, 1619, p. 32.
    Translation in Walter Hoffmann-Axthelm, *History of Dentistry,* Quin-
    tessence, Chicago, 1981, p. 142.
2. Pierre Dionis, *A Course of Chirurgical operations, Demonstrated in the
    Royal Gardens at Paris,* 2nd edn, Tonson, London, 1733, p. 334.
3. Christopher Breward, *The culture of fashion: A new history of fashion-
    able dress,* Manchester, Manchester University Press, 1995, p. 77.
4. Ibid., p. 84.
5. At the end of the seventeenth century, over 50 per cent of the Parisian
    nobility had fortunes exceeding 50 000 *livres* while barely 20 per cent
    had 100 000. See Daniel Roche, *The culture of clothing: dress and
    fashion in the 'ancien régime',* translated by Jean Birrell, Cambridge,
    Cambridge University Press, 1994, p. 96.
6. Ibid., p. 185.
7. Ibid.
8. Jean de la Bruyère, *The Characters, or the Manners of the Age, by
    Monsieur de la Bruyère, of the French Academy. Made English by
    several hands,* Bullord, London, 1699 (English translation of French
    edition of 1688), p. 188.
9. Ibid., pp. 53–4.
10. Jean Baptiste Poquelin de Molière, *Les Précieuses ridicules,* Paris, 1683;
    cited in Richard Corson, *Fashions in makeup from ancient to modern
    times,* Peter Owen, London, 1972, p. 165.
11. There were many others. *La galante* was worn in the middle of the
    cheek, *L'impudent* or *l'effrontée* on the nose, *la discrète* on the lower lip,
    la baiseuse beside the mouth and *la silencieuse* between the mouth and
    the chin. See ibid., p. 167.
12. Ibid., p. 187.
13. Roy Genders, *History of Scent,* Hamish Hamilton, London, 1972,
    p. 129.
14. Corson, *Fashions in makeup,* p. 187.
15. Ibid., p. 197.
16. Michael and Ariane Batterberry, *Fashion: The mirror of history,*
    Columbus, London, 1982, p. 169.
17. Corson cites Mme de Genlis's remark to a gentleman on having permit-
    ted him to watch whilst she applied her patches: 'Well, what do you
    think of that! Would you not take me for a girl of twenty?' Corson,
    Fashions in makeup, p. 211.
18. Genders, *History of Scent,* p. 130.
19. Daniel Roche, *The People of Paris: an essay in popular culture in the
    eighteenth century,* Berg, Leamington Spa, 1987, p. 153.
20. Ibid.
21. Lady Mary Wortley Montague, *Letters of the Right Honourable Lady
    Mary Wortley Montague: Written, during her Travels in Europe, Asia*

    and Africa, to Persons of Distinction, Men of Letters, &c. in different Parts of Europe. T. Becket and P. A. De Hondt, London, 1763, Letter XLIX, to the Lady R————, Paris, 10 October 1718.

22. Corson, *Fashions in makeup*, p. 215.
23. La Bruyère, *Characters*, pp. 53–4.
24. Ibid., p. 353.
25. Pierre Fauchard, *Le Chirurgien Dentiste, ou Traité des Dents*, 2nd edn, Mariette, Paris, 1746, vol. I, title page.
26. Fauchard, *Das Herrn Pierre Fauchard Frantzösischer Zahn=Arzt, Oder Tractat Von den Zahnen*, Rudigern, Berlin, 1733, title page.
27. Fauchard, *Le Chirurgien Dentiste*, vol. I, p. 60.
28. Ibid., pp. 61–2.
29. Ibid., p. 62.
30. Ibid.
31. Letter of 9 July 1714, from A. Geffroy, *Madame de Maintenon, d'après sa correspondance*, vol. II, p. 352, in Alfred Franklin, *La vie privée d'autrefois*, vol. 14, *Variétés chirurgicales*, p. 167.
32. Fauchard, *Le Chirurgien Dentiste*, vol. II, p. 189.
33. Fauchard, *Le Chirurgien Dentiste*, vol. I, p. 63.
34. Ibid.
35. Ibid., p. 219.
36. Ibid., p. 377.
37. Ibid., p. 379.
38. Dionis, *A Course of Chirurgical operations*, p. 335.
39. Fauchard, *Le Chirurgien Dentiste*, vol. II, p. 3.
40. Ibid., p. 4.
41. '(a) Espéce de microscope' (Fauchard's note). Fauchard, *Le Chirurgien Dentiste*, vol. I, p. 73.
42. Geraudly, *L'Art de conserver les dents*, Mercier, Paris, 1737. On his title page, Geraudly describes himself as 'GERAUDLY, Chirurgien-Dentiste, Valet de Chambre de S.A.S. le Duc d'Orleans, & seul privilégié du Roy de France'. He also gives thanks to the family of the Duc d'Orléans for 'l'honneur qu'elle me fait de m'employer en qualité de Chirurgien-Dentiste'. Ibid., epitre, p. iv.
43. Robert Bunon, *Essay sur les maladies des dents, ou l'on propose les moyens de leur procurer une bonne conformation dès la plus tendre Enfance, & d'en assurer la conservation pendant tout le cours de la vie*, Briasson, Chambert, de Hansy, Paris, 1743, p. 170. Bunon describes himself as 'Chirurgien-Dentiste, à Paris'.
44. Ibid., p. vi.
45. Fauchard, *Le Chirurgien Dentiste*, vol. I, p. 351.
46. See Chapter Five, p. 122.
47. Fauchard, *Le Chirurgien Dentiste*, vol. II, p. 112.
48. Ibid., p. 113.
49. Fauchard, *Le Chirurgien Dentiste*, vol. I, p. 370.
50. Ibid., p. 371.
51. Ibid.
52. Ibid., p. 368.
53. Ibid., p. 369.
54. *Gabelles* = salt tax.
55. Fauchard, *Le Chirurgien Dentiste*, vol. I, p. 359.

56. Ibid.
57. Ibid., p. 361.
58. Ibid.
59. Ibid.
60. Ibid.
61. Ibid., p. 354.
62. Ibid., p. 355.
63. Ibid.
64. Ibid., p. 357.
65. Dionis, *A Course of Chirurgical operations*, pp. 341–2.
66. Ibid., p. 342. For details of Guillemeau's paste, see Chapter Three, p. 57.
67. Fauchard, *Le Chirurgien Dentiste*, vol. II, p. 215.
68. Ibid., pp. 215–6.
69. Ibid., p. 217.
70. Ibid., chapter XIV: *Maniére de blanchir les os des jambes de bœuf qui servent ainsi préparez, à faire des dents, ou partie de dentiers artificiels.*
71. Ibid., p. 260.
72. Ibid., p. 271.
73. Ibid., p. 283.
74. Ibid., pp. 283–4.
75. Ibid., p. 284.
76. Ibid., p. 339.
77. Ibid.
78. Ibid.
79. Ibid.
80. Ibid., p. 340.
81. Similar to that shown in Figure 6.1, but with a much smaller row of teeth.
82. Fauchard, *Le Chirurgien Dentiste*, vol. II, p. 352.
83. Ear-rings. Ibid., p. 289.
84. Ibid.
85. A 'happy cough'. Ibid., p. 290.
86. 'Je ne sçai si on a depuis remédié à ce vuide, ni comment on l'a pû faire; mais il faloit que cette Dame eût une forte envie d'avoir la bouche garnie, pour souffrir une opération si cruelle & même comprendre qu'un Dentiste tant soit peu jaloux de sa réputation, l'ait ainsi exposée, surtout à Paris, où tant d'habiles gens de toutes sortes de professions se trouvent, & concourent par leur travail à l'ornement de cette grande Ville.' Ibid.
87. Louis Sébastien Mercier, *Tableau de Paris*, Amsterdam, 1782 (nouvelle édition), vol. V, p. 74.
88. Ibid.
89. The allocation of a specific date to the ennoblement of the king's *dentiste* is problematic. The Archives Nationales contain papers relating to the *lettres d'anoblissement* awarded to two royal *dentistes*: Jean-François Capperon in 1745 and Etienne Bourdet in 1767. Whilst the *lettres* confirming Bourdet's subsequent ennoblement are held in the *Archives*, there is no record of those confirming Capperon's. However, while modern French writers such as François Vidal identify Bourdet firmly as the first *dentiste* to have gained ennoblement ('Bourdet est annobli. Jusqu'alors, jamais pareille distinction n'avait été donnée à un dentiste.' Vidal (ed.), *Histoire d'un diplôme*, CDF, 1993, p. 36), Georges Dagen's

earlier uncovering of papers relating to Capperon indicates that he was indeed awarded such an honour by the king more than twenty years before, confirmed or not. See Georges Dagen, 'Lettres de Noblesse accordées à Caperon et à Bourdet par Louis XV', *La Semaine Dentaire*, 28 February 1926, 198–200. We shall also see that in Bourdet's letters of ennoblement the king made specific reference to those awarded to Capperon.

90.   The French historian Alfred Franklin noted that to cure the king's toothache d'Aquin 'employait l'essence de girofle et celle de thym; quand il se formait un abcès, il appliquait sur la joue un cataplasme de mie de pain'. Franklin, *Variétés chirurgicales*, p. 167.

91.   J. A. le Roi, *Journal de la Santé du roi Louis XIV*, Paris, 1862, p. 162.

92.   It should be noted that there is no firm evidence to the effect that this is, in fact, a painting of a *dentiste*. It could equally well, be of a barber. However, the seated gentleman is neither 'soaped' nor draped in a towel, and the rather well-dressed man standing behind him holds his jaw in the manner suggested by Fauchard for one about to work on the teeth.

93.   Le Roi, *Journal de la Santé*, p. 164.

94.   Trabouillet, *État de la France pour 1712*, vol. I, p. 178, cited in Franklin, *Variétés chirurgicales*, p. 167.

95.   Franklin, *Variétés chirurgicales*, p. 167.

96.   Fauchard, *Le Chirurgien Dentiste*, vol. II, p. 339. See p. 171.

97.   Fauchard, *Le Chirurgien Dentiste*, vol. II, p. 339.

98.   Colin Jones, 'The *Médecins du Roi* at the End of the *Ancien Régime* and in the French Revolution', in Vivian Nutton (ed.), *Medicine at the courts of Europe, 1500–1837*, Routledge, London, 1990, pp. 209–61, 210.

99.   A detailed study of the structure of the French nobility would be inappropriate here, but for contemporary writings on the French nobility in the *ancien régime*, see G. A. de la Roque, *Traité de la Noblesse, et de toutes ses differentes espéces*, bound with *Traité de la Noblesse et de son origine, suivant les préjugés rendus pour des commissaires députés pour la vérification des Titres de Noblesse* (nouvelle édition), Le Boucher, Paris, 1735; François A. Aubert de la Chesnaye-Dubois, *Dictionnaire de la Noblesse de France*, 1770–78 (12 vols); Père Anselme de Sainte Marie, *Histoire généalogique et chronologique de la maison royale de France, des pairs, grands officiers de la couronne et de la maison du roy, et des anciens barons du royaume; avec les qualitez, l'origine, le progrès et les armes de leurs familles; ensemble les statuts et le catalogue des chevaliers, commandeurs, et officiers de l'ordre du Saint Esprit*, 1726–33 (9 vols). See also the entry under *Noblesse* in the *Encyclopédie, ou Dictionnaire Raisonné des sciences, des arts et des métiers, par une societé de gens de lettres* compiled by Diderot and d'Alembert, Paris, 1757. Useful secondary sources include Guy Chaussinand-Nogaret, *The French nobility in the eighteenth century: From feudalism to enlightenment* (Eng. trans.), CUP, Cambridge, 1985; Norbert Elias, *The Court Society*, Blackwell, Oxford, 1983; Jean-François Solnon, *La Cour de France*, Librairie Arthème Fayard, Paris, 1987 and Ruth Kleinman, 'Social Dynamics at the French Court: The Household of Anne of Austria', *French Historical Studies*, 16 (3), 1990, 517–35.

100.   La Roque, *Traité de la Noblesse, et de toutes ses differentes espéces*, pp. 54–5.

101. Ibid., p. 55.
102. Jean-Pierre Goubert, *The Ancien Régime: French society 1600–1750*, Weidenfeld and Nicolson, London, 1973, p. 166.
103. La Roque, *Traité de la Noblesse et de son origine*, p. 400.
104. La Roque, *Traité de la Noblesse, et de toutes ses differentes espéces*, p. 54.
105. But they could also be expensive. The *Encyclopédie* of Diderot and d'Alembert states under the entry for *noblesse par lettres* that the many needs of the state would thus reduce ministers to finding resources in the greed men have for honours: one example given is that of Richard Graindorge, a famous beef merchant of Pays d'Auge in Normandy, who was obliged in 1577 to take *lettres de noblesse* for a fee of 30 000 *livres*.
106. Chaussinand-Nogaret, *The French nobility in the eighteenth century*, p. 32.
107. Fiscal privilege is now often held to have been the greatest advantage conferred by nobility: because in principle the nobleman served the king by bearing arms or giving counsel, he was generally exempt from the direct taxation of the *taille* – the badge of the commoner – but there were important exceptions. Areas such as Languedoc, for example, were *pays de taille réelle*, in which both noble and commoner were obliged to pay taxes on any non-privileged land which they possessed (see Colin Jones, *Charity and bienfaisance: the treatment of the poor in the Montpellier region, 1740–1815*, CUP, Cambridge, 1982, pp. 37–8). The financial system of the *ancien régime* was highly complex, but as Jean-Pierre Goubert has said succinctly, 'On the whole, the nobility was only slightly affected by taxation.' Goubert, *The Ancien Régime*, p. 165.
108. Ibid., p. 180.
109. Ruth Kleinman, 'Social Dynamics at the French Court: The Household of Anne of Austria', *French Historical Studies*, 16 (3), 1990, 517–35.
110. Chaussinand-Nogaret, *The French nobility in the eighteenth century*, p. 2.
111. See note 99.
112. Kleinman, 'Social Dynamics at the French Court', p. 521.
113. See J.-F. Bluche, *L'origine des magistrats du parlement de Paris au XVIIIe siècle*, Fédération des sociétés historiques et archéologiques de Paris et de l'Ile de France, Paris, 1956, p. 21.
114. *Encyclopédie*, entry under *Noblesse par Lettres*.
115. The following requirements and regulations are all referred to in La Roque, *Traité de la Noblesse et de son origine*, p. 400.
116. Goubert, *The Ancien Régime*, p. 185.
117. Letters of renewal, literally 'past one year' (Fleming and Tibbins, *Grand Dictionnaire*).
118. Kleinman, 'Social Dynamics at the French Court', p. 519.
119. *Encyclopédie*, entry under *Noblesse par Lettres*. No reason is given for the various revocations and reinstatements of nobility.
120. *Journal de la Santé du Roi Louis XIV*, ed. J.-A. Le Roi, Paris, 1862, pp. 166–75, 395–405, cited in Gelfand, *Professionalizing modern medicine*, p. 34.
121. Jean Devaux, *Index funereus* (1714), p. 100; cited in Alfred Franklin, *La vie privée d'autrefois*, vol. 12, *Les Chirurgiens*, p. 143.
122. Dionis, *A Course of Chirurgical operations*, p. 222.

123. Ibid.
124. Such as Jacques de la Cuisse and his father-in-law François Bouchet. See Franklin, *Variétés chirurgicales,* p. 86.
125. Ibid., p. 94.
126. For discussion of the work of the midwife and the *accoucheur,* see Jacques Gélis, 'Sages-femmes et accoucheurs: l'obstétrique populaire aux XVIIᵉ et XVIIIᵉ siècles', *Annales Économies Sociétés Civilisations,* 32 (5), 1977, 927–57 and Mireille Laget, 'Childbirth in Seventeenth- and Eighteenth-Century France: Obstetrical Practices and Collective Attitudes', in Robert Forster and Orest Ranum (eds), *Medicine and Society in France: Selections from the Annales,* vol. 6, The Johns Hopkins University Press, Baltimore, 1980, pp. 137–76. Adrian Wilson's writings on man-midwifery, principally 'William Hunter and the varieties of man-midwifery', in W. F. Bynum and Roy Porter, *William Hunter and the eighteenth-century medical world* (CUP, Cambridge, 1985, 344–69) and Adrian Wilson, *The Making of Man-Midwifery: Childbirth in England, 1660–1770* (UCL Press, London, 1995) give a useful insight into the differing implications of involving the surgeon or the man-midwife in seventeenth- and eighteenth-century Britain. Although the story of the rise of the *accoucheur* in France is not within the scope of Wilson's book, his analysis of the fashionable component of the man-as-midwife is nevertheless of value to the story of the making of the *dentiste.*
127. 'Encore que l'anoblissement et les autres titres d'honneur que nous accordons soient le plus ordinairement la récompense des services que nos sujets nous rendent dans la profession des armes'. *Lettres d'anoblissement accordées à Julien Clément,* reproduced in Franklin, *Variétés chirurgicales,* p. 95. The quotations which follow in this paragraph are all taken from this source.
128. 'Et pour lui donner encore un témoignage plus authentique de notre estime, nous lui permettons d'ajouter auxdites armoiries une fleur de lis d'or sur champ d'azur'. *Lettres, Clément,* in Franklin, *Variétés chirurgicales,* p. 95.
129. Variously spelt 'Capperon', 'Caperon' or 'Capron'. I shall use the form 'Capperon', as in the records held in the Archives Nationales, where appropriate.
130. Archives Nationales (A.N.), Z1 A: 607, cited in Georges Dagen, 'Lettres de Noblesse Accordées à Caperon et à Bourdet par Louis XV', *La Semaine Dentaire,* 28 February 1926, 198–200.
131. 'Une Dame de la premiére condition'. Fauchard, *Le Chirurgien Dentiste,* vol. II, p. 339.
132. Ibid.
133. Entry for 24 November 1742 in Barbier, *Chronique de la Régence et du regne de Louis XV (1718–1763), ou Journal de Barbier,* Charpentier, Paris, 1857 edn, vol. VIII, p. 199.
134. 'Enquête de noblesse faite par nous Augustin Guillier, conseiller du Roy ... à la requête de Jean-François Capperon, Chirurgien-Dentiste du Roy, sur les lettres de noblesse à luy accordées par Sa Majesté, au mois de Décembre mil sept cent quarante cinq, sur lesquelles j'ai obtenu des lettres de surrannation ' A.N., Z1 A: 607, in Dagen, 'Lettres de Noblesse,' p. 199. The date of this *enquête* is 31 May, 1759: the reasons for this apparent delay are not clear.

135. A.N., Z1 A: 607, in ibid.
136. A.N., Z1 A: 607, in ibid. Dagen chooses to interpret Bandezy's title as 'Maître à danser'.
137. A.N., Z1 A: 607, in ibid.
138. See page 179.
139. A.N., Z1 A: 607, in Dagen, 'Lettres de Noblesse,' p. 199.
140. A.N., Z1 A: 607, in ibid.
141. *Lettres de noblesse* accorded to Etienne Bourdet, A.N. P/2597.
142. M. Bourdet, *Recherches et observations sur toutes les parties de l'art du dentiste*, Herissant, Paris, 1757, vol. I, title page.
143. Vidal, *Histoire d'un diplôme*, p. 52. *Odontologie*, for Vidal, means the work of the *dentiste*.
144. Hoffmann-Axthelm, *History of Dentistry*, p. 210. According to Franklin, Mouton, despite his name, 'faisait une belle peur à ses royales clientes'. Franklin recounts one particular episode, recorded in the memoirs of the Duc de Luynes, in which Mouton had declared that one of the king's daughters needed to have a tooth removed: 'M. Mouton avoit prononcé qu'il falloit arracher une dent à Mme Victoire. Cette sentence, confirmée par la Faculté et approuvée par le Roi, étoit sans appel.' Mm. Victoire, who was 'plus pieuse que brave', was not keen, and resisted all attempts to persuade her to undergo the operation. After two days of prevarication and fruitless attempts at persuasion, the *dentiste* eventually managed to perform the extraction. His unhappy patient was restrained by the king on one side, and the queen on the other. Duc de Luynes, *Mémoires*, 17 April 1748, vol. IX, p. 11, in Franklin, *Variétés chirurgicales*, p. 170.
145. Bourdet, *Recherches*, vol. I, p. ix.
146. Ibid., p. viii.
147. Ibid.
148. Ibid., p. x. A reading of the *Recherches et observations* will reveal a liberal sprinkling of references to Fauchard's work, perhaps most noticeably in the chapters which deal with the operations for the teeth and the construction of artificial ones. In the latter part of volume II, for example, Fauchard's name appears on pp. 203, 223, 226, 240, 243, 244, 255, 265 and so on.
149. Bourdet, *Recherches*, vol. II, heading to chapter V.
150. Ibid., p. 2.
151. Ibid., p. xvi.
152. Ibid., p. xii.
153. Ibid., pp. ix–x.
154. Ibid., p. 207.
155. Ibid.
156. Bourdet, *Recherches*, vol. II, p. 47. Bourdet, unlike Fauchard, did not publish the names of his patients.
157. Vidal, *Histoire d'un diplôme*, p. 52.
158. Hoffmann-Axthelm, *History of Dentistry*, p. 210.
159. Vidal, *Histoire d'un diplôme*, p. 56. According to the *Almanach Royal* for 1788, both Bourdet and Dubois-Foucou were 'Parmi les Chirurgiens-Jurés' of Paris. Dagen, *Documents pour servir à l'Histoire de l'Art dentaire en France, principalement à Paris,* Editions de La Semaine Dentaire, Paris, 1925, p. 326.
160. A.N., Z1 A: 611, in Dagen, 'Lettres de Noblesse,' p. 199.

161. A.N., Z1 A: 611, in ibid., p. 200.
162. A.N., Z1 A: 611, in ibid.
163. A.N., Z1 A: 611, in ibid., p. 199.
164. A.N., Z1 A: 611, in ibid., p. 200.
165. A N., Z1 A: 611, in ibid.
166. *Recherches et observations* would, for example, in 1790 become the first book on the teeth to be published in Russian. Hoffmann-Axthelm, *History of Dentistry*, p. 210.
167. *Lettres de noblesse* accorded to Etienne Bourdet, A.N. P/2597, p. 16.
168. Ibid., p. 17.
169. Ibid., p. 16. Unfortunately, I have not succeeded in uncovering evidence relating to any actual treatment Bourdet may have performed for either the king or the members of the royal family.
170. Ibid., p. 16.
171. Ibid.
172. Ibid., p. 17.
173. Michelle Caroly, *Le corps du Roi-Soleil: grandeur et misères de sa majesté Louis XIV*, Imago, Paris, 1990, p. 137.
174. Elias, *The Court Society,* p. 149.
175. Ibid., p. 132.
176. Ibid., p. 79.
177. There is 'no long shelf of books' regarding the life of Louis XV. Olivier Bernier, *Louis the Beloved: The Life of Louis XV,* Doubleday & Company Inc., New York, 1984, preface.
178. François-Marie Arouet Voltaire, *The Age of Lewis XIV,* Faulkner, Dublin, 1752 (Eng. trans.), vol. I, pp. 2–4.
179. Voltaire, *The Age of Lewis XIV,* vol. I, p. 4.
180. Voltaire, *The Age of Lewis XIV,* vol. II, p. 19.
181. Ibid., p. 28–9.
182. I do not intend to discuss the king's influence on 'French absolutism'. In an attempt to avoid possible confusion, I shall not use the term 'absolute' in connection with my discussion of the personal power of the king's body.
183. David Parker, *The Making of French Absolutism,* Edward Arnold, London, 1983, p. 136.
184. Ibid., p. 150.
185. Ibid.
186. P. Anderson, *Lineages of the Absolutist State*, NLB, London, 1974, p. 86.
187. Elias, *The Court Society,* pp. 117–18.
188. Bernier, *Louis the Beloved*, p. 24.
189. Duc de Luynes, *Mémoires sur la cour de Louis XV*, Paris, 1860, vol. I, p. 263; in Bernier, *Louis the Beloved*, p. 90.
190. Peter Burke, *The Fabrication of Louis XIV,* Yale University Press, New Haven, 1992, p. 87.
191. Ibid.
192. Balzac, *Aristippe,* 1658, p. 221, cited in Marc Bloch, *The Royal Touch: Sacred Monarchy and Scrofula in England and France*, Routledge & Kegan Paul, London, 1973, p. 196.
193. 'The king touches you, God cures you.' Burke, *The Fabrication of Louis XIV,* p. 43. Burke notes, however, that later in the eighteenth century

the king's statement became a little more cautious, taking the form 'Le roi te touche, Dieu te guérisse – '*may* God cure you.' Burke, *The Fabrication of Louis XIV*, p. 131.

194. Bloch, *The Royal Touch*, p. 203.
195. Ibid.
196. Ibid., p. 204.
197. Burke, *The Fabrication of Louis XIV*, p. 90.
198. Elias, *The Court Society*, p. 63.
199. Ibid., p. 17.
200. The king liked to be asked for lodgings at Versailles. Elias notes that the diarist Saint-Simon said in a summary of Louis XIV's life, written after his death, that 'He [Louis] had countless apartments installed at Versailles, and he was flattered to be asked for one.' Ibid., note to p. 80.
201. Jacques Gélis, 'Sages-femmes et accoucheurs: l'obstétrique populaire aux XVIIᵉ et XVIIIᵉ siècles', in *Annales Économies Sociétés Civilisations*, 32 (5), 1977, 927–57, 947.
202. For an analysis of Hecquet's strong religious beliefs, see Laurence Brockliss, 'The medico-religious universe of an early eighteenth-century Parisian doctor: the case of Philippe Hecquet' in Roger French and Andrew Wear, *The medical revolution of the seventeenth century*, CUP, Cambridge, 1989, pp. 191–221.
203. J. Etienne, Paris, 1708.
204. Hecquet, *De l'indécence*, list of chapters.
205. Ibid., p. 9.
206. J. Devaux, *Index funereus*, p. 112, cited in Franklin, *Les chirurgiens*, Paris, 1893, p. 11.
207. Mireille Laget, 'Childbirth in Seventeenth- and Eighteenth-Century France: Obstetrical Practices and Collective Attitudes', in Robert Forster and Orest Ranum (eds), *Medicine and Society in France: Selections from the Annales*, vol. 6, The Johns Hopkins University Press, Baltimore, 1980, pp. 137–76, 158.
208. Jacques Gélis, *Accoucheur de campagne sous le roi soleil: le traité d'accouchement de G. Mauquest de la Motte*, Edouard Privat, Toulouse, 1979, p. 29.
209. Pierre Dionis, *Traité général des accouchemens. Qui instruit de tout ce qu'il faut faire pour etre habile accoucheur*, d'Houry, Paris, 1724 (2nd edn), p. 448. We shall see that Dionis saw the *accoucheur*, as he did the *dentiste*, as a surgeon who had chosen to practise one particular part of surgery only.
210. Ibid. However, Jacques Gélis notes that this phenomenon was, to some extent, confined to northern France. See Gélis, 'Sages-femmes et accoucheurs', p. 948.
211. *Dictionnaire de Bayle*, 1720, vol. ii, p. 1468 (marginal note), cited in Franklin, *Variétés chirurgicales*, p. 96.
212. Philip Thicknesse, *Man-midwifery analysed: and the Tendency of that Practice detected and exposed*, 2nd edn, Davis and Caslon, London, 1765.
213. Thicknesse, *Man-midwifery analysed*, pp. 3–4. My emphases.
214. G. M. la Motte, *Traité complet des accouchemens naturels, non naturels, et contre nature, explique dans un grand nombre d'observations et de*

reflexions sur l'art d'accoucher, d'Houry, Paris, 1722 (English translation: *A general treatise of midwifery*, Tomkyns, London, 1746).

215. F. Mauriceau, *Traité des maladies des femmes grosses*, Paris, 1668 (English translation by Hugh Chamberlen: *The accomplisht midwife*, London, 1673). This was reissued as *The diseases of women with child* in 1683, 1697, 1710, 1716, 1718, 1727, 1736 and 1752.

216. See Chapter Five.

217. See p. 183 ff.

218. *Lettres*, A.N. P/2597, p. 16.

219. In the present work I shall, of necessity, limit my sources to printed material. Some archive work has been performed in recent years which relates to those 'received' to practice on the teeth in a few provincial surgical *communautés*, and I am grateful to writers such as Dr Pierre Baron of the *Société Française d'Histoire de l'Art Dentaire* with whom I have enjoyed much personal communication regarding the range of such material. From these conversations, and from my own research, it would seem that little thorough archive work has been carried out on records relating to *dentistes* and *chirurgien dentistes* in Paris since the 1920s (see Georges Dagen, *Documents pour servir à l'Histoire de l'Art dentaire en France, principalement à Paris,* Editions de La Semaine Dentaire, Paris, 1925). Whilst I shall draw on the valuable evidence provided by modern workers such as Baron (principally for Lyon, but also for Paris) and Xavier Deltombe (Rennes), it is clear that the archive picture of the *dentiste* in Paris, built on the record provided by legal documents, trade records, advertisements and other similar material awaits much further work.

220. Wilson, *The Making of Man-Midwifery*, p. 5. In his work on man-midwifery in England, Adrian Wilson uses the publication of original midwifery treatises in this way. In doing so, he presents a strong argument for the rise of man-midwifery in England after 1733, taking as his foundation the large number of original English treatises on the subject which followed that date.

221. In the preface to his book, Fauchard refers in passing to the surgeon Hémard's *Recherche de la vraie Anatomie des dents* of 1582 and the apothecary Martin's *Dissertation sur les dents* of 1679 (see *Le Chirurgien Dentiste*, vol. I, p. x) as the only books worthy of note to have been written on the subject of the teeth in particular. However, he suggests that both are limited in their extent, and neither deals with the operations for the teeth: throughout his own writing he takes Dionis's *Cours d'opérations de Chirurgie* as the previous authority (for example, vol. I, p. 205).

222. *Journal des Sçavans*, December 1756, vol. 2, p. 2518, in Bourdet, *Recherches*, vol. I, p. vii.

223. Louis Sébastien Mercier, *Tableau de Paris*, Amsterdam, 1782 (nouvelle édition), vol. V, p. 75. In this large twelve-volume work the chapter entitled *dentistes* follows immediately after that concerning another body of specialist surgeons, the *accoucheurs,* in volume V.

224. 'Les habiles dentistes s'attachent plus à conserver les dents qu'à les extirper. Ils n'arment plus si fréquemment leurs mains de l'acier douloureux. Le plus étonnant dans son art se nomme Catalan, rue Dauphine.

A la légèreté de la main, il a réuni les observations les plus judicieuses et les plus fines; enfin il est créateur d'une espèce de merveille.

Il vous fera (tant en cette partie ses connaissances anatomiques sont étendues), il vous fera, dis-je, un ratelier complet avec lequel vous broyerez tous les aliments sans gêne et sans efforts. Il a su deviner le jeu de la mastication; il a su l'imiter à un tel point de perfection que cela m'a paru d'un mérite trop rare et de trop grande utilité pour qui'il me fût permis de taire ici et le nom et l'éloge de l'artiste.' Mercier, *Tableau de Paris*, vol. V, p. 75.

225. Pierre Dionis, *The Anatomy of Humane Bodies*, Bonwick, London, 1703, p. 1.
226. Pierre Laudet, 'Two dental experts from Toulouse: the Delgas', in *Dental practice in Europe at the end of the eighteenth century: transactions of the Paris meeting, September 1994* (ed. Christine Hillam), pp. 44–9, 46. Despite Laudet's title, he notes that records relating to Guillaume Delga describe him as an officially received surgeon and *not* an *expert*. In 1793, Delga described himself in an advertisement as 'Citoyen Delga neveu, chirurgien-dentiste'. *Journal des affiches du département de la Haute-Garonne et de l'Armée des Pyrénées*, 17 April 1793, cited in Laudet, 'Two dental experts', p. 46.
227. Pierre Baron in particular has performed a thorough search of those surgical guild records for Paris which have survived, but has so far uncovered no new material relating to the treatment of teeth (personal communication). No detailed study has, as yet, been made of the extensive newspaper archives for this period, nor of other potential sources such as legal documents.
228. Fauchard, *Le Chirurgien Dentiste*, vol. I, p. 362.
229. Fauchard, *Le Chirurgien Dentiste*, vol. II, p. 189.
230. Ibid., p. 149. These are, of course, Fauchard's titles, which he has applied retrospectively; but in doing so, he is implying the existence of a particular type of practitioner.
231. Ibid., p. 201.
232. Fauchard, *Le Chirurgien Dentiste*, vol. I, p. 416.
233. *Compte des recettes faites pour l'école du Collège Royal de Saint-Côme à Paris, depuis le 1er octobre 1757 au 1er novembre 1758. Chapitre X, à cause du droit de visite et de confrérie de MM. des Experts.* Reproduced in Besombes and Dagen, *Pierre Fauchard*, p. 82.
234. See Georges Dagen, *Documents pour servir à l'Histoire de l'Art dentaire en France, principalement à Paris*, Editions de La Semaine Dentaire, Paris, 1925, p. 322.
235. Jeze, *Tableau de Paris*, 1761: facsimile of p. 6, in Dagen, *Documents*, p. 323.
236. Facsimile reproduced in Besombes and Dagen, *Pierre Fauchard*, p. 6.
237. Dagen, *Documents*, pp. 324–5.
238. 'Book of minor surgical practice', *Archives Municipales de Lyon*, HH49, in Pierre Baron, 'Dental experts in Lyon at the end of the eighteenth century', in *Dental practice in Europe at the end of the eighteenth century: transactions of the Paris meeting, September 1994* (ed. Christine Hillam), pp. 27–34. It should be noted that by the use of 'expert' Baron is not intending to pass judgement on the nature of the individual's practice.

239. Baron alternates freely between the titles of 'dental expert' and 'dentiste' in his descriptions. However, as I have shown, it is significant that practitioners such as Auzebi (admitted in 1763) referred to themselves as *chirurgien dentistes* (see Baron, 'Dental experts in Lyon', p. 30).
240. Ibid., p. 29.
241. Ibid., pp. 29–30.

Bibliography

Manuscript source

Lettres de noblesse accordées à le Sieur Estienne Bourdet, donné à Versailles, le 18 Juin 1768. Archives Nationales, P/2597.

Printed primary sources

Anon., *Fun upon Fun, or the Humours of a Fair, giving a description of the curious Amusements in Early Life: Also an account of a Mountebank Doctor and his Merry Andrew.* J. Lumsden, Glasgow, n.d. (*c.* 1810).

—————., *The Harangues or Speeches of several celebrated Quack-Doctors in Town and Country.* J. Thomson, London, 1762.

—————., *The Harangues or Speeches of several Famous Mountebanks in Town and Country.* T. Warner, London, n.d. (*c.* 1725).

Anselme, (père) de Sainte Marie, *Histoire généalogique et chronologique de la maison royale de France, des pairs, grands officiers de la couronne et de la maison du roy, et des anciens barons du royaume; avec les qualitez, l'origine, le progrès et les armes de leurs familles; ensemble les statuts et le catalogue des chevaliers, commandeurs, et officiers de l'ordre du Saint Esprit,* 1726–33 (9 vols).

Arnaud de Ronsil, Georges, *Memoires de Chirurgie, avec quelques remarques historiques sur l'etat de la Médicine & de la Chirurgie en France & en Angleterre.* J. Nourse, London, 1768.

Bourdet, Etienne, *Recherches et observations sur toutes les parties de l'art du Dentiste.* Herissant, Paris, 1757.

de la Bruyère, Jean, *The Characters, or the Manners of the Age, by Monsieur de la Bruyere, of the French Academy. Made English by several hands.* Bullord, London, 1699.

Bunon, Robert, *Essay sur les maladies des dents, ou l'on propose les moyens de leur procurer une bonne conformation dès la plus tendre Enfance, & d'en assurer la conservation pendant tout le cours de la vie.* Briasson, Chaubert and de Hansy, Paris, 1743.

Carracioli, Charles, *An Historical account of Sturbridge, Bury, and the most famous fairs in Europe and America; interspersed with anecdotes curious and entertaining.* Fletcher and Hodson, Cambridge, 1773.

Desault, Pierre-Joseph, *Oeuvres Chirurgicales, ou exposé de la doctrine et de la pratique de P.-J. Desault* (Compiled by X. Bichat). Méquignon, Paris, 1812.

Dionis, Pierre, *The Anatomy of Humane Bodies improv'd, According to the circulation of the Blood and all the modern discoveries. Publicly demonstrated at the Theatre in the Royal Garden at Paris by Mr Dionis, Chief Surgeon to the late Dauphiness, and to the present Dutchess of Burgundy.* Translated from the 3rd edn, Bonwick, London, 1703.

————., *Cours d'opérations de Chirurgie, démontrées au Jardin Royal.* t'Serstevens et Claudinot, Bruxelles, 1708.

————., *Cours d'opérations de Chirurgie, démontrées au Jardin Royal.* 4th edn, d'Houry, Paris, 1740.

————., *A Course of Chirurgical operations, Demonstrated in the Royal Gardens at Paris.* Translated from the Paris edn, Tonson, London, 1710.

————., *A Course of Chirurgical operations, Demonstrated in the Royal Gardens at Paris.* 2nd edn, Tonson, London, 1733.

————., *Traité général des accouchemens. Qui instruit de tout ce qu'il faut faire pour etre habile accoucheur.* 2nd edn, d'Houry, Paris, 1724.

Fabricius, Hieronymus ab Aquapendente, *Opera Chirurgica.* Venice, 1619.

Fauchard, Pierre *Le Chirurgien Dentiste, ou Traité des Dents, ou l'on enseigne les moyens de les entretenir propres & saines, de les embellir, d'en réparer la perte & de remédier à leurs maladies, à celles des Gencives & aux accidens qui peuvent survenir aux autres parties voisines des Dents.* Pierre-Jean Mariette, Paris, 1728.

————., *Le Chirurgien Dentiste, ou Traité des Dents, ou l'on enseigne les moyens de les entretenir propres & saines, de les embellir, d'en réparer la perte & de remédier à leurs maladies, à celles des Gencives & aux accidens qui peuvent survenir aux autres parties voisines des Dents.* 2nd edn, Pierre-Jean Mariette, Paris, 1746.

————., *Das Herrn Pierre Fauchard Frantzösischer Zahn=Arzt, Oder Tractat Von den Zahnen.* Rudigern, Berlin, 1733.

de la Faye, *Principes de Chirurgie.* Paris, 1738.

Fabricius Hildanus, Wilhelm, *Observationum et curationum chirurgicarum centuriæ.* Basileæ, 1606.

de Garengeot, René Jacques Croissant, *Traité des Operations de Chirurgie, suivant la Méchanique des Parties du Corps Humain, la Théorie & la Pratique des Chirurgiens de Paris les plus sçavans & les plus experimentés.* Cavelier, Paris, 1720.

————., *Nouveau Traité des instrumens de chirurgie les plus utiles, et de plusiers nouvelles machines propres pour les maladies des Os.* Scheurleer, The Hague, 1725.

————., (Garengeot, Renatus James Croissant), *A Treatise of Chirurgical Operations, according to the mechanism of the parts of the humane body, and the theory and practice of the most learned Surgeons in Paris*. Revis'd and corrected by Mr St Andre, Woodward, London, 1723.

Geraudly, Claude Jacquier, *L'Art de conserver les Dents*. Mercier, Paris, 1737.

Guillemeau, Jacques, *The Frenche Chirurgerye, or all the manualle operations of Chirurgerye, with divers, & sundrye Figures, and amongst the rest, certayne nuefownde Instrumentes, verye necessarye to all the operations of Chirurgerye*, 1597 (trans. from the Dutch by A.M.).

Hécquet, Philippe, *De l'indécence aux hommes d'accoucher les femmes, et de l'obligation aux femmes de nourrir leurs enfans. Pour montrer par des raisons de physique, de morale et de médecine que les mères n'exposeroient ni leurs vies ni celles de leurs enfans en se passant ordinairement d'accoucheurs et de nourrices*. J. Etienne, Paris, 1708.

Le Clerc, Charles Gabriel, *The Compleat Surgeon: or, the whole art of surgery explain'd in a most Familiar Method*. Eng. trans., Freeman, Walthoe, Goodwin, Wotton and Parker, London, 1701.

Le Dran, Henry-François, *Traité des operations de chirurgie*. Charles Osmont, Paris, 1742.

————., *The Operations in Surgery of Mons. Le Dran, Senior Surgeon of the Hospital of La Charité, Consultant Surgeon to the Army, Member of the Academy of Surgery at PARIS, and Fellow of the Royal Society at LONDON. Translated by Mr Gataker, Surgeon*. 4th edn, Hawes, Clarke and Collins, London, 1768.

Mauquest, Guillaume, Sieur de la Motte, *Traité complet de Chirurgie, contenant des observations & des reflexions sur toutes les Maladies Chirurgicales, & sur la maniere de les traiter*. Huart, Paris, 1722.

Mauriceau, François, *Traité des maladies des femmes grosses*, Paris, 1668.

————., *The Diseases of Women with Child, and in Child-bed: As also the best means of helping them in Natural and Unnatural LABORS*. Trans. by Hugh Chamberlen, 2nd edn, John Darby, London, 1683.

Mercier, Sebastien, *Tableau de Paris*. Amsterdam, 1782.

Montague, Lady Mary Wortley, *Letters of the Right Honourable Lady Mary Wortley Montague: Written, during her Travels in Europe, Asia and Africa, to Persons of Distinction, Men of Letters, &c. in different Parts of Europe*. Becket and De Hondt, London, 1763.

Owen, William, *Owen's Book of Fairs, being an authentic account of all the Fairs in England and Wales*. Owen, London, 1773 (6th edn).

Paré, Ambroise, *Les Oeuvres d'Ambroise Paré, conseiller et premier chirurgien du roy.* 8th edn, Nicolas Buon, Paris, 1628.

————., *Les Oeuvres* ... 11th edn, P. Rigaud, Lyons, 1652.

————., *The Workes of that famous Chirurgion Ambrose Parey. Trans-lated out of Latine and compared with the French by Thomas Johnson.* Cotes and Young, London, 1634.

Pomet, Pierre, *A Compleat History of Druggs, written in French by Monsieur Pomet, chief druggist to the late French King Lewis XIV.* Bonwicke and Wilkin, London, 1725.

de La Roque, Gilles André, *Traité de la Noblesse, et de toutes ses differentes espéces.* Nouvelle édition, Le Boucher, Paris, 1735.

————., *Traité de la Noblesse et de son origine, suivant les préjugés rendus par les commissaires députés pour la vérification des Titres de Noblesse.* Le Boucher, Paris, 1735.

Scultetus, Johannes, *The Chyrurgeon's Store-House.* English trans. by E. B. John Starkey, London, 1674.

Thicknesse, Philip, *Man-midwifery analysed: and the Tendency of that Practice detected and exposed.* 2nd edn, Davis and Caslon, London, 1765.

da Vigo, Giovanni, *The most excellent workes of Chirurgerye, made and set forth by maister John Vigon, heed Chirurgien of our tyme in Italie, translated into english. Whereunto is added an exposition of stravnge terms and unknowen symples, belongyng to the acte.* Edward Whytchurch, 1543. Facsimile reprint published by Da Capo Press, Amsterdam and New York, 1968.

Voltaire (François-Marie Arouet), *The Age of Lewis XIV.* Faulkner, Dublin, 1752 (Eng. trans.).

Publications concerning official papers

D'Olblen, le Blond, *Statuts et Réglemens généraux pour les communautés de Chirurgiens des Provinces. Donnés à Marli [sic] le 24 Février 1730.* Nouvelle édition, Delaguette, Paris, 1754.

————., *Statuts et Réglemens généraux pour les maîtres en Chirurgie des provinces du Royaume. Donnés à Marly le 24 Février 1730.* 5th edn, Didot, Paris, 1772.

Verdier, Jean, *La Jurisprudence particulière de la Chirurgie en France, ou Traité Historique et Juridique Des Établissemens, Réglemens, Po-lice, Devoirs, Fonctions, Honneurs, Droits & Priviléges, des Sociétés de Chirurgie & de leurs supôts; Avec les Devoirs, Fonctions & autorité des Juges à leur égard.* D'Houry et Didot, Paris, 1764.

Printed secondary sources

Anderson, P., *Lineages of the Absolutist State*. NLB, London, 1974.

Barbier, E. J. F., *Chronique de la Régence et du regne de Louis XV (1718–1763), ou Journal de Barbier.* Charpentier, Paris, 1857.

Baron, Armelle and Pierre, *L'Art dentaire à travers la Peinture.* ACR, Paris, 1986.

Batterberry, Michael and Ariane, *Fashion: The mirror of history.* Columbus, London, 1982.

Bennion, Elisabeth, *Antique Medical Instruments.* Sotheby Parke Bernet, London, 1979.

————., *Antique Dental Instruments.* Sotheby's, London, 1986.

Bernier, Olivier, *Louis the Beloved: The life of Louis XV.* Doubleday & Company, New York, 1984.

Besombes, André, and Dagen, Georges, *Pierre Fauchard, Pere de l'Art Dentaire Moderne (1678–1761) et ses contemporaines.* Société des Publications Médicales et Dentaires, Paris, 1961.

Bloch, Marc, *The Royal Touch: Sacred Monarchy and Scrofula in England and France.* Routledge & Kegan Paul, London, 1973 (translated from *Les Rois thaumaturges*, Max Leclerc et Cie, 1961).

Bluche, J. F., *L'origine des magistrats du parlement de Paris au XVIIIᵉ siècle.* Fédération des sociétés historiques et archéologiques de Paris et de l'Ile-de-France, Paris, 1956.

Branca, Patricia (ed.), *The Medicine Show: Patients, Physicians and the Perplexities of the Health Revolution in Modern Society.* Science History Publications, New York, 1977.

Breward, Christopher, *The culture of fashion: A new history of fashionable dress.* Manchester, Manchester University Press, 1995.

Brockliss, Laurence, *French Higher Education in the Seventeenth and Eighteenth Centuries: A Cultural History.* Clarendon Press, Oxford, 1987.

Brockliss, Laurence and Jones, Colin, *The Medical World of Early Modern France.* Clarendon Press, Oxford, 1997.

Burke, Peter, *The Fabrication of Louis XIV.* Yale University Press, New Haven, 1992.

Bynum, William F. and Porter, Roy (eds), *William Hunter and the eighteenth century medical world.* Cambridge University Press, Cambridge, 1985.

Campbell, John Menzies *Dentistry Then and Now.* Private publication, Glasgow, 1981 (3rd edn, first published 1963).

Caroly, Michelle, *Le corps du Roi-Soleil: grandeur et misères de sa majesté Louis XIV.* Imago, Paris, 1990.

Chaussinand-Nogaret, Guy, *The French nobility in the eighteenth cen-*

tury: from feudalism to enlightenment. Cambridge University Press, Cambridge, 1985.

Colyer, Frank J., *John Hunter and Odontology.* Claudius Ash, London, 1913.

Corson, Richard, *Fashions in makeup from ancient to modern times.* Peter Owen, London, 1972.

Cunnington, Cyril W. and Phyllis, *Handbook of English costume in the eighteenth century.* Faber & Faber, London, 1972 (2nd edn revised: first pub. 1957).

Dagen, Georges, *Documents pour servir à l'Histoire de l'Art dentaire en France, principalement à Paris.* Editions de La Semaine Dentaire, Paris, 1925.

Darnton, Robert and Roche, Daniel (eds), *Revolution in print: the press in France, 1775–1800.* University of California Press, Berkeley, 1989.

Eamon, William, *Science and the secrets of nature: books of secrets in medieval and early modern culture.* Princeton University Press, Chichester, 1994.

Eckart, Wolfgang and Geyer-Kordesch, Johanna (eds), *Heilberüfe und Kranke im 17. und 18. Jahrhundert die Quellen und Forschungssituation.* Münster, 1982.

Elias, Norbert, *The Court Society.* Blackwell, Oxford, 1983.

Franklin, Alfred, *La vie privée d'autrefois: Arts et métiers, modes, mœurs, usages des parisiens du XIIᵉ au XVIIIᵉ siecle d'après des documents originaux ou inédits,* vol. 2, *Les Soins de Toilette: Le Savoir-vivre.* E. Plon, Nourrit et cⁱᵉ, Paris, 1887.

————., *La vie privée d'autrefois: Arts et métiers, modes, mœurs, usages des parisiens du XIIᵉ au XVIIIᵉ siecle d'après des documents originaux ou inédits,* vol. 11, *Les Médecins.* E. Plon, Nourrit et cⁱᵉ, Paris, 1892.

————., *La vie privée d'autrefois: Arts et métiers, modes, mœurs, usages des parisiens du XIIᵉ au XVIIIᵉ siecle d'après des documents originaux ou inédits,* vol. 12, *Les Chirurgiens.* E. Plon, Nourrit et cⁱᵉ, Paris, 1893.

————., *La vie privée d'autrefois: Arts et métiers, modes, mœurs, usages des parisiens du XIIᵉ au XVIIIᵉ siecle d'après des documents originaux ou inédits,* vol. 14, *Variétés chirurgicales.* E. Plon, Nourrit et cⁱᵉ, Paris, 1893.

————., *La vie privée d'autrefois: Arts et métiers, modes, mœurs, usages des parisiens du XIIᵉ au XVIIIᵉ siecle d'après des documents originaux ou inédits,* vol. 21, *La vie de Paris sous la Régence.* E. Plon, Nourrit et cⁱᵉ, Paris, 1897.

French, Roger, and Wear, Andrew (eds), *The medical revolution of the seventeenth century.* CUP, Cambridge, 1989.

Geison, Gerald L. (ed.), *Professions and the French State, 1700–1900*. University of Pennsylvania Press, 1984.

Gelfand, Toby, *Professionalizing modern medicine: Paris surgeons and medical science and institutions in the eighteenth century*. Greenwood, Westport, 1980.

Gélis, Jacques, *Accoucheur de campagne sous le roi soleil: le traité d'accouchement de G. Mauquest de la Motte*. Edouard Privat, Toulouse, 1979.

Genders, Roy, *History of Scent*. Hamish Hamilton, London, 1972.

Goubert, Pierre, *The Ancien Régime: French society 1600–1750*. Weidenfeld and Nicolson, London, 1973.

Guerini, Vincenzo, *A History of Dentistry from the Most Ancient Times until the End of the Eighteenth Century*. Lea and Febiger, Philadelphia, 1909.

Hackwood, Frederick, W. *Inns, Ales and Drinking Customs of Old England*. Bracken, London, 1987.

Hillam, Christine, *Brass Plate and Brazen Impudence: Dental practice in the provinces, 1755–1855*. Liverpool University Press, Liverpool, 1991.

Hoffmann-Axthelm, Walter, *History of Dentistry*. Quintessence, Chicago, 1981.

Jones, Colin, *The charitable imperative: hospitals and nursing in ancien régime and revolutionary France*. Routledge, London, 1989.

La Berge, Ann, and Feingold, Mordechai (eds), *French medical culture in the nineteenth century*. Rodopi, Amsterdam, 1994.

Latham, Robert (ed.), *The Shorter Pepys*. Unwin Hyman, London, 1990.

Le Roi, Joseph Adrien, *Journal de la Santé du Roi Louis XIV de l'année 1647 à l'année 1711 ecrit par Vallot, d'Aquin et Fagon*. Durand, Paris, 1862.

Lindsay, Lilian, *A Short History of Dentistry*. John Bale, Sons and Danielsson, London, 1933.

———., *The Surgeon Dentist* by Fauchard, translated into English by Lilian Lindsay, Butterworth, London, 1946.

Margairaz, Dominique, *Foires et marchés dans la France préindustrielle*. Editions de l'École des Hautes Études en Sciences Sociales, Paris, 1988.

Morley, Henry, *Memoirs of Bartholomew Fair*. Chapman and Hall, London, 1859.

Nutton, Vivian (ed.), *Medicine at the courts of Europe, 1500–1837*. Routledge, London, 1990.

Parker, David, *The Making of French Absolutism*. Edward Arnold, London, 1983.

Perrot, Jean-Claude, *Genèse d'une ville moderne: Caen au XVIIIe siecle*. Mouton & Co. and École des Hautes Études en Sciences Sociales, Paris, 1975.

Porter, Roy, *Health for sale: Quackery in England, 1660–1850*. Manchester University Press, Manchester, 1989.

Ramsey, Matthew, *Professional and popular medicine in France, 1770–1830: the social world of medical practice*. Cambridge University Press, Cambridge, 1988.

Ring, Malvin E., *Dentistry: An illustrated history*. Harry N. Abrams, New York, 1985.

Roche, Daniel, *The People of Paris: an essay in popular culture in the eighteenth century*. Berg, Leamington Spa, 1987.

————., *The culture of clothing: dress and fashion in the 'ancien régime'*. Translated by Jean Birrell, Cambridge University Press, Cambridge, 1994.

Smith, M., *A Short History of Dentistry*. Allan Wingate, London, 1958.

Solnon, Jean-François, *La Cour de France*. Librairie Arthème Fayard, Paris, 1987.

Starsmore, Ian, *English Fairs*. Studies in Industrial Archæology, Thames and Hudson, London, 1975.

Taton, René (ed.), *Enseignement et diffusion des sciences en France au XVIIIe siècle*. Hermann, Paris, 1964.

Vess, David M., *Medical revolution in France, 1789–1796*. Florida State University, Gainesville, 1975.

Vidal, François (ed.), *Histoire d'un diplôme*. Le Chirurgien Dentiste de France, Paris, n.d. (*c.* 1993).

Webster, Charles, *The health services since the war*, vol. I. *Problems of health care: the National Health Service before 1957*. HSMO, London, 1988.

Wilson, Adrian, *The Making of Man-Midwifery: Childbirth in England 1660–1770*. UCL, London, 1995.

Woodforde, James, *A Country Parson: James Woodforde's diary, 1759–1802*. Oxford University Press and Century, Oxford and London, 1985.

Articles and papers from books and periodicals

Baron, Pierre, "Dental experts" in Lyon at the end of the eighteenth century', in *Dental Practice in Europe at the end of the eighteenth century: transactions of the Paris meeting, September 1994* (ed. Christine Hillam), pp. 27–34.

Chaussinand-Nogaret, Guy, 'Nobles médecins et médecins de cour au

XVIIIᵉ siècle', *Annales Économies Sociétés Civilisations*, 5, 1977, 851–7.

Chevalier, Albert, 'Un charlatan du XVIIIᵉ siècle: Le Grand Thomas', *Mémoires de la société de l'histoire de Paris et de l'Ile-de-France*, 7, 1880, 61–78.

Dagen, Georges, 'Lettres de Noblesse accordées à Caperon et à Bourdet par Louis XV', *La Semaine Dentaire*, 28 February 1926, 198–200.

Deltombe, Xavier, 'The Rennes Guild of Surgeons at the end of the 18th century', in *Dental Practice in Europe at the end of the eighteenth century: transactions of the Paris meeting, September 1994* (ed. Christine Hillam), pp. 38–43.

Gelfand, Toby, 'The "Paris Manner" of dissection: student anatomical dissection in early eighteenth-century Paris', *Bulletin of the History of Medicine*, XLVI (2), 1972, 99–130.

————., 'Medical Professionals and Charlatans: the *Comité de salubrité enquête* of 1790–1', *Histoire sociale — Social History*, XI (21), 1978, 62–97.

Gélis, Jacques, 'Sages-femmes et accoucheurs: l'obstétrique populaire aux XVIIᵉ et XVIIIᵉ siècles', *Annales Économies Sociétés Civilisations*, 32, (5), 1977, 927–57.

Goubert, Jean-Pierre, 'L'art de guérir. Médecine savante et médecine populaire dans la France de 1790', *Annales Économies, Sociétés, Civilisations*, 32 (5), 1977, 908–26.

Hamy, Ernest Théodore, 'Recherches sur les origines de l'enseignement de l'anatomie humaine et de l'anthropologie au Jardin des Plantes', *Nouvelles Archives du Muséum d'Histoire Naturelle*, 3rd series, 1895, vol. III, 1–30.

Henry, John, Book review of W. F. Bynum and Roy Porter (eds), *Companion Encyclopædia of the History of Medicine*, in *British Journal for the History of Science*, September 1995, vol. 28, pt. 3, no. 98, pp. 379–81.

King, Roger, 'Curing toothache on the stage? The importance of reading pictures in context', *History of Science*, 33, 1995, 396–416.

Kleinman, Ruth, 'Social Dynamics at the French Court: The Household of Anne of Austria', *French Historical Studies*, 16 (3), 1990, 517–35.

Laget, Mireille, 'Childbirth in Seventeenth- and Eighteenth-Century France: Obstetrical Practices and Collective Attitudes', in Robert Forster and Orest Ranum (eds), *Medicine and Society in France: Selections from the Annales*, vol. 6, The Johns Hopkins University Press, Baltimore, 1980, 137–76.

Laudet, Pierre, 'Two dental experts from Toulouse: the Delgas', in *Dental practice in Europe at the end of the eighteenth century:*

transactions of the Paris meeting, September 1994 (ed. Christine Hillam), pp. 44–9.

Meynell, Guy, 'Surgical Teaching at the Jardin des Plantes During the Seventeenth Century', *Gesnerus*, 51, 1994, parts 1 & 2, 101–8.

Prinz, Hermann, 'Pierre Fauchard and His Works', *The Dental Cosmos*, **LXV** (8), 1923, 827–30.

Shapin, Steven, 'Discipline and bounding: the history and sociology of science as seen through the externalism-internalism debate', *History of Science*, 30, 1992, 333–69.

Stanley, Alan, 'Dentistry — The Dependence upon Medicine and Surgery for its Professional Status', *British Dental Journal*, **176**, (12), 25 June 1994, 448–50.

Viau, Georges, 'The Manuscript of Fauchard', *The Dental Cosmos*, **LXV** (8), 1923, 823–6.

————., 'The Life of Pierre Fauchard (1678–1761)', *The Dental Cosmos*, **LXV** (8), 1923, 797–808.

Walsh, J. J., 'Fauchard, the Father of Modern Dentistry', *The Dental Cosmos*, **LXV** (8), 1923, 809–23.

Unpublished sources

Hargreaves, Anne S., 'The provision of practical dental treatment in England from the 14th to the mid-18th centuries', unpublished Ph.D. thesis, University of Newcastle-upon-Tyne, 1996.

Kilpatrick, Robert, 'Nature's Schools: The Hunterian revolution in London hospital medicine 1780–1825', unpublished Ph.D. thesis, University of Cambridge, 1989.

Reference sources

Almanach Royale, année bissextile M.DCC.LXVIII. Le Breton, Paris, 1768.

Biographie Universelle Ancienne et Moderne, ou Histoire, par ordre Alphabétique, de la vie publique et privée de tous les hommes qui se sont fait remarquer par leurs écrits, leurs actions, leurs talents, leurs vertus ou leurs crimes. M. Michaud (ed.), Thoisnier Desplaces, Paris, 1852.

de la Chesnaye-Dubois, François A. Aubert, *Dictionnaire de la Noblesse de France*, 1770–78 (12 vols).

Cotgrave, Randle, *A Dictionarie of the French and English Tongues, 1611.* Facsimile edition, Scolar Press, Menston, 1968.

Encyclopédie, ou Dictionnaire Raisonné des sciences, des arts et des métiers, par une societé de gens de lettres. Diderot et d'Alembert. Briasson, David, Le Breton, Durand, Paris, 1757.

Supplément à l'Encyclopédie, ou Dictionnaire Raisonné des sciences, des arts et des métiers, par une société de gens des lettres. Diderot et d'Alembert. Briasson, David, Le Breton, Durand, Paris, 1776.

Fleming and Tibbins, *Grand Dictionnaire Français-Anglais et Anglais-Français.* 6th edn, Paris, 1841.

Furetière, Antoine, *Dictionnaire Universel, contenant géneralement tous les mots françois, tant vieux que modernes et les termes de toutes les sciences et des arts.* The Hague, 1690.

———., *Dictionnaire Universel, contenant géneralement tous les mots françois, tant vieux que modernes, et les termes des sciences et des arts.* The Hague, 1727.

Hooper, *Lexicon Medicum.* 4th edn, Longman, Hurst, Rees, Orme & Co., London, 1820.

James, R., *A Medicinal Dictionary, ... together with a History of Drugs.* Osborne, London, 1743.

Johnson, Samuel, *Dictionary of the English Language.* Strahan, London, 1755 (facsimile edition, New York, 1967).

Larousse, *Grand Dictionnaire Français-Anglais Anglais-Français.* Larousse, Paris, 1993.

Oxford English Dictionary, 2nd edn, Clarendon, Oxford, 1989.

Rey, Alain (ed.), *Dictionnaire Historique de la Langue Français.* Dictionnaires Le Robert, Paris, 1992.

Richelet, Pierre, *Dictionnaire François.* Geneva, 1685.

———., *Dictionnaire François.* Amsterdam, 1732 (nouvelle édition).

Index